Behind the Wire: The Road to Oflag VII-B Eichstätt

Behind the Wire: The Road to Oflag VII-B Eichstätt

The PoW Diaries of Captain John Blomfield Dixon, 1940-45

Paul Johnson

FRONTLINE BOOKS

First published in Great Britain in 2025 by
Frontline Books
An imprint of Pen & Sword Books Limited
Yorkshire – Philadelphia

ISBN 978 1 03612 144 0

A CIP catalogue record for this book is
available from the British Library

Typeset by Mac Style
Printed in the UK by CPI Group (UK) Ltd, Croydon, CR0 4YY.

Pen & Sword Books Limited incorporates the imprints of After
the Battle, Atlas, Archaeology, Aviation, Discovery, Family History,
Fiction, History, Maritime, Military, Military Classics, Politics,
Select, Transport, True Crime, Air World, Frontline Publishing, Leo
Cooper, Remember When, Seaforth Publishing, The Praetorian Press,
Wharncliffe Local History, Wharncliffe Transport, Wharncliffe True
Crime and White Owl.

For a complete list of Pen & Sword titles please contact

PEN & SWORD BOOKS LIMITED
47 Church Street, Barnsley, South Yorkshire, S70 2AS, England
E-mail: enquiries@pen-and-sword.co.uk
Website: www.pen-and-sword.co.uk
or
PEN AND SWORD BOOKS
1950 Lawrence Road, Havertown, PA 19083, USA
E-mail: uspen-and-sword@casematepublishers.com
Website: www.penandswordbooks.com

For Jo.

Loves eternal flame still flickers.

Contents

Acknowledgements

I wish to express my deepest gratitude to the following people, who not only inspired this book but have assisted greatly in its creation: Allan and Mary McNab, Jill Campbell, Doug Banks of Colourising History, Greg Crane, Dave Hineson, Martin Mace of Frontline Books, Eve Martin, Steve Rogers of The War Graves Photographic Project, and John West (@JohnWestAuthor).

Abbreviations

Some of the following abbreviations and phrases are those used at the time and are not considered appropriate today.

AA	Anti-Aircraft
AEF	Allied Expeditionary Force
AFV	Armoured Fighting Vehicles
ARP	Air Raid Precautions
ASO	Assistant Section Officer
ATS	Auxiliary Territorial Service
Bar	Bar to medal
BBC	British Broadcasting Corporation
BEF	British Expeditionary Force
Bosche	Germany army
C of E	Church of England
CBE	Commander of Most Excellent Order of the British Empire
CO	Commanding Officer
DDT	Dichlorodiphenyltrichloroethane (insecticide)
DoW	Died of Wounds
DSO	Distinguished Service Order
e.g.	For example
ERY	East Riding Yeomanry
Goon/goons	German guard/guards at PoW camps
GSW	Gun Shot Wounds
HQ	Headquarters
IRC	International Red Cross
Japs	Japanese
Jerry/Jerries	German Soldier/Soldiers
KIA	Killed in Action
KRRC	King's Royal Rifle Corps
LMG	Light Machine Gun
MC	Military Cross
MID	Mentioned In Dispatches

MG	Machine Gun
NCO	Non-Commissioned Officer
No.	Number
NZ	New Zealand
NZDC	New Zealand Dental Corps
NZYMCA	New Zealand Young Men's Christian Association
OBLI	Oxfordshire and Buckinghamshire Light Infantry
OC	Officer Commanding
OCTU	Officer Cadet Training Unit
OKW	Oberkommando der Wehrmacht (German army)
PMC	Post-Mortem Company (a theatre production)
PoW/PoWs	Prisoner of War/Prisoners of War
PT	Physical Training
QM	Quartermaster
RA	Royal Artillery
RAC	Royal Air Corps
RAF	Royal Air Force
RAOC	Royal Army Ordnance Corps
RASC	Royal Army Service Corps
REME	Royal Electrical and Mechanical Engineers
RHQ	Regimental Headquarters
RM	Royal Marines
RN	Royal Navy
RNVR	Royal Naval Voluntary Reserve
RSM	Regimental Sergeant Major
RTR	Royal Tank Regiment
SAS	Special Air Service
SBMO	Senior British Medical Officer
SBO	Senior British Officer
SHAEF	Supreme Headquarters Allied Expeditionary Force
SHQ	Section Headquarters
SIS	Secret Intelligence Service
SMMT	Society of Motor Manufacturers and Traders
SMO	Senior Medical Officer
SOE	Special Operations Executive
SOS	Save Our Sole
SQMS	Squadron Quartermaster Sergeant
SS	*Schutzstaffel* (Nazi paramilitary organisation)
SSM	Squadron Sergeant Major
TA	Territorial Army

TAB	Typhoid A & B inoculation
TB	Tuberculosis
TD	Territorial Decoration
TEWT	Tactical Exercise Without Troops
Tommy/Tommies	British Soldier/Soldiers
TSM	Troop Sergeant Major
UK	United Kingdom
US	United States
USA	United States of America
USDC	United States Dental Corps
USMC	United States Marine Corps
VB	Völkischer Beobachter (Nazi Newspaper)
WAAF	Women's Auxiliary Air Force
WD	Westminster Dragoon
WO	Warrant Officer
Wops	Derogatory term for people of Italian origin
WRNS	Women's Royal Naval Service
WW1/WWI	First World War
WW2/WWII	Second World War
Yanks/Yankee	Americans/American
YMCA	Young Men's Christian Association

Translations

Akute Luftalarm	Acute air raid warning
Auf wiedersehen	Goodbye
Autobaun	German motorway
Bauersloaf	Farm loaf (bread)
Bauernwurst	Sausage
Blitzkrieg	Lightning war
Croix de Guerre	French military medal
Fallschirmjäger	Paratroopers
Fall Gelb	Assault on France, Belgium and the Low Countries
Gebirgsjäger	Light Infantry Troops
Gefangenschaft	Captivity
Gestapo	German Secret Police
Hauptman	Captain
Kommandant	(Commandant) German commander
Kommandantur	German military headquarters
Kriegie	Military slag for a PoW
Kriegiedom	PoW camp
Kultur	Culture
Lebensraum	Territory the Nazi's believed was required for natural development
Luftwaffe	German air force
Oberkommando der Wehrmacht (OKW)	German army
Oberleutnant	First Lieutenant
Oberst	Group Captain
Oberstabsartz	Medical Officer
Oflag	Camp (for PoWs)
Offizierslager	Prisoner of war camps for officer
Ostfront	Eastern Front
Reich	Nazi German state
Reichsmarks	German currency
Schaft	Slang term for *Gefangenschaft* (captivity)

Schutzstaffel (SS)	Nazi paramilitary organisation
Sonderfürher	Special leader
Stuka	German Junkers Ju 87 dive-bomber aircraft.
Unteroffizier	Junior Non-Commissioned Officer
Volkstrum	Nazi national militia

Introduction

When I was first asked to look at a collection of material belonging to a British officer, who had been a PoW in Germany during the Second World War, I really wasn't expecting to find the wealth of history that was to be laid out before me. A series of scrapbooks, folders, maps, photographs and documents surrounded a small pile of well-worn booklets, in which, written in almost microscopic script, were the daily musings of a young soldier, whose life had been placed on hold following his capture during the retreat to Dunkirk. While many diaries and letters from service personnel who served throughout the Second World War survive in quite large numbers, both in national and local archives, rarely are they so detailed as those of John Blomfield Dixon, whose home was in the Hertfordshire town of Ware.

Having lived what could be described as a fairly privileged life, the prospect of war would see him enlist as a private in 22nd Battalion, Royal Tank (Westminster Dragoons) Regiment, at that time part of the Territorial Army. With the outbreak of the Second World War he became a newly appointed junior officer in the British Army, and was then attached to the East Riding Yeomanry in May 1940. His story may never have been known, if it were not for a single entry in the battalion war diary coupled with his voracious appetite, in the early days of his capture, in diarising his thoughts and feelings, which describe his training, life during the retreat, his humiliating capture by the enemy at the culmination of the Battle of Cassel and the long arduous journey through a variation of *Offizierslagers*, which would, ultimately, lead him to Oflag VII-b, a PoW camp located in the small picturesque Bavarian town of Eichstätt, Germany.

The ebb and flow of entries across John's five years of captivity are clearly dictated by both his mood and circumstance, and that of those around him. Influenced by long tedious days, miserable food shortages, his thoughts for home, the woman he desperately loved, his hatred for both captors and captives, the killing of his comrades on and off the battlefield, the tireless efforts and disasters of escape, and his passion for the theatrical life, which was borne out on dusty prison camp stages, all of which help to provide a picture of his experiences and emotions. A personal narrative, written as it happened, describe both times of great optimism and terrible pessimism. Although the arrival of mail and Red Cross parcels were well received, they were often coupled with the burden of censorship and the theft of contents, bringing despair to longed-for news from home, and a break from the monotony of German rations. The weather, which produced marvellous summers for sunbathing and playing games, also brought terribly harsh winter conditions, impacting greatly upon the life of PoWs. The parting of friends and the deaths of comrades also took its toll, all of which is reflected in his writing. The text in this book is mainly derived from John Blomfield Dixon's diary entries and reflects the language of that era, which may not align with contemporary standards. The decision to continue reading is up to you. Understandably, as you read through the much handled pages of the Dixon diaries, there is a good deal of repetition concerning many aspects of daily camp life, something John eludes to in his final diary, which is an attempt to summarise his previous journals and describe the latter part of his captivity. Therefore, in an effort to provide the reader with as wide a perspective as possible, I have combined many of the salient entries with a narrative lifted from both historic official records of the period, and the recollections of men who both served or were imprisoned with John. His diaries are complimented by a series of annotated photographs, some of which have not been seen before, providing a brief glimpse of life prior to his enlistment and detailing, where possible, those fellow officers who appear before the lens, helping to tell the story of captivity and the desperate desire for freedom. As time progressed, the longing to escape the monotony of camp life led many PoWs to make ever desperate attempts to break out of their surroundings, and John provides a vivid insight to the outcome of these, often disastrous efforts, occasionally berating his comrades for the inconvenience it brings upon those who were left behind. The morale of the PoWs was often boosted by these escape attempts, along with a show of opposition, which emboldened them to make further shows of disobedience, generally succeeding in causing upset and irritation to the camp administration, which John details to throughout his chronicles.

During his incarceration, not only did he have the opportunity to continue his education, through a series of correspondence courses, but also to immerse himself in his love of the theatre. Playing mainly female characters, something he would eventually come to hate, he would participate in a large number of plays, pantomimes and theatrical events, some of which were performed for the very first time. He records his thoughts and feelings in respect of both the production, producers, cast and audience, and his words are coupled with a series of images showing the event.

As the war progressed, the PoWs were subjected to wild and inaccurate rumours, often brought to them by men who had just been captured in locations such as Crete, the Western Desert and Dieppe. John, who could read, write and speak German lays out these reports, as well as the propaganda relayed to the PoWs through both the German and Allied press, all of which paints an often distorted picture of the wars progression. Notification of Allied landings in France is something that was repeated on more than one occasion, but the Normandy landings in June 1944 brought a sudden realisation to John and his comrades that freedom may become a reality. However, the frustration and anxiety of anticipated release run through his entries during that period, all of which culminate in a terrible disaster at the very moment liberty appears upon the horizon. Liberation, once attained, brings its own frustrations on the journey home, borne out in the final diary entries and supplemented by a post-war summary of his long awaited arrival back to his mother arms.

In the post war period, John remained in the service of the British Army, as a member of the Intelligence Corps until his retirement in 1948 with the rank of captain. Having survived his long incarceration, he married in 1947, but he and his wife did not bring children into the world and, following her death in 2010, and his own in 2013, the vast assortment of material passed to his niece. The desire of his family, through this publication, is not only to share the collection of diaries, photographs and ephemera, but also to memorialise those with whom he shared his incarceration and who were denied the opportunity to bring their own stories to the fore.

In closing this brief introduction, it is perhaps only right that the final comment comes from the words of John who said, 'Anyway, we survived, and now try to recall the memories of those far off days, that we hope will never come again.'

Captain John Blomfield Dixon of the Royal Tank (Westminster Dragoons) Regiment, attached to East Riding Yeomanry, 1918–2013. Remember him. (*Both courtesy of The J B Dixon Collection*)

Chapter 1

The Early Years

I was born on Sunday, 29 December 1918, in a nursing home at Clapton, East London, the second child of William Thomas and Emily Kate Dixon (née Blomfield), and given my birth was within the sound of bow bells I aways regarded myself as a cockney. This was despite the fact my family lived in Hazelmere Road, Winchmore Hill, a suburb of North London. My father worked as a mechanical Engineer for Ingersoll Rand & Co., an American company producing rock drills, who were based in Queen Victoria Street, London. My mother, who in later life was occasionally and rather sarcastically referred to as the Duchess of Ware, was a native of Colchester, Essex, where her father ran a successful wholesale confectionary business. One of six children, she married my father on 9 June 1908 at St Botolph's church in the town. Only death would part them.

I had three siblings. My elder brother, William Fortune Dixon, who was a huge nine years older than me, my sister, Alice Elinor, who was seven years older and was always known to me as Elinor, and [my younger brother] Richard Sutton Dixon, known to me as Dick, who arrived a year after my birth. In 1920, just prior to my second birthday, a new home beckoned, and our family moved to a large house at 103 New Road, Ware, Hertfordshire. I can vividly recall the layout of the enormous property, the staff who worked for my parents and the joyous times we had together. The house had been built in 1889 as a home for the headmaster of Ware Grammar School, Walter New. The entrance was through two large brick gateposts covered in some sort of cement or plaster. A gravel path led to the front door, which was up quite a high flight of stone steps leading into the hall. A telephone hung on the wall close to a large dining room and an equally large drawing room. Opposite this was a small sitting room where I recall spending many happy hours sitting listening to the BBC on a crystal radio set, which was in this room because the large aerial came from a high flagpole in the garden. There was a conservatory with steps that led down to the garden, where and I remember sitting in the early 1920s, watching an eclipse of the sun through smoked glass with my sister and her school friends, the Morlings, who lived in the row of houses further down the road. It seems incredible but we had a cook, housemaid, parlour maid and a gardener. In addition to this, there was Mrs Hart who came in to do the laundry and, of course, there was our dear nanny, Dora Kreischer, a Dutch woman who used to call father 'Daddypa' and mother 'Daddyma'. In our early years, Dick and I were pushed around the town of Ware in an enormous pram which was nicknamed 'The Dixon Bus'.

My memories of life at New Road are very fragmented but I recall how, at mealtimes, I was forced to eat chocolate pudding, which I hated, and how we were given something called Radio Malt, horrible stuff, which I think was supposed to build us up! There were parties at 103, particularly at Christmas. These would be held in what was known as the long room, where mother used to hang partridges supplied by her father. There

A family photograph of the house at 103 New Road, Ware, Hertfordshire. The home of the Dixon family between 1920 and 1926. (*Courtesy of The J B Dixon Collection*)

would be a big Christmas tree in the corner, and our Uncle Jim would be a big source of fun as he led a conga of twenty or more people trailing across the room and around the house. Our family was odd in a way, as it was really two families. William and Elinor were that much older and, with him at prep school and then St Peter's in York, and her at Ware Grammar School, we had little contact really, until much later in life.

Whilst at New Road we had a car, an American open tourer called a 'Dixie Flyer'. There was a hood which pulled right over the top and I recall one memorable trip to Colchester to see granny and grandpa in which William was driving. In the town of Bishops Stortford, Hertfordshire, there is a fairly steep hill and, as we headed downward, the pin came out of the footbrake and the car shot down the hill nearly knocking down a postman. We finally came to a stop and had to sit very still whilst William fetched a mechanic, who repaired the damage. Mother also drove and I remember there was a Dixon chorus every time we went over a hump bridge and reached the other side of 'Thank you

Photograph of a 'Dixie Flyer' owned by the Dixon family in the 1920s. (*Courtesy of The J B Dixon Collection*)

Mum'. It seems that, due to an unfortunate accident, she did not drive for very long. I have happy memories of this time.

In 1926 we moved house again, into what would be our long-term home at High Oak Lodge, which is in High Oak Road, Ware. It was actually number 27 but the number was never used. The entrance was through a tall wooden gate in the middle of long high fence. The grounds were enormous and on summer nights you were almost overwhelmed by the smell of wisteria, which grew on the pergola. There was an immense chestnut tree some distance from the house and steps that led up to the front door. Going inside, immediately to the left was the sitting room, a little further down the wide hall was what would later be known as the 'school room', in front of which stood a huge grandfather clock, so lovingly polished by our home help, Violet Bearman. Dick and I were still quite young and, for a while, on Sunday mornings we would go along to our parents' bedroom and climb into bed with them. Father would tell us stories about the lady with the large hands and the small feet (mother). There was also another story, about finding a butler's tray, which had been left behind a door and how grateful the tray was for being found. Mother used to make Dick and me lie down on our backs for an hour every afternoon, I have no idea why this was or what it was supposed to do. I was also fitted with some sort of insert for my shoes. Presumably this was to try and correct my flat feet. Much good did it do, however, as I had the flattest of feet for the rest of my life.

High Oak Lodge, Ware. It was actually number 27 but the number was never used. (*Courtesy of The J B Dixon Collection*)

About this time, we also began to make friends of our own age. I think the first, apart from the Kipling boys who used to live close to us in New Road, were Hugh and Guy Colson, the sons of the local bank manager. There was also a boy called Michael Baylis, a lad with a hare lip, who did not live in Ware but came to stay with his aunt, Mrs Chapman, a funny wizened old lady who lived in a big house further up High Oak Road. We used to go up there to play, and I remember Mrs Chapman had a wonderful music box, which she allowed us to listen to. It played a variety of tunes. The other boys, Hugh and Houston Andrews, both wore shorts though they were, of course, some years older than us. In the cottages further up High Oak Road, which boarded onto our field, there lived a troop of girls who appeared to form a band and seemed a danger to us. Before going to sleep I used to make up stories about how we fought with them and thwarted their 'dastardly deeds'.

Dick and I were now growing up fast, and mother decided that we had to start reading. The first 'comic', which we had, was 'Chicks Own' designed especially to teach the young to read. I always remember the opening page, which read, 'The sun shines, the wind is up, I will fly my kite'. We then progressed to more exciting comics such as 'The Rainbow', 'Puck' and finally 'Modern Boy'. I kept every single copy of this particular magazine, as my brother William said we would grow out of it, but when I came home after the [Second World War], I found mother had given them all away. After starting us reading our parents decided we needed a governess. I think this was about 1927 and a Miss Allum was brought in to teach us. She was a very kind and patient lady, or rather a girl, as she was quite young, and taught us Latin, history, geography, English and arithmetic. She also began to teach me to play the piano, as we had an old upright in the school room on which Elinor used to play 'Charmaine' and 'Shepherd of the Hills', to which we used to sing along. Soon after we started, other parents heard about this and approached mother about their children joining the 'school'. The first two to join were Hugh and Guy Colson, but they didn't last long as father heard Guy say the word 'bugger', which was anathema to him, and they were quickly shot out of the door!

Every year we would to be taken away on a holiday that used to last about a month, at least that was in the palmy days before the depression hit. Before World War One, and before my time it seems from photographs, Worthing was the favourite place. After the war [First World War] we seem to have changed to Clacton and Southwold, where we always stayed in lodgings not hotels. Father gave us his fishing rods, which Dick and I used to fish for dabs off the pier. Although we did not have any great success, on one occasion we caught quite a few and took them back to the lodgings where we had them for supper. In Clacton, there was a big book shop not far from the front and it was there that I was introduced to the books of Edgar Rice Burroughs. I used to devour avidly the paperback books about Tarzan but the ones that used to thrill me most were those about Mars and the adventures on that planet of John Carter, 'Lord of Barsoom'.

So, we come to 1929, the big year of change. William graduated from the Camborne School of Mines as a mining engineer and went off to East Africa. Just before going he acquired a dog, a smooth haired black and white mongrel terrier which was christened 'Ben', after the character William played in the amateur dramatics at Camborne. He was a lovely little animal and we adored him. He lived for many years and only died during the war [Second World War].

Elinor also was on the move, as she was sent abroad by mother to Abbeville in France, where she taught English in a girl's school and also learnt French. For me the big crunch came when I was sent off to prep school at Heath Brow in Boxmoor, Hertfordshire, where William had been many years before. Mother took me over in a taxi with Dick and Peter Pavier and I remember having to wear a straw boater and mackintosh for the journey. On arrival at the school, we met the headmaster, Mr Eastwood, and his wife and then mother left and, for the first time I was on my own. How I hated it, and how homesick I was. I was shown to the dormitory, which was right at the top of the house, with the landing lit by a gas flare. There were only twelve to thirteen boys in the school at this time and Morris, Cox, Morrison, Grierson and Maiden are the names of a few whom I remember. Apart from Mr Eastwood, there were other masters, Fletcher-Jones who came from Jersey and wore plus fours, and an older man Patrick or 'Snowball' as he was called due to his white hair. He found it impossible to keep order in any class and was given a hell of a life by all the boys. The only thing he was good at was reading stories to us in the evening, and I particularly remember 'King Solomon's Mines', which kept us enthralled. I used to come down to breakfast, not in tears, but so terribly homesick I could not eat anything, and the only food I remember was porridge with golden syrup. The school played football, which I had never played before and, for my sins, I was made goalie, as there were only just enough of us to make a team. Our first match was against Lockers Park which we lost 12–0,

William and Emily Dixon with the family dog, Ben, at High Oak Lodge, Ware, on the day of their only daughter's wedding in 1933. (*Courtesy of The J B Dixon Collection*)

what a goalie! Eventually they put Grierson in goal who made a better job of it, and I used to play full back.

Every Sunday we had to dress up in stiff Eton collars and, wearing boaters, were marched down the road to the church at the bottom of the street. It was here, next door to the church, that we had use of the swimming pool, a horrible thing fed from the nearby river – quite dirty, cold and full of leeches. I was taught to swim hanging in a rubber inner tube suspended from a pole. Just inside the entrance to the school was a large wood floored area that could have once been a gym. This was used as a skating rink for roller skates. I had none but was lent a pair occasionally and whizzed around precariously. At this time, I became friendly with Barry Grierson whose parents were in Malaya. On one occasion I was invited round for lunch. Grierson also had a sister who was at the girl's school next door to Heath Brow. Sadly, she died of some illness, though I do not know what. Another friend I made later was John Potts who also had an uncle living nearby and again I was invited for lunch. On Sunday afternoons we used to go out on rambling walks. On one occasion I was approached by a chap called Morris, a rather effeminate individual, who asked if he could walk with me as Maiden and Morrison, two quite horrible bullies, had said they were going to beat him up and stuff shit in his mouth. I must say I was a bit afraid myself then, as they were big boys, but actually nothing happened.

At last, the end of term came, and I came home for Christmas. I was so thankful to be there, it was a wonderful time. We would hang out our stockings on Christmas Eve and my favourite in them was the sugar mice, either pink or white. We would then come down to breakfast but were not allowed into the school room where the tree was, since all the presents were piled under it. However, we could hand in our own small, and usually quite useless, presents for mother or father to join the pile. Then we went to church, and sometimes Dick and I would go on ahead and on arrival take up our places in our reserved pew. One could always tell when mother arrived because she immediately, upon entry, would clear her throat like a trumpet. Afterwards we were then allowed into the school room to open the presents, and what a pile they used to be – so good were mother and father to us. Mother was an exceptional cook, and how she was able to cook the turkey in that coal-fired oven in the kitchen I'll never know. This, of course, was followed by the usual Christmas pudding which, weeks before, mother had steamed in the clothes boiler at the end of the passage. They had little silver objects in them wrapped up in grease proof paper, a sixpence or threepenny bit. Christmas was also not complete without a large ham, which sat on the side table in the dining room, masses of mince pies and, of course, Christmas cake all made by mother. Christmas time was also panto and showtime. Father was wonderful, he used to take us every year to the theatre. I remember seeing Nellie Wallace as the Widow Twankey in *Aladdin*. Nat Jacklin was another name I remember, he used to come on stage, throw up some white pieces of paper above his head like snow, and shout, 'God! what a night'. We were also taken to see *Where the Rainbow Ends* where, at the end of the show, the children held prisoner by the wicked magician managed to make and hoist a flag and St George appeared in a great flash of light and defeated the magician. *Maskelyne and Devance* was another show, but this time it was one of magic and illusion. We were also taken to the *Bertram Mills Circus* at Olympia. For all of these shows, we were always taken up and back by taxi, usually provided by a local man, Mr Girling. Dick and I were also 'Gugnuncs', which was a children's club run by the *Daily Mirror* and based on the comic strip of Pip, Squeak and Wilfred. 'Gugnuncs' had a secret code to contact one another and, once, there was an enormous rally in the Albert Hall, to which mother took us. Much to our disappointment there was no sign of Wtskowski the Russian agent from the comic strip who was always planting bombs with his sidekick Popski, and whose plans were always foiled by either Pip, Squeak or Wilfred.

It was from this time onwards that we started getting visits by French girls whom Elinor knew from the school where she was teaching. They did not all come at once but the names I remember were, Simone Peschet, Yvonne and Edith de Blangy and Susanne Bethouard. I cannot remember whether it was the next term or the one after that we came back to find that Mr Eastwood, the headmaster, had died and his place had been taken by a Mr Meneer, who was the son of Mrs Eastwood by a previous marriage. 'Beery', as he was immediately nicknamed, was a tough old character who had lived in Australia for many years. He had served in the Australian artillery during the First World War and told us hair raising war stories. His wife was a former Miss Jellicoe and related to the famous admiral [George Jellicoe]. The school staff also changed. Fletcher Jones and Patrick left and were replaced by an Irishman, whose name I cannot remember and a certain Mr O'Neale. The latter had a bull nosed Morris car which was always reluctant to start. So, we used to push it to the nearby hill, give it a shove and as soon as the engine started, all jump on and ride on the running boards down to the bottom. How we never had an accident I will never know.

The arrival of the Meneer's brought an influx of new lads, in particular the three Kitto boys, John, Peter and Norman. John was my age, and we became great friends. Peter was more or less the same age as Dick, who had also now arrived at the school. Suddenly a great witch hunt was started. I think it was initiated by the Irish master who had noticed rude words written up in the outside lavatories and had heard boys talking about sex. We were all summoned to interviews with 'Beery' who asked us what we knew about the matter and told what a filthy thing sex was and that we must never talk about it again. One was made to feel very uncomfortable about the whole matter, and this attitude affected me for the whole of my life. One chap, Jackson, who was seen grinning after he came out of the interview was asked to leave. Mrs Meneer was very arty and introduced amateur dramatics to the school. I took the part of Hubert in *King John*, where I was supposed to be putting out the eyes of young Prince Arthur played by Barry Grierson. We also had a Christmas nativity play, in which I was one of the Three Kings. It was all great fun and set me off on the path of amateur dramatics, which would be put to good use in my years of incarceration. About 1930, rumours began to circulate about a possible move of the school and eventually, around 1931 or early 1932, we did go to an enormous house and grounds called Shendish at Kings Langley, Hertfordshire. It was a dream location, the gardens were extensive and wonderful to wander in. By this time John Kitto and I had become great friends, and both he and Peter used to come and stay at High Oak Lodge. John and I became joint head boys, and I was actually beginning to enjoy school life.

The next stage was to be St Peter's in York, and I had to take a scholarship exam. After the papers were submitted, I was given a roasting by 'Beery' because I had spelt 'translation' in this fashion. In the end I did not get a scholarship but was given, rather reluctantly, a small exhibition. When the result was announced I had a letter from a firm of photographers who had seen the notice of my award and wanted to photograph me. Proudly, I showed this to 'Beery' who immediately punctured my pride by saying that I did not do very well, so no photograph. Around the same time, for some reason, mother decided to employ a German girl to teach us boys German. I have no idea why. Anyhow, Truda arrived, I cannot remember her surname. We got on very well, but I don't think we learnt much German. She was not particularly beautiful, but a blonde, and caused quite a sensation in Ware. She was desperate to find a husband to give her British nationality because her mother was half Jewish and she was scared stiff of going back to Germany. Eventually, she married a Singhalese, which was a shame, but they went back to Ceylon where she had a baby boy and became very interested in gemmology, in which she eventually became an expert.

John (left) and Richard 'Dick' Dixon with their dog, Ben. (*Courtesy of The J B Dixon Collection*)

The final end of term at Shendish came in the summer of 1932 and after the holidays I went up to St Peter's in York. Suffice to say, with the exception of the last year, I was not a happy man, and I did not enjoy my stay there. I was a long, long way from home and whilst other boys' parents called fairly regularly, mother came up only twice in my four years there, and father only at the end of my last term. In addition, other boys seemed to have lots of money to buy sweets and extra food, whereas I had very, very little. Mother came up on the occasion of my confirmation in 1933, when I was confirmed by Dr Temple, the Archbishop of York. It was quite an occasion. I was in the school choir for some reason, but enjoyed myself there because we used to get out of prep to go to choir practice. Also, later when I became more senior and was supposed to sing bass, I had a nice little corner in the choir stall where I could go to sleep during the sermon. I really could not sing bass properly but as I sat just in front of Buzz Barby, the chaplain, I used to follow him. In my last year at school, I was a school monitor and with this privilege began to enjoy life a bit more. But, in retrospect, I felt my last year was a complete waste of time. I had passed all my exams and it would have been better if I had left earlier and been sent to Europe to learn a foreign language. Again, amateur dramatics were a great source of pleasure, and, except for the first term, I appeared in the school play every year.

So then to adult civilian life. I had no idea what I wanted to do. I went for several interviews, one of which was to Powers Samas, an early computer type firm, but none of them came to anything. Eventually, I was accepted by the Society of Motor Manufacturers as a trainee manager for the motor industry. The offices were at 83 Pall Mall, London, and I was first put into the overseas department under Alan Oliver Tookey, where I earned 25 shillings per week. The idea was that we should study for our B. Com degree and then be passed out into industry. I entered a course at the London Polytechnic but found the going very hard and failed my first exam. After a while, I was passed down to the statistical department, where I found life more congenial. There were quite a number of other chaps all doing the same thing, Vic Norlock, Henry Beckwith and three or more others whose names I have forgotten. I became a great pal of Vic who was a sub-lieutenant in the RNVR and he used to invite me along to nights on HMS *President*, which was great fun. Sadly, he contracted tuberculosis and had to leave the service, so did not serve in the [Second World War]. We used to play bridge during the lunch hours when we ate Eddie's lunches, which cost sixpence and consisted of two sandwiches, a piece of cake and a piece of fruit. When we were feeling flush, we used to go to the Brasserie at Lyons' Corner House in Coventry Street, where one could get a three-course lunch plus coffee for 1/6 pence. I'm afraid I did not do much work on my exam. Instead, I used to go to the cinema or wander around London on the evenings I was supposed to go to classes. I would catch the 12.04 pm train from Liverpool Street to Ware and mother would leave me Ovaltine in a thermos flask, with some sandwiches. Late in 1937, the Society of Motor Manufacturers and Traders decided to move to Hobart House in Grosvenor Place where we had offices on the first floor but you could go up on the roof and look over into the gardens of Buckingham Palace. The SMMT also ran an amateur dramatic society and I used to appear in all their plays, which ran for two or three nights at the Fortune Theatre. After Vic Norlock fell ill, he passed to me the secretaryship of the Number Plate Manufacturers' Association, which gave me a welcome income of £25 per year.

In 1938, I took the plunge and joined the Territorial Army becoming 7889568 Private Dixon, with the 22nd Royal Tank (Westminster Dragoons) Regiment. Their headquarters were in Elverton Street, not far from Victoria Street, and were great fun. At the same time, Geoff Whyntie, who had joined SMMT, also joined the Territorial Army, serving with the London Scottish. In March 1939, the Territorial Army was doubled in size, and I persuaded Peter Kitto to join the Royal Tank (Westminster Dragoons) Regiment as well. The Regiment then became 22nd Royal Tank (Westminster Dragoons) Regiment, and I became a trooper. We went to annual camp at Warminster and, as Peter had a car, we travelled down in it and used it while we were there. It was rather a riotous camp, and, on one occasion, I was given the task of driving one of the medium tanks but was unable to get it going, so the corporal in charge had to take it over. I don't think he realised that I had not yet passed a driving test!

Chapter 2

Very Basic Training

I was in the office on the afternoon of Friday, 1 September 1939, after Germany had invaded Poland, when I was told that the Territorial Army was being mobilised and I had to report to Regimental HQ immediately. I said goodbye to everybody, including Colonel McLagan the head of SMMT, and went round to Elverton Street, where I was told to come back the next morning. This I did, and was then kitted up and told to report again early on Monday. Geoff Whyntie and I had booked a holiday together for ten days in the south of France starting on the 9 September [1939], but of course this never happened.

On Sunday, 3 September [1939], I sat in front of the radio blancoing my equipment and finally listening to [Prime Minister Neville] Chamberlain saying we were now at war with Germany. Mother was rather upset but put on a brave face. It was on Monday, 4 September 1939, that I took the train to London and reported to HQ, where we were formed up and marched to Waterloo Station and then entrained for Blackdown, Dorset, where we were installed in uncompleted militia huts as No. 101 OCTU. Life at first was very strange, but helped by the fact that most of the people were known to me. We were formed into three companies. 'A' Company, collective training for the more experienced, plus two recruit training companies 'B' and 'C' of which I and my friends joined number one section of the

Trooper John Blomfield Dixon in the garden of High Oak Lodge, Ware, Hertfordshire, while serving with the 102nd Officer Training Unit, October 1939. A few months later he would be commissioned into the Royal Tank (Westminster Dragoons) Regiment at the age of 21.

former. The work was spasmodic at first, but gradually settled down into a routine of general principles of map reading, military law, gas etc. After two weeks in huts we were moved into barracks with the departure of Royal Berkshires, and after the first month, leave began to come in ever increasing quantities until it became an acknowledged fact that one obtained it every weekend unless on duty, which was very seldom.

During this time, often referred to as the 'Phoney War' period, I became great friends with Eric Duncan and when on courses at weekends we used to go over to Southbourne. I rode on the pillion of his motorbike, and we stayed in a hotel there. We met the Parry family in the hotel, who had been evacuated from London. A mother, an elder daughter about 14 years old named Betty, and two twin sisters. The father used to come down at weekends. We enjoyed their company and used to have the most hair-raising parties with our instructors all of whom got very drunk. Looking back, one is ashamed of the amount of leave one really did have at that time. In the third week, I left for a course at Bovington Camp, Dorset. Work here was much more strenuous, starting at 8.30 am in the morning and lasting until about 9.00 or 10.00 pm at night. The course consisted of four weeks into which was crammed some twelve weeks of work. Two weeks on general principles, one week on the A9, one week on the A13 Cruiser and the last week TP and exams and driving on both vehicles. The first I thought to be quite a useful tank, but underpowered and therefore difficult to handle. The second was definitely a step in the right direction, with a high-powered engine, delight full suspension, providing a good platform and very easy to handle. Both of course, in the light of after experience, had ridiculously little armour. Our weekend leaves were spent mostly at the Grange Hotel in Bournemouth, as it was too expensive to go home every week and hardly worth it from a time point of view. Eric's wife came down and we spent some evenings together. I left Bovington on the 11 November 1939 for Lulworth. Things were much slacker here and the week involved mostly practical work. Ammunition, of course, was ridiculously short, and we got very little firing practise. The instructors too did not strike me as well informed. Again, the course lasted four weeks but with no exam at the end. On Friday, 8 December 1939 I left Lulworth for home and a spot of weekend leave. Eric and I went by motorbike home from Waterloo, returning to Blackdown on the Sunday. The following morning, I started the wireless course, which was the worst organised course of the lot. Again, it lasted for four weeks, during which we learned little that we did not already know and spent most of the time running about in V8s or going over to Woking. Since our day finished at roughly 3.00 pm, we found ourselves on ten days Christmas leave from 21 December [1939]. I went to several shows and celebrated my twenty-first birthday at home, returning back to work on New Year's Day 1940. I started the last lap of the course on 15 January 1940. Six weeks tactical training, and one of the most interesting phases of our instruction. But ideas at that time were very hazy it seemed to me that there was not any definite direction as to how tanks should be used, apart from a few obvious principles. I then went on a fortnights leave on 27 January [1940], to allow a change over at Bovington, and on 12 February [1940] I began 'I' tank tactics. This was very much to my liking and something into which I should very much like to go. The course finished up with an exam, which as we were the first to pass out of the recruit companies was more in the nature of an experiment than anything else and we left for home on leave on 9 March [1940]. The course naturally finished up with a farewell party for the officers and the results of this in the barracks very nearly led to disaster. I managed to pass out Class 'B', but wished later that it might have been 'C' as in that case my future history might have been very different. As regards to the course as a whole, training was very sketchy. The technical training on the whole was good and I think we learned a lot, but of course owing to the compressed nature took quite a little assimilation. The other portion of the training left much to be desired although we were of course training for war, there were many duties of officers which were not dealt with at all. This may be put down admittedly to the newness of the scheme and also to the lack of training of those who were supposed to be training us. Leave too was ridiculous, and one realises now that a little more hard work would have been preferable and also continued checks on our knowledge, with a deal more delegation of authority in order to accustom us to leadership. Great preparations also occurred during these days as regards uniform, which required numerous expeditions to London.

The period from the beginning of March until April 1940 was one continued long holiday. Shortly after

The *London Gazette* of 9 March 1940 lists the cadets of 102nd OCTU who were commissioned as subalterns. Amongst them are John Blomfield Dixon and the men who were to serve with him in the East Riding Yeomanry, some of whom would never return from their deployment to France. (*Courtesy of The J B Dixon Collection*)

> The undermentioned Cadets, from 102nd Officer Cadet Training Unit, to be 2nd Lts. 9th Mar. 1940:—
> Tpr. Donald Marshal HALL (124420).
> Tpr. Peter Errington Guy LOBB (124425).
> Tpr. John Blomfield DIXON (124415).
> Tpr. Basil Fuller GODFREY (124419).
> Tpr. James HERRATT (124422).
> Tpr. Frederick William Edward JAMES (124424).
> Tpr. David Robert PETERS (124427).
> Tpr. Ian Ellerthorpe PHILP (124428).
> Tpr. Kenward Winton PHILP (124429).
> Tpr. Norman Townes PLOUGH (124430).
> Tpr. Norman Henry BONNER (124437).
> Tpr. Leonard Thomas BRABROOK (124411).
> Tpr. Gerald Anthony BUSBY (124412).
> Tpr. Charles Wilfred COYTE (124413).
> Tpr. Florimond Louis DESBOTTES (124414).
> Tpr. Eric Forster DUNCAN (124416).
> Tpr. Harold Heath DUPONT (124417).
> Tpr. Peter Holland GODDARD (124418).
> Tpr. Sydney John HENNINGS (124421).
> Tpr. Vincent Andrew HOLLOM (124423).
> Tpr. Lowther Henry MOORMAN (124426).
> Tpr. Philip Morgan PUDDICOMBE (124431).
> Tpr. Frederick Charles SCARBOROUGH (124432).
> Tpr. Ronald Walter STEPHENS (124433).
> Tpr. John Dudley STOWARD (124434).
> Tpr. Patrick Andrew TOMLIN (124435).
> Tpr. Albert Percy TURNER (124436).

being Gazetted, I received orders that I was to join the 51st Training Regiment at Catterick on 1 April, which was later postponed until 6 April. All my friends we're going to Westminster, so I was dearly disappointed when I learned this and also that the training regiment was a cavalry unit. Our arrival at Catterick was with a great deal of trepidation upon our past, but really unnecessary. After the preliminary settling in I was given a section of militia to take over, who had just started their training. It is laughable to think that I had such a position. I hardly knew anything myself and, as we were left entirely on our own and given no help except a copy of a timetable to adhere too, it was difficult to know exactly where to start. Still, after three or four weeks I had them under me. Whether I taught them anything or not is a rather stupid question to start worrying about now. Although officers are supposed to show initiative, it was a little difficult to get a grip of things, especially as we were given no help on top of our meagre training. But this was not to last long. No sooner had we begun to settle down than all of us received orders to proceed to France on attachment to the East Riding Yeomanry. At that time, of course, we were delirious with delight and could hardly think for excitement. We were given forty-eight hours leave and had to be back on the 27 April. We finally left Catterick on the evening of the 30 April and set sail for France from Southampton the next day.

Apart from those officers who would join John Blomfield Dixon in the East Riding Yeomanry and become casualties of the fighting in the retreat to Dunkirk, two other cadets of 102nd OCTU would lose their lives, both serving with elements of the special forces.

In October 1943, Captain James Herratt was posted to the Albanian Section of the Special Operations Executive. He had originally been recruited for operations, but became the section's welfare officer when no field employment was found for him. His duties were to deal with the welfare of operational personnel. He sent out books, mail and other comforts to the missions in Albania, censored personal mail meant for home and tried to deal with endless minor crises like finding and despatching new spectacles to

Gravestone of Captain James Herratt, 2nd County of London Yeomanry (Westminster Dragoons). He died on 26 September 1944, aged 29 and is buried in Bari Cemetery, Italy. (*Courtesy of The War Graves Photographic Project*)

replace pairs broken in the field. Tragically, after the Albanian Section moved to Bari in Italy, Jim Herratt, was rushed to hospital on 21 September 1944, dangerously ill with poliomyelitis. He succumbed to the illness five days later.

Peter Goddard was killed in action on 3 September 1944, as a consequence of what some regard as rather reckless behaviour. He was in command of a three man team who were in the small village of Tannay. Whilst eating lunch in a café with members of the Marquis, the sound of artillery could be heard in the distance. This came from a German armoured column, who were attacking a Marquis enclave north of nearby Ouagne. It appears the partisans rashly decided to make a frontal assault on the enemy and Goddard offered to support them, by attacking the German column from the rear. As two of his men, Lilley and Howe, turned a bend at the hamlet of Plessis, they found the Germans in front of them, who then began firing a flak gun at them. As shells smashed into the distant buildings, Goddard, who had arrived at the same location, announced he was going to capture the gun. Lilley, who had seen no sign of the Maquis, warned Goddard against this move, but Goddard insisted. Grabbing the single Vickers from the driver's side of Lilley's jeep, he shouted 'You cover me', and sprinted down a ditch. Despite covering fire being provided by Lilley, Goddard was spotted by the Germans who enfiladed him before he had gone 100 yards, killing him instantly. His body was taken to Tannay and interred in the communal cemetery, where it remains today.

Lieutenant Peter Holland Goddard, 'C' Squadron, 1st Special Air Service Regiment. He was killed in action on 3 September 1944 during Operation Kipling and is buried in the Tannay Communal Cemetery, France. (*Courtesy of Special Forces Roll of Honour*)

The grave of Lieutenant Peter Holland Goddard. (*Courtesy of The War Graves Photographic Project*)

Chapter 3

With the BEF: A Diary of Combat

Wednesday, 1 May 1940

Arrived at Le Havre at about 10.00 am having lost the convoy in transit. We were hurried off the boat and onto a train for the RAC base camp at Bonnieres. Here we caught up with some of the other former Westminster Dragoons who had been at Warminster. They were leaving on attachments in the morning. Norman Bonner amongst them. As the camp had only just been started there was practically nothing doing. One day we were taken out on a TEWT by a cavalry major and even with our meagre knowledge managed to get him all confused. I was given the job of censor officer, quite a tedious job as most of the letters were very ordinary. There was, however, one which was griping at the British Army and its officers and taking a very pro-German attitude as well as making treasonable remarks. The chief censor officer had the chap up, gave him a rocket and warning, then tore up his letter.

The unit war diary for the East Riding Yeomanry records the arrival of four subalterns from the Royal Armoured Corps Base Depot on Sunday, 5 May 1940, Bonner, Brabrook, Coyte and Dupont. Second Lieutenant John Blomfield Dixon is listed as arriving the following day.

Wednesday, 8 May 1940

Received orders today to join the ERY tomorrow. Very excited and all the others very jealous. Threw the hell of a party in the evening and Jim Herratt (ex-WD) had to put me to bed.

Thursday, 9 May 1940

Left after lunch in a 30cwt with three other ranks. Had to call at various HQs to deliver messages. Finally arrived at Irvy-la-Bataille and found only the QM and RSM at home. Most of the others were on an exercise. Had tea at RHQ and then had a short interview with the adjutant and the colonel. I was assigned to 'B' squadron under Major Wade and found Coyte and Dupont there. My billets were about 1 mile away, and I had great difficulty in getting in as the landlady was shocked by my dirty valise. I had dinner in the mess and afterwards was left alone with the squadron French liaison officer, Bouganowski, as the others were on night driving. I had my last bath but the geyser would not work properly.

At 9.00 pm on 9 May [1940], the code word 'Danzig' was relayed to all German army divisions, beginning what was known as '*Fall Gelb*', the assault on France, Belgium and the Low Countries. Commonly referred to as the *Blitzkrieg* or the Battle of France, German forces launched their offensive into the Netherlands and Belgium. On the morning of 10 May [1940], *Fallschirmjäger* executed surprise landings at The Hague, on the road to Rotterdam and against the Belgian Fort Eben-Emael which helped the advance of German ground forces. The French command reacted immediately, sending the 1st Army Group north in accordance with their plan, which committed their best forces, diminishing their fighting power by the partial disorganisation it caused and their mobility by depleting their fuel stocks.

For the men of the East Riding Yeomanry an intense period of continuous movement now began, one that would see them in combat with the fast-advancing enemy and would bring about the loss of a number of their officers and men. John Blomfield Dixon, a supernumerary officer with the regiment, would find himself amid the resulting chaos, recording the daily events as best he could.

Friday, 10 May 1940
Arrived at SHQ in time to hear that the blitz had started. George Wade told me that I was being transferred to 'C' Squadron at Nantilly. Duly arrived there after tea where I was very warmly welcomed. The OC is Major Radcliffe and there is a very different atmosphere to 'B' Squadron. Was given a billet in the mess with Len Brabrook who had arrived earlier.

Saturday, 11 May 1940
Attached to No. 5 troop under John Cockin. This is a carrier troop and both Len and I are really superfluous. The troop in which Len finds himself is commanded by a TSM, a very invidious position. Neither of us have any training in this type of vehicle or in divisional cavalry work. We both of us were trained on A9s and A13s as part of an armoured regiment. I was issued with a .38 revolver but only three rounds available and no lanyard! Nothing very much happening, so Len and I went over to the base camp to see if they had any equipment to spare such as binoculars and more ammunition.

Sunday, 12 May 1940
Squadron TEWT work done. Finished up in a restaurant high up overlooking the [river] Seine, sitting in the sun and drinking champagne cocktails provided by Geoffrey Ratcliffe. Parachute scare in the evening.

Monday, 13 May 1940

Dick Hudson set off in charge of the Forward party. I went over to the Base Camp to try again for some binoculars but no luck. Others there all very excited and wanted to know what we were doing but we were under orders not to say anything. I think they realised we were off, but we were told that we were going further forward for advanced training. I actually believed it! Along with the Fife and Forfar Yeomanry we now formed the 1st Armoured Reconnaissance Brigade.

Tuesday, 14 May 1940

At the last minute I was transferred from the rail to the road party and left in company with the other Squadron road parties. We went via Beauvais, and all along the route the people came out to cheer us. We had to keep a sharp look out for aircraft and the roads were filled with streams of expensive looking cars, refugees with hand carts, bicycles and on foot, all fleeing from Belgium. We passed a large number of war cemeteries and place names made familiar by the last war. Stopped for the night at a small village of Ascq 1 mile or 2 from the Belgian border, where the inhabitants were terrified of us because they thought we would attract the bombers.

Wednesday, 15 May 1940

Left behind with Bernard LeMaitre, the squadron's French liaison officer, to settle up with the Mairie.

Drove in his own private car escorted by four motor cyclists and arrived at Chéreng, south-west of Lille in the afternoon. Settled into a small but very comfortable billet and the landlady was kindness itself. She couldn't do enough for me, and I got her to do some laundry. During the night there was an air-raid and the AA fired straight over the top of the house.

Thursday, 16 May 1940

Rail party arrived last night, and today was spent digging trenches. Our first sight of aircraft.

About fifty Germans raided Tournai during the afternoon. French AA very inaccurate but our fighters brought down one, the pilot of which jumped, but his parachute failed to open, and he made a nasty hole in the ground. Roadblocks and guards set out at night, and we were warned to prepare for an 'exercise' early next morning.

Friday, 17 May 1940

Roused at 4.00 am and told my batman to pack. Orders to move came at 5.30 am for the 'exercise' and we left Chéreng at 7.30 am, the landlady waving me tearful farewell from the pavement. I was completely superfluous as I was under the command of John Cockin still, taking the place of one of his Lance Corporals who was away on leave, and found myself in charge of a carrier. Passed through Tournai and arrived at some woods north of Ath at about 10.30 am. Here 'C' Squadron stayed for the remainder of the day and by this time I realised that this was no exercise. All day long we could hear the rumble of gunfire away to the west. Refugees on foot poured past us all day long, in contrast to the hundreds of cars which had passed us on our way up.

Saturday, 18 May 1940
Stand to at 3.00 am. Spent the day cleaning Brens and sleeping. I kept guard at night turn by turn with the men. Orders came to move at 4.30 pm and we went to woods north of Wadlincourt. Just before reaching them German bombers passed over on the way to Tournai and machine gunned us. We shifted ourselves pretty rapidly as we thought they might come back and strafe us again. CO's conference at 11.00 pm in Wadlincourt. The Germans had apparently broken through the French line, and we had to hold the Blaton Canal until further orders. The Fifes were supposed to be on our right and the 12th Lancers on our left. Neither of them actually turned up.

Sunday, 19 May 1940
Took up position on Blaton Canal at 1.00 am. 'B' Squadron troops doubling up with ours. No. 5 Troop had the bridge at Grandglise. My carrier was in a farmyard on the left. At a house just below the bridge John Cockin decided to take up a position and we upset the inhabitants badly when we said that we should have to knock a hole in the wall. It was very eerie but luckily there was hardly any traffic, as in the dark we were unable to distinguish the nationality of the vehicles. At 3.00 am we were recalled back nearly as far as Wadlincourt, where we bivouacked in a field and had breakfast. We were surrounded by cows all in extreme agony with swollen udders and mooing like mad. At 6.00 am we suddenly received orders to go back to our original positions but this time without 'B' Squadron. John Cockin first gave me a position in a house the other side of the canal, very comfortable with a good field of fire, but no sooner had we got the guns in position and barricaded, than he changed his mind and put me on a bridge to the left of the main one that had only just been discovered. My men and I spent ages trying to work out a satisfactory position as we were rather exposed. The sun was boiling hot and eventually I let the others go to sleep while I kept watch. This bridge was part of a deserted gas works and it was queer to be there with hardly a sound and not a soul stirring. Saw vague figures moving in the distance once or twice but it was too far to

distinguish them. At 11.30 am troops withdrew independently. Still no sign of the Germans although we heard afterwards that our troop was followed at a distance by German armoured cars. Attacked by a German fighter (ME109) which in turn was shot down by two Spitfires. Crossed the river at St Antoine and at 3.00 pm arrived back at Chéreng, which was now completely deserted. Long streams of vehicles kept on passing through and finally at about 8.00 pm the whole Regiment lined up and we set off for some woods southwest of Phalempin. When darkness set in there was chaos. Most of us had had our last sleep on 17th and in addition to this had covered enormous mileages. The roads were thick with traffic and halts were frequent. At one halt both the driver and I fell asleep, waking up with a start to find the road ahead completely empty. By dint of hard driving and entire luck we caught up with the others further on.

Monday, 20 May 1940

Arrived at the woods absolutely exhausted at about 2.00 am and immediately fell asleep in our vehicle with no guard at all. Fortunately, nobody found this out and it seems others did the same. Several lost sheep turned up during the day having lost the way or had breakdowns. Spent the whole day in the woods resting and digging trenches. Had a much-needed bath in a stagnant pool. Constant alarms of aircraft. Heard the tragic news that John's brother Phil

Second Lieutenant Philip Maitland Cockin was killed by friendly fire on 18 May 1940, his tank being struck by a shell from a British anti-tank unit. His burial location is unknown, and his name is recorded on Column 5 of the Dunkirk Memorial. (*Both courtesy of The J B Dixon Collection*)

(Cockin), of 'A' Squadron, had been shot up and killed by our own anti-tank gunners when returning from patrol.

Tuesday, 21 May 1940

Stood to at 3.00 am. Did some more digging. Mills bombs, anti-tank mines and the squadron library suddenly arrived. Sudden orders to stand to and move at 1.00 pm, which were cancelled almost immediately. Got the wireless working for the one and only time and listened to the news. Heard that the Germans were in Arras and Abbeville and realised that things were getting a bit serious. One of the things that stands out in one's mind once again is the number of cows deserted in the fields and bellowing in pain from distended udders. We have done our best to relieve them whenever it was possible and we had the time, but there are literally hundreds of them. I have come to the conclusion that I do not like milk straight from the cow! Orders came to move again at 11.30 pm.

Wednesday, 22 May 1940

Moved through Seclin and Lille at 4.00 am and arrived at some woods near Victe at about 10.30 am. '8' did a 'demonstration of force' in the afternoon. Greatly troubled by artillery which shelled the woods all afternoon. Observation being given by a balloon which sailed serenely undisturbed in the sky in front. Luckily there were no casualties. At 7.30 pm received urgent orders to move, and on coming out of the wood encountered a very frightened Brigadier who asked frantically for Major Radcliffe. He said the Germans had broken through our lines and that 44th Division Headquarters was surrounded. Geoffrey took it all very quietly and soon had us moving out quickly on separate roads with orders to clear each one and then report to him further on. Apart from quite heavy shelling and a little desultory small arms fire there were no Germans actually to be seen. No. 5 Troop took up rear guard position spread out with the rest of the Squadron to withdraw 44th Division and they came through us gradually all during the night with very little disturbance.

Thursday, 23 May 1940

The division having passed through us, we withdrew ourselves at 2.00 am to a village some miles east of Courtrai where we dug in again. No sign of the Germans, however, and at 7.00 am we went back through Courtrai where the bridges were already mined and went into bivouac in some woods to the east of the Gheluvelt-Menin road. On the way we stopped at a shop and bought some chocolate and bread as our supplies were running low. Spent the remainder of the day resting again.

Friday, 24 May 1940

At 12.00 pm left for Hazebrouck. When nearly there we were stopped on the main road to Lens and La Bassee to take up defensive positions, as German tanks and armoured cars were reported to have broken through. This proved to be false and we at length proceeded on our way to take up defensive positions on the railway line north-west of Hazebrouck. The road into the town ran dead straight and the Germans were bombing the town like mad. A great pall of smoke rose over it and explosions shook the air. We passed '8' at the side of the road (they were going into reserve). Bill Coyte told me later that he never expected to see me again, and I must say the thought of going through that lot was not making me feel very happy. Luckily our road skirted the side of the town, so we managed to avoid most of the bombing. On reaching the railway John and I took sides of a level crossing. We mined the road, greatly inconvenienced by the protestations from the crossing keeper who said mines exploding would break his windows. German aircraft were very much in evidence, more than we had seen up to date, and we had to lie very low.

Saturday, 25 May 1940

Up most of the night as the men were so tired, felt I had to give them a bit of rest. Squadron after squadron of German aircraft passed over the positions during the day and bombed the surrounding towns. Shortly after mid-day, reconnaissance planes came over and proceeded to write our positions in the sky. We expected dive bombers or artillery shortly after, but nothing happened and at 4.00 pm we were withdrawn to a farm north of St Sylvestre.

Sunday, 26 May 1940

Spent the morning doing much needed maintenance. It was impossible to do much, but we managed to tighten up some tracks and make other superficial adjustments. At 5.00 pm the squadron was sent out on patrol, our troop going to the Forêt de Clairmarais north of the Forêt de Nieppe. Our objective was to locate the armoured forces of the Germans who were known to be somewhere in the region. My carrier led and, owing to a faulty bit of map reading, which did not become apparent.

until later, I led the Troop to a wood which was actually a small adjunct just north of Clairmarais. This was the one and only time I ever had a map in my hand. It only meant that we had not come as far as we ought to have done by about 300 yards, but I was very shamefaced when it became apparent. As events turned out it was just as well, as otherwise we should have run into the same German anti-tank nest which hit Harold Hopper. I went ahead on foot to reconnoitre and coming round a corner I saw some French civvies in the road. They saw me at the same time and literally scuttled back into a house. We pushed on up to the house in the carrier and got out to see if we could find out any information. I saw them peeping round the curtains at us and when they saw we were British they came out very excitedly and told us that German reconnaissance vehicles had been through many times. So, we pushed on and arrived at the wood we should have been in the first place. As we arrived, we heard the sound of heavy firing further along the road we had just left. It was mainly small arms fire but also what sounded like a 2-pounder. However, we didn't pay much attention and John and I left the carriers in the charge of Sergeant Clare and set off on foot through the wood. Alongside we found tracks by the hundreds of a very large size and decided that this was hardly the sort of stuff that could be tackled by carriers. It was here that my map reading error became apparent as there was a gap of about 300 yards between our wood and the real Clairmarais. While we were debating whether to go back for the carrier or cross the gap on foot we were attracted by shots from the rear. Sergeant Clare was evidently excited about something, and we hurried back to learn that Geoffrey had rung up to order us back at once. We got back so far to a road junction on the return route and were here ordered to take up temporary defensive positions. It was here that we learnt that Harold's Troop had met an anti-tank nest; his front carrier had been knocked out and the other two escaped with casualties. Eventually we arrived back at the farm at about 8.00 pm.

Monday, 27 May 1940
Started to do a bit more maintenance. Continuous firing all the way around us during the morning but nobody seemed to be worried or do anything about it. We were told later it was aircraft machine gunning. At Just before 11.00 am four ambulances passed along the side road leading to St. Sylvestre. About two minutes later they came racing back with the news that German tanks were just entering the village. Shells now began to arrive from what seemed all directions and Geoffrey shouted, 'Get out everybody as fast as you can.' Thank God all the tracks were back on, and with a good deal of undignified scuffling everybody did get out and shot down to the left, which joined up with the Steenvoorde road. Troops were split up all over the place but about three complete carrier troops, of which we were one, were together and we got into a field on the side of the Steenvoorde road. We were immediately shelled and decided to move to a wood just the other side of Steenvoorde. 'B' Echelon caught it badly as they were nearest the Germans. On arriving at the wood, Roger Waterhouse, who was the senior, sent out scouts to pick up what information they could about the rest of the squadron. They came back with the news, which they had

obtained from a Military Policeman, that our vehicles had been seen moving up the road to Dunkirk. We were just about to follow when a despatch rider from Geoffrey arrived and summoned us to join him urgently on the Steenvoorde-Cassel road. On coming up to the position we were heavily shelled and had to scatter. I put my carrier behind a house and in so doing lost touch with the others. I reconnoitred on foot until I found them and was given a lift on the track guard of another carrier to SHQ. Had a very bumpy and unpleasant ride as it was difficult to hold on and, in addition, we were being machine gunned by the Germans. Found John at last and we took up our positions on the side of the road and spent a very uneventful afternoon, except for being fired on once or twice from the rear. At 7.00 pm we withdrew with our carriers and harboured in a field west of the Mont de Recollet. At 8.00 pm we were told to load up one carrier with all the weapons and ammunition and proceed up to the side of the Mont. Having arrived here the carrier was unloaded, and we dug weapon pits on the far side of the hill and were told that we were to defend these to the last man and last round. The positions were very bad as there was no field of fire. Although the ground fell right away in front of us so that it was almost impossible to attack from the front, there were trees all round and at the bottom so that any attacker had plenty of cover. It rained heavily during the night and was most unpleasant.

Tuesday, 28 May 1940

All during the night German verey lights were going up continuously and with daybreak they shelled us slowly but continuously all morning. At 12.00 pm we were withdrawn to the previous harbour and given orders to move to Bergues with the Welsh Guards in order to hold off German attacks from that quarter. No move took place, however, and we sat still for the next hour in the pelting rain. Finally, orders came through that we were to move into Cassel, while the Fife and Forfars went back to Bergues. We were very disappointed as the only time the Fifes had been in action had been on the Ath front and since then we had done all the dirty work. Brigade HQ went with the Fifes, and we were attached to 145 Brigade under Brigadier Somerset. At 3.00 pm we moved into Cassel and took positions alongside the main road, which ran up to the top of the hill and facing down the valley. The town was devastated. Dead bodies lay about all over the place and burnt-out trucks and debris covered the side of the road. Behind our position was a small hovel in which the troop slept while a guard was kept in the weapon pit facing down the valley. We were all soaking wet and managed to get a fire going. It was very difficult to keep awake when on guard.

Wednesday, 29 May 1940

On guard all day long. Could see German vehicles moving in the distance and they dive bombed Steenvoorde. Food supplies were running short, but we were lucky to find a dump with all sorts of delicacies on which we gorged ourselves. At 2.00 pm I was detailed to take out a patrol in conjunction with the Ox and Bucks to look for Germans in the wood to the south-west. On arrival at the Ox and Bucks HQ I immediately had to take cover from some short but heavy shelling. Then we set out and the plan was that my troops would cover the Ox and Bucks from the château while they went into the wood. This we did, but it involved lying amongst numerous dead horses whose bodies were extremely bloated and the smell was ghastly. Sergeant Clare and I were together, he with his rifle and me with a revolver. If the Germans had arrived, we hadn't got much to hit back with, but I thought it better that we should be separated from the Bren in order to give it some form of cover. The cellars of the château were swarming with refugees who came out furtively at intervals to fetch water. There was no result from the patrol, however, and after about an hour the Ox and Bucks came back, and we all returned under another short spell of shelling. At 8.00 pm we received orders to move at midnight. The whole Brigade was moving by a certain route to rendezvous on the canal surrounding Dunkirk. I only received a very hurried version of these orders so that all I knew was the approximate route, the rendezvous and the possibility that the enemy might be met enroute. I had no map or compass. We were to be the last to leave Cassel and all vehicles other than the carriers were to be destroyed. The infantry started coming out at dark and from then until midnight they came past our positions in a long stream.

Thursday, 30 May 1940

Just after midnight we climbed into our carriers and proceeded out of Cassel. Progress was very slow as the infantry were in front of us. By the time day broke we had not gone more than 2 to 3 miles and on reaching Winnezeele heavy firing broke out in front. Nobody knew what was happening and the entire column came to a halt, finally getting off to the side of the road. From here the regiment started to go over the fields with only a vague idea as to what was actually happening. We were continually engaged from every side by some kind of fire and the squadrons became inextricably mixed. We were held up by enemy fire round Le Droogland, and 'C' Squadron deployed to the west of the road. Our troop observed a small German anti-tank gun firing from about 600 yards away. We fired several bursts of Bren at it, which appeared to knock it out. At about 6.00 am we halted and made rendezvous with Geoffrey Radcliffe

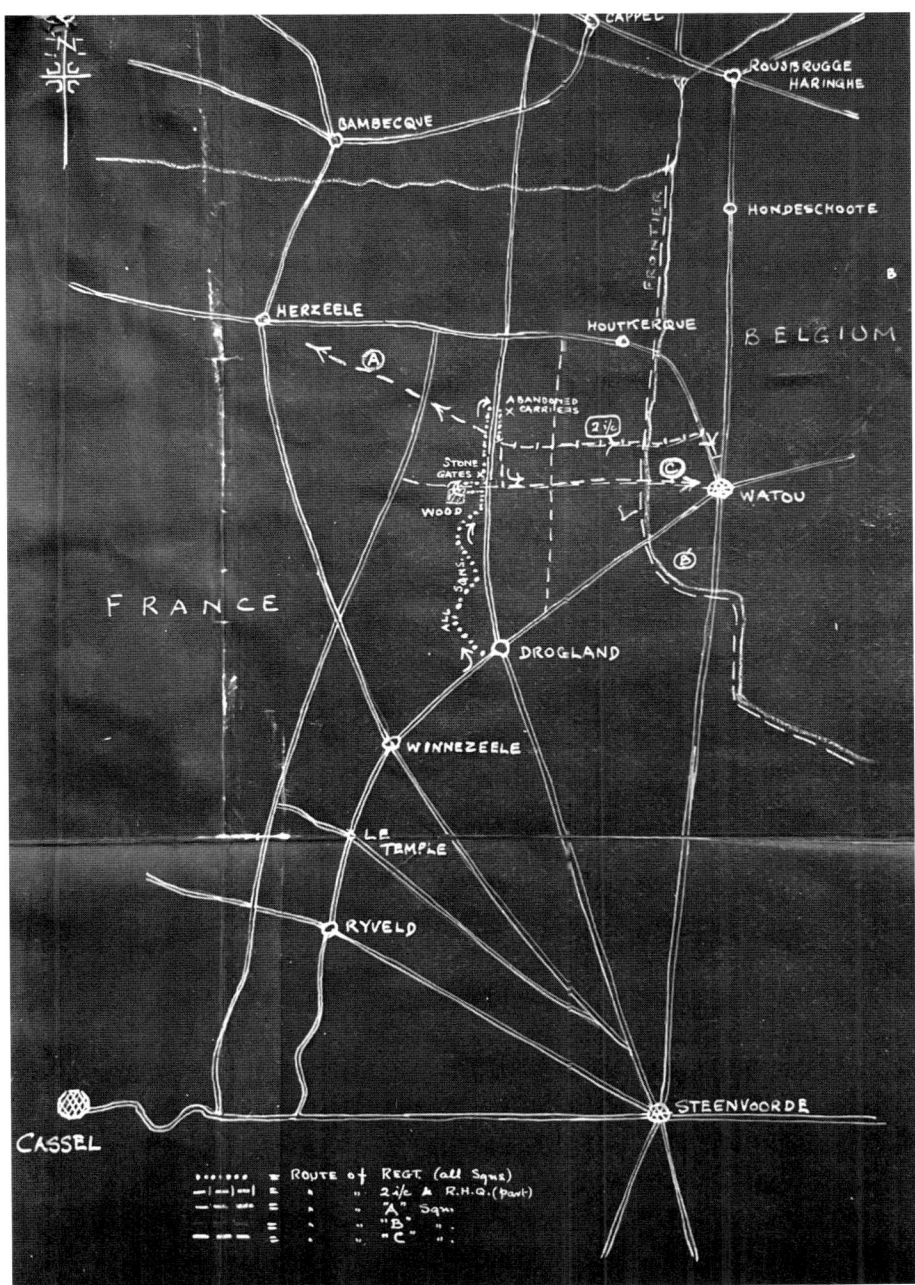

The Final Assault. This map, taken from the unit war diary of the East Riding Yeomanry, shows the location of 'C' Squadron on 30 May 1940. The lack of communication prevented the senior officers from understanding what had taken place that morning. The diary of John Blomfield Dixon fills in a number of gaps, including what happened to the commander of No. 5 Troop, John Cockin. (*Courtesy of The National Archives – WO167/457*)

in a wood west-south-west of Watou. It was decided that the squadron would separate, and each troop would make its own way as best they could. Geoffrey then went off at high speed on his own and was not seen alive again. No. 5 Troop accompanied by No. 6 Troop attempted to work round Watou to the west towards Houtkerque. I followed John Cockin but at about 6.45 am we came under heavy enemy fire and John considered it advisable to change direction and attempt a route to the East of Watou. By this time, we had picked up all sorts and kinds of other regiments, who were either riding on or following the carriers. We also appeared to have lost two of the carriers from No. 6 Troop. Proceeding east towards Watou, and having crossed a stream, we turned north. Once again, we were fired on and Trooper Short was hit in the ankle.

John headed towards a road entering Watou from the south-east. We were in extended echelon from the left and the two carriers in front of me ran straight onto the road, followed further to the right by my carrier and that of Sergeant Clare. Anti-tank guns fired somewhere from the front and John's carrier and the other disappeared in a cloud of smoke. My carrier and that of Sergeant Clare plunged head first into a deep ditch at the side of the road and stuck. The force of the impact threw me and the gunner, Trooper Cyril Dodsworth, out of the carrier into the middle of the road where we had bullets whizzing over

As he saw it. British troops captured on 30 May 1940, stand gloomily in the village square at Watou, Belgium. It was amidst this scene that John Blomfield Dixon helped to carry the wounded Trooper Short to a dressing station, after which he was held captive in a local house, fearing that he was about to be shot. (*Courtesy of John West, http://140th-field-regiment-ra-1940.co.uk*)

our heads from a machine gun further down the road. We rolled into a ditch on the opposite side and lay there for a few seconds. I felt for my revolver, but this had gone. Having no lanyard, it must have fallen out of the holster. Almost immediately Germans came over the top of the bank and took us [as] PoWs. What humiliation!

We were marched into the village of Watou. As Trooper Thomas McCeag Shortt was badly wounded, we carried him on a table, together with another wounded chap, to the dressing station. From here we were led to the square where all the other PoWs were gathered. Norman Bonner, who had been nicked by a bullet on his right thumb, was the first one I recognised and from him I learnt

Second Lieutenant Leonard Thomas Brabrook (Centre) was amongst the subalterns who were attached to the ERY with John Blomfield Dixon at the beginning of May 1940. Described by Norman Bonner as 'one of the nicest men I had ever met', he was killed in action on the day John Blomfield Dixon was taken as a PoW. Originally buried at Watou in a small cemetery created for civilian victims of an earlier air raid, his body was reinterred at Hotton War Cemetery, Belgium, on 22 January 1948. (*Photo courtesy of John West*)

Trooper Thomas McCeag Shortt, the badly wounded soldier John Blomfield Dixon helped to carry on a table, would eventually succumb to his injuries on 23 December 1940. Trooper Short was transported to Stalag IX-C near Bad Sulza, Germany. Here was a large hospital in the town of Obermaßfeld, south-west of Erfurt. There was a smaller hospital Reserve-Lazaret IX-C(b) at Meiningen, which is where he died and was originally buried. His body was reinterred in the Berlin 1939–1945 War Cemetery, Germany, on 19 March 1948. (*Courtesy of The War Graves Photographic Project*)

that John Hodgson was also a PoW. Of the others from the regiment, one could learn nothing, except that it was thought a good many had been killed though nothing definite. I was depressed as hell and had no food into the bargain. All my kit had been lost in the carrier or been taken from me. Norman, however, had a tin of Libby's bully beef and his emergency ration, which he very kindly shared with me. Later on, officers were separated from the men and moved into a house where we could get water. Here we were joined by Colonel Thompson and Brian Reid and I quite expected to be put against a wall and shot, as parties of men were continually being marched away followed by what seemed to be firing in the distance. However, in the evening officers were moved by lorry to Steenvoorde. The guards on my lorry were not as generous as on some of the others, but they did give me a small piece of bread to eat. The last of my cigarettes had gone. At Steenvoorde we were put in a deserted café, which had been rather badly bombed. Here we spent the night being lucky enough to pick up spoons and forks, but knives were not allowed, although I managed to find a pair of scissors. Casualties in our squadron alone that morning were very heavy. At the time I thought that I was the only one left alive of the officers, out of nine in the squadron. Major Radcliffe, Captain Sissons and lieutenants Hudson, Cockin and Brabrook were all killed. What the losses amongst the men were we still do not know but 'missing' lists received over a year later put the figure at over 25 per cent and they were probably much higher.

In his report detailing the withdrawal to Dunkirk, the commanding officer of the East Riding Yeomanry, Colonel William Douglas Baird Thompson DSO MC CdG lists the names of officers of the regiment, but does not include the names of those subalterns who were attached to the East Riding Yeomanry, one of whom, Second Lieutenant Leonard Thomas Brabrook, would lose his life during the attempt to reach the Belgian coast.

The official records for the East Riding Yeomanry show that only 9 officers and 215 other ranks were evacuated from Dunkirk. They disembarked at several different Channel ports in England and were attached to a variation of units until they were eventually collected together at Bovington Camp, Dorset. Of those officers who had joined the regiment along with John Blomfield Dixon, Second Lieutenant Leonard Brabrook had been killed in action on 30 May 1940, second lieutenants Charles Wilfred Coyte and Harold Heath Dupont had made it home and Second Lieutenant Norman Bonner marched with them into captivity.

Chapter 4

Entering Captivity

Friday, 31 May 1940

At 4.00 am we were roused and started on an 8km march to Hazebrouck. Everywhere there were signs of destruction, burnt out vehicles and bomb holes. On arrival in the town we were searched again and shoved into a cellar by a very loud-mouthed NCO, a bullying man who snatched sticks from some of the British officers and flung them across the street. Norman and I managed to obtain water bottles here and I made a sort of towel and some soap. After a while we were taken upstairs and put into a schoolroom. We were very hungry and at about noon we were given a very thin soup with lumps of uneatable fat in it, as well as some large Belgian biscuits, which had a rather bitter taste. About 2.00 pm we were on the move again and at about 7.00 pm arrived at Lillers after a 23km foot march. Here we sank tired into a field but were almost immediately loaded into lorries and taken to a farm at Hesdin. Here we had most pleasant surprise. A woman on the farm gave us some milk for a start and the camp commandant, who was not expecting us, split his men's rations with us and we got one third of a loaf of bread each and nearly a full tin of meat paste with lashings of rum and tea! It was wonderful and after a night spent on straw in a barn, we had ersatz coffee the next morning and the remains of the last night's rations. Norman's wound had, by now, turned septic and was dressed by the medial officer, Major Lawson.

Saturday, 1 June 1940

After breakfast we were sent by lorry to Arras where we were quartered in the memorial chapel of a French barracks and given some stew and a small portion of bread. Almost immediately, however, we were shifted and marched 29km to Lecluse. It was a dreadful trip. The guards lost their way and we seemed to go on and on and round in circles. When at last we did arrive, we found ourselves in a large open air camp which was divided into barbed wire pens. These were occupied by French, Belgian and Colonial troops. The smell was appalling but were so tired we just dropped where we stood and went to sleep.

Sunday, 2 June 1940

Hot as blazes today again. About 11.00 am we were given a dish of macaroni from large wine barrels on carts, and I managed to keep the bowl. My belongings are growing as I had also been able to obtain a cup and a makeshift towel, which I shared with Norman. He and I discussed the possibility of escaping from the line of march. Unfortunately, we had no food, which was possibly not insuperable, but we had no map, no compass and not the faintest idea what was happening, and therefore in which direction to head. In addition, we had noticed that after each halt a posse of guards were sent back along the route. So, we decided to leave it until a better opportunity arose and we might be better prepared. In the afternoon the British and French officers, about thirty of us, were taken by transport to Cambrai and there transferred to larger vehicles and, together with other ranks, carried on to Avesnes. Here the camp was situated in an old cotton wool mill and the guards were real L of C Prussian types. Our tin hats were literally knocked off our heads as we entered the mill, and we were shouted at and abused the whole time. We found some other English officers there too, but they were shut up in a coal shed. There were also Frenchmen, but they would not allow us to move in with them. So, we had to spend the night in the open on bales of cotton wool, which wasn't too bad. Norman and I were given a small portion of tinned tongue and some bread and then managed to get some thin stew. Our clothes by this time were getting decidedly beasty as we had had no proper wash for days.

Monday, 3 June 1940

Dick's birthday! I remembered it the first thing when I woke up. I wonder what they are all doing? What a long time it seems since this time last year. For the first time in captivity, I'm beginning to get a bit homesick. I suppose the initial shock has now worn off and I am coming to face with reality.

Today we marched 26km to Rance. The march lasted six hours with only one five-minute halt.

On the way, every now and then, great JU52s would lumber overhead so low it seemed one could almost touch them. It made one realise how well prepared the Hun were. We were quartered in a girl's school. On the way I managed to get a piece of rhubarb, which I shared with Norman. At the school we all managed to get a complete wash and soon afterwards we were put on transport and shifted. This was a most pleasant ride, if one can use such a term. We were approaching the Ardennes and the scenery was marvellous. Once we stopped for an hour and a half in a village where the inhabitants were most kind. Norman and I managed to get some milk and an egg, which we ate raw. Saunders also got some jam, which tasted marvellous on what bread we had left. This behaviour was not unusual from the civilians but usually they were shouted at and roughly pushed out of the way by the guards and the offerings dashed to the ground. Our journey passed through Dinant, which was beautiful, and we decided that, should it be possible, we would visit it after the war with Eric Duncan, Ken and Ian Philp.

(Note: these were all ex-Westminster Dragoons with whom Norman and I were commissioned. Eric and Ken got back to England and went out to the desert where they were both killed. Eric (Eric Forster Duncan) as a Captain with an MC and Bar and Ken (Kenward Winton Philp) as a major with a DSO. Ian (Ian Ellerthorpe Philp) was wounded with the RTR in France but also got back.)

We eventually arrived at a coal yard in Laignon and here officers and troops were herded together.

It was utterly filthy, no proper sanitary arrangements and shit all over the place. The night was bitterly cold, and we spent it lying on cobbles on our greatcoats. It was here we learnt why the French and Belgians were being treated better than us. The German High Command order is that treatment shall be first Belgians, second French and third British because we 'willed the war'.

The 'Cassel 21'

It is worth mentioning here that prior to 2 June 1940, there were twenty-one British officers who had all been captured at the same location and had been thrown together at Watou. We called ourselves the 'Cassel 21' and the roll is as follows:

Colonel William Douglas Baird Thompson, East Riding Yeomanry.
Colonel Edward Maurice Blunt Gilmore, Gloucestershire Regiment.
Major William Faithful Anderson, Royal Engineers.
Major John Reed Hodgson, East Riding Yeomanry.
Major John George Lawson, Royal Army Medical Corps.
Major Henry Lindsay Mercer, Royal Artillery.
Captain Cecil Arthur Hood, Royal Artillery.
Captain Peter Mackenzie, Royal Engineers.
Lieutenant George Denys Ireland, Cheshire Regiment.
Lieutenant Norman Robert Lansdell, Royal Army Medical Corps.
Lieutenant Reginald Lewis Sanders, Royal Engineers.
Lieutenant Philip Lionel E Skipworth, Royal Engineers.
Second Lieutenant Norman Henry Bonner, East Riding Yeomanry.
Second Lieutenant Donald Budd, Royal Artillery.
Second Lieutenant Joan Boucicault de Tiffield Calthrop, Royal Sussex Regiment.
Second Lieutenant John Blomfield Dixon, East Riding Yeomanry.
Second Lieutenant Wilfred Roderic Hord Forbes, Royal Artillery.

Second Lieutenant George Henry Douglas Greene, Green Howards.
Second Lieutenant F.W. Hislop, Cameronians (Scottish Rifles) (91536
    Cheshire Regiment).
Second Lieutenant Lowley, Royal Artillery.
Second Lieutenant Brian Robert Tyrer Reid, East Riding Yeomanry.

Tuesday, 4 June 1940

We got some stew and bread late in the morning and after sitting about in the blazing sun for some while were marched 25km to Jemelle passing through Rochefort another pleasant town, which we thought we'd like to visit later. During this time the Belgians were proving very troublesome straggling all over the road and generally being a bloody nuisance. Some of our own officers too were rather tiresome in their efforts to buy jam and butter, and other goods from the local inhabitants. Their behaviour made one feel sometimes that you wished they did not belong to your lot. Incidentally, I forgot to mention above that we marched through Rochefort singing and whistling *It's a long way to Tipperary* and other similar tunes. The Jerries were astonished to see a crowd of PoWs singing on the march and it seemed to get some of them very angry. It was great fun and did our spirits good.

At Jemelle we were separated from the men and put in an old café where we spent quite a comfortable night but were given no food.

Wednesday, 5 June 1940

Never have I had such a bath as today. The dirt of weeks rolled off as we managed to bathe in a fast-running river quite close to our prison. It was icy cold but marvellous. The only pity was that we had no clean clothes to put on afterwards. We had some soup about midday, which wasn't too bad but not nearly enough. A great deal of trouble was caused again by officers buying things from the inhabitants as everyone rushed in a panic trying to get their share of what there was not much of anyway. The resultant scrum and shouting was not very pleasant. The French were foremost in this and got more than their fair share. Eventually owing to the fact that the civilians complained that vegetables were being stolen out of their gardens, we were all marched out of the building and back to the men's camp where, after sharing a tin of tongue, [which] the colonel had in his possession, we spent a bitterly cold night in spite of the fact that we all huddled together.

Thursday, 6 June 1940

Early in the morning we received some soup and as we marched off were given a third loaf of bread and some very good cheese. The countryside was beautiful, woods and trees stretching away into the distance and the weather was still boiling hot. Water was our main problem and some of the men were drinking from all sorts of pools and streams and later got serious dysentery. The road mounted higher and higher until at last we arrived at a temporary camp at [Barrière de Champlon] after about 24km. The camp was right up in the hills, and we had marvellous view for miles. The commandant was very decent and allowed us to buy from the inhabitants. The Cassel 21 crowd got 1lb of butter and about a cup of milk each. The latter was supposed to have coffee in it but there was little sign. Our six Ery's (Colonel Thomson, Major Hodgson, Brian Reid, Norman Bonner, Lindy Leslie and me) heated up the milk and with the butter and bread and a small piece of potato each made a very good meal. The colonel also made some soup out of some Oxo cubes and biscuits, which he shared with us. We went to sleep feeling particularly full for once.

Friday, 7 June 1940

About 4.00 am we were roused and given bread and some bacon fat, and marched off at 5.20 am, on what turned out to be our last day in Belgium. It was good to get going when the weather was cool, and we were especially glad as the road switch backed all the way and would have been particularly trying in the very hot weather. Trees were in blossom, which made me think of home, and the fruit that would probably just be ripening. Fruit and chocolate are what we miss most I think with meat running a good third. Eventually, after about 23km, we arrived at Bastogne, where we were shoved into a very dirty yard near the station. A vile little NCO was in charge and after a bit we were marched out to the side of the line. Here we were left all day with nothing to eat or drink except that which we had saved. Eventually about 9.00 am we were bundled into cattle trucks. There were sixty-five of us squashed into ours, which was supposed to hold forty, and told we were off to Germany. What a hell of a journey. I shall never forget it. We were so tightly squashed that one could hardly breathe. If one had fallen over, I doubt if he could ever have got up. The cursing and grunting as we swayed with the movement of the train never stopped. Some people appeared to sleep but Norman and I were awake the whole night. You just had to tie a knot in it unless you wanted to pee down someone else's leg.

Saturday, 8 June 1940

About 4.00 am we arrived at Trier and with never to be forgotten thankfulness got out of our boxes, despite the fact that we were now in Germany. Everywhere was a sea of red and black Nazi flags. Fortunately, at that time of the day very few people were about but those that were glared at us, and we glared back. Up and up, we were marched through the town until we reached the camp right up on the side of a hill and overlooking the river Moselle. Here we were separated from the men who were quartered in huts, and we were marched off to an artillery barracks nearby where we had rooms and bunks to sleep in. It was a fairly new German barracks and had that smell about it, which was to me to become a sort of trademark for Germany, of what I think was ersatz rubber. Soon we were lined up for breakfast, which consisted of coffee, bread and jam. We were so hungry we thought it simply marvellous but as time went on one noticed that the jam had no sweetness and the coffee, of course, no sugar, but at that moment it was nectar. At 12.00 pm we were marched up to the main camp for some soup and afterwards back again to sleep. During the afternoon a certain number were allowed to go to the canteen to buy things and we managed to get razors and something they called soap, some writing paper and toothbrushes. In the evening there was another meal of coffee, bread, margarine and cheese. I wrote my first letter home and gave a list of stuff I would like sent out. Whether it went or not I don't know yet. (Note: by this time, we had marched over 100 miles on foot and travelled a further 200 miles by truck and train. I had not shaved for twelve days and had not brushed my teeth or smoked for ten days. Norman and I had very little small kit between us and our personal belongings consisted of a trooper's greatcoat each, a respirator haversack containing two water bottles, a fork and spoon each, a drinking cup and a small china bowl, a rough homemade towel and a piece of soap. To have a proper wash in running water, a shave and clean ones teeth was grand.)

Sunday, 9 June 1940

Sunday and the weather still remains fine, and the view is marvellous. I missed communion service I'm sorry to say, but there was a service later at which I managed to arrive halfway through. Funny how in such circumstances one tends to turn more to religion. I suppose it is comforting to think that maybe there is someone to turn to in adversity. The food was not more or less the same though not quite so lavish as before and no margarine. Beginning to feel rather ill with a tummy upset. Excessively tired into bargain and no energy. I want to sleep the whole time. I expect it is the unaccustomed eating. Homesickness is coming on again too. Not so much the type that one used to get at school but a longing nostalgia for England in general and all the things we have and used to do. I think the humiliation of the position as a captive is also beginning to tell. To be wounded or killed one expected. To be taken [as a] PoW never entered one's head nor was it ever mentioned, so it is a situation for which one is completely unprepared and the ignominy of it is difficult to bear, though at least we are alive.

Monday, 10 June 1940

Nothing much to report. We are right up on the hills running along the edge of the Moselle Valley and the air is so fresh. One can see people working in the fields and walking about. Slept most of the day and read a bit from a cheap thriller that I managed to borrow. Some of the chaps left today, including Brian Reid and Major Hodgson but the colonel is still with us.

Wednesday, 12 June 1940

Very wet today for the first time since Cassel. The whole room managed to get to the canteen as we thought we might be leaving. Had a couple of beers. As soon as we arrived back, we were gathered together and stood about in a downpour of rain for a bit. They then put us under shelter and finally marched us off to the station. Here we waited for a few hours and then, wonder of wonders, were put in actual carriages with only eight in each compartment and given some bread and cheese. Calthrop had some French mustard, which we spread liberally on the cheese and bread. The night passed slowly as I could not sleep for a pain in my shoulders, but on the whole the journey was comparatively comfortable.

Thursday, 13 June 1940

At 5.30 am we arrived at Mainz and the troops carriages were moved off. After about two hours our carriages were moved on to Mainz-Sud station and there we detrained and were led to a camp about 200 yards away. This was an old barracks, built around 1914, which we understood later was known as the Citadel. Although there was nothing really wrong with it, it had quite a depressing atmosphere. There were already a large number of French officers including about eight or nine generals. They gave us a meal and then a list of our names was taken, and we were given printed cards to send home. About fifty of us, Norman and I included, were separated and led off to a large house nearby, it looked quite pleasant and was covered with climbing plant, although the windows were barred. Here we were put into comfortable rooms and left. Norman and I were together in a room at first and then he was taken away. I was given a plate of potatoes to eat and then lay down to sleep. After a while I was woken and feeling still rather dozy was given a small piece of sausage, and some margarine and bread, and then led downstairs. Here I left my kit and was then led into a room where it seemed I was to be interrogated. The interrogator was quite a pleasant German who asked me some basic questions about the regiment to which he obviously knew the answers. Various other questions followed about various types of tanks, which I refused to answer. He then asked if I thought a successful invasion of England could be made. Naturally, I said 'no', and when he asked 'why', I said that they would never be able to get past the navy. That was the end of that, and I was then led off for delousing and finally put into rooms in the main camp.

Friday, 14 June 1940

Roll call at 8.00 am this morning. Ersatz coffee to drink, which was quite sweet, and the remains of the sausage to eat. An airman who arrived today bucked us up tremendously with news of [Prime Minister Winston] Churchill's speech and what was happening in England. Later we were again depressed to learn that Paris [in France] had fallen. Two hot meals today of potato, and odds and ends at 12.30 pm and 7.00 pm. We were also paid our first ten days' war pay. Norman and I got 24 Lagermarks each. This was not normal currency but a kind of 'chit', which could only be used in the prison camps. Kept on parade for two hours in the evening roll call as two officers were missing. Finished off the day with some cold potato and bread.

Heard that one of the French generals had committed suicide.

Saturday, 15 June 1940

Had a very disturbed night last night, suffering bad dreams and was also woken by an air-raid alarm. It's raining like stink and I breakfasted on remains of cold potato. Then stood for two hours in a queue for canteen and managed to get cigarettes and a knife. A hot meal consisting of potatoes, *sauerkraut*, cheese, margarine and bread were issued. At 2.00 pm we were paraded and handed in blankets. Issued with a further ration of bread and some very good sausage. Marched off to station and loaded into cattle trucks but only about twenty in each and they had seats so quite comfortable. Lindy Leslie was left behind. We passed through Würzburg during the night.

Sunday, 16 June 1940

Spent quite a good night. The journey went very slowly though and only speeded up in the morning. The country is getting more wooded and mountainous. At Siegelsdorf we stopped for an ablution and were told we were eating in about two hours. I then foolishly finished off my ration of cheese, sausage and bread – my God it was good! At Nürnberg we had some soup and a slice of bread, but I was still hungry and wished they'd give us some more bread and cheese. Talk about *Lebensraum* – the country here is as open as I have ever seen. Villages at very infrequent intervals and long, long stretches of beautiful countryside. Everything so marvellously clean and some of the town's most picturesque with the sugar loaf towers. Hunger is the worst pang though. I could eat and eat. Oh, for some of the second helpings that I have refused in the past. To think of the

Casualties of war. Some of the officers of the East Riding Yeomanry who were killed in action during the Battle of Cassel. (Above left): Second Lieutenant John Furley Cockin, who was killed in action on 30 May 1940, aged 20. His carrier disappeared in a pall of smoke in front of John Blomfield Dixon. He is buried at Hotton War Cemetery, Belgium. (Above centre): Second Lieutenant Richard Lawrence Hudson, who was killed in action on 28 May 1940, aged 22. He is buried at Hotton War Cemetery, Belgium. (Above right): Captain Thomas Edward Beswick Sissons TD, who was killed in action on 30 May 1940, aged 30. He is buried in the Hotton War Cemetery, Belgium. (*Courtesy of The J B Dixon Collection*)

number of times I've said 'No, I don't like second helpings.' I think the hunger is probably worse because one is sitting with nothing to do. We felt hungry on the march but were kept occupied by having to press on. Our next stop was Regensburg where we halted for about seven hours. Food was not forthcoming until quite late and then it was only soup and a slice of bread, which left me even hungrier. Quite a long conversation with one of the sergeants of the German guard and some railwaymen. They were Bavarian and seemed quite decent. However, this contact was stopped by a Nazi official as [it was] not considered proper.

When we left Cassel I had no idea that there was an evacuation going on. It made one even angrier to think that if we, instead of the Fife and Forfars, had pushed off earlier we might have got back. In fact, we also learnt that the orders for the brigade to retreat to the coast were delayed by about six hours as the despatch rider lost his way. As a result, the brigadier decided to delay our pull-out for a further twelve hours and move out at night. What a difference those extra hours would have made. When at Laufen, I also learnt that the

Major Geoffrey Minto Radcliffe TD MID, who was killed in action on 29 May 1940, aged 39. He is buried at Hotton War Cemetery, Belgium. (*Courtesy of The J B Dixon Collection*)

Hotton War Cemetery, Belgium. The bodies of the officers and men who were originally buried in the Watou temporary cemetery were removed in January 1948 and transported over 250km to their final resting place. (*Courtesy of The J B Dixon Collection*)

Regimental 'B' Echelon had left some time before us. With them had gone Harry Dupont and Bill Coyte, though they had no authority to do so, and the colonel was hopping mad at what he called this 'disgraceful behaviour'. If they felt as useless as I did, I am not now surprised at their action. If I had had the opportunity, I would have done the same. We were all completely wasted for what we were doing and might as well have been lance corporals. Bill Coyte certainly got back as he was with the 2nd Regiment for some time. I don't know about Dupont.

Chapter 5

Life at Laufen

We arrived at Laufen Am Salzach at about 8.00 am on Monday, 17 June 1940 and were marched to the camp known as Oflag VII-c/h, which we later learned was the former summer palace of the Archbishop of Salzburg. A massive building, just like a castle, about four stories high, built round a central courtyard and situated right on the banks of the river Salzach, which had been the border between Germany and Austria. The view of course was wonderful and, from the ablutions next to our room, one could look over the valley of Salzburg and further on to the Alps In the morning and the evening there were the most wonderful dawns and sunsets that I have ever seen. They were reflected in the river, and in spite of our unhappy circumstances I never failed to be thrilled by the sight. The camp was run by about six German officers, two NCOs plus additional camp guards. The attitude of the staff towards us was governed by the behaviour of Dr [von] Frey, the German commandant, who, on the slightest excuse, turned down any suggestions made by the SBO, Brigadier Claude Nicholson.

Monday, 17 June 1940

Upon arrival we were given a loaf of bread and some coffee. The loaf had to last five days! Interrogations and searching followed after which they shaved all our hair off, a typical bit of Hun degradation for the British. Batches of us were then marched off to be deloused, showered and issued with shaving and washing soap together with eating utensils. Two soup meals today, and some potatoes in their skins. Finally, we were split up into ranks and allocated to rooms. Norman and I stuck together and there were fifty-two of us in our room, which was No. 84 on the top floor beside the ablutions, where we were to spend the next eight months of an awful existence.

At first, the rooms, and the accompanying latrines, were tremendously overcrowded as the camp was suitable for about 600 officers, but actually contained 1,200, with some rooms holding as many as 100 officers. We slept on triple-deck bunks, with palliasses, sheets and two blankets and to fall from the top to the bottom was no joke. There was no dining hall, and messing in over-crowded rooms was a discomfort. There were no books, of course,

A unique photograph shows John Dixon having his head shaved upon arrival at Laufen POW Camp. (*Courtesy of the J B Dixon Collection*)

and one spent one's time either lying on their beds asleep, which helped pass the time and fight hunger, walking or drinking beer in the bar when money was available. Parcels were received at varying times and were opened by the German authorities in the presence the recipient. No tin, wrapper or box was

John Blomfield Dixon is seen here before (left) and after (right) having his head shaved. The photographs, attached to his PoW Card, provide a graphic reminder of those men and women who were held captive by the Nazi regime. (*Both courtesy of The J B Dixon Collection*)

ever given to the recipient, all foodstuffs etc. had to be received in plates and bowls. Grey flannel trousers, golfing jackets and any clothes similar to civilian were confiscated. Grey flannel trousers were sent away by the Germans and dyed khaki to prevent their use as civilian escape clothing.

Most of us were so weak that climbing the stairs was an effort and there were no games to be played as, in the first place, there was no equipment and, secondly, no one felt strong enough. Some brave minded spirits used to do PT, but for myself it wasn't worth the effort as it made one so hungry. The rations supplied by the Germans were handed over to the British cook-house staff, which made itself responsible for the cooking and distribution. The exercise field was very small and handball was the only game we were able to play.

Things at Laufen very much settled down throughout the remainder of July 1940, but I was very worried about the air raids on England and tried hard not

Oflag VII-c Laufen Castle, in southeastern Bavaria. The Oflag existed only for a short time. In early 1942 all the officers were transferred to Oflag VII-b in Eichstätt. The castle was then used as an internment camp Ilag VII for men from the Channel Islands. Laufen was eventually liberated by the Third United States Army on 5 May 1945. (*Courtesy of The J B Dixon Collection*)

to believe the German reports, but it is difficult at times to keep an optimistic outlook. Among the other considerations in the first few months of captivity, those that blaze in capital letters, are food and cigarettes. No matter at what stage of the war one is captured they are the first considerations, and I do not think that I am exaggerating when I say that we of France and Norway had the hardest lot of all. Cigarettes were issued at the rate of two per day and after a while changed from the German brand to a particularly terrible Polish type, made mostly of sweepings I should think. Understandably, food also remained a concern and ration levels varied considerably. Red Cross issues gradually grew bigger, mostly bulk stuff, jam, condensed milk and cheese etc., but a great help to eke out our German rations. The Germans also helped a little by selling us plums and apples, at exorbitant prices. Recreation at this time consists of makeshift concerts and piano recitals, with any number of lectures besides. But life began to settle into a daily routine that, whilst not entirely comfortable, became bearable for most of the PoWs. These were early days and there remained a strong belief that the war would soon be over, and those held in captivity would be released. When the winter came and no clothes parcels had arrived, the Germans issued great coats but refused to help with anything else. Some officers went very short throughout the winter. During these few months, however, part of the exercise field was flooded, giving us a skating rink and two curling rinks. Skates and curling stones were bought and despite the difficulty of having 950 officers wanting to use such a small bit of ice at the same time, it afforded us the best fun and exercise we had.

Throughout the months of captivity at Laufen, the days melted into one and another, and so did the diary entries, but still there were a few salient moments.

Friday, 28 June 1940
We were called out for parade at 7.45 am today and made to stand in the garden for three hours whilst a series of officers were searched. Another seven new officers were allotted to our room, bringing it to a total of eighty-seven, which is absolutely overcrowded. However, we are at last now able to buy toilet roll from the canteen, which we have to share between four of us!

Wednesday, 3 July 1940
Today, I went into hospital with follicular tonsillitis. It was quite a good rest, but with hardly any equipment it was no more really than an ordinary room, which was less crowded than others. During the time I was in the infirmary the remnants of the 51st Division and Major General Fortune arrived. The latter was a fine chap and throughout all our associations with him proved an absolute tower of strength. The attitude of the Germans at this time was of course that

of the complete subjugation. None of our requests were ever acceded to and on the slightest protest small 'privileges', which in a civilised country would have been regarded almost the natural necessities of life, were withdrawn.

When we left Cassel I had no idea that there was an evacuation going on. It made one even angrier to think that if we, instead of the Fife and Forfars, had pushed off earlier we might have got back. In fact, we also learnt that the orders for the brigade to retreat to the coast were delayed by about six hours as the despatch rider lost his way. As a result, the brigadier decided to delay our pull out for a further twelve hours and move out at night. What a difference those extra hours would have made. When at Laufen, I also learnt that the Regimental 'B' Echelon had left some time before us. With them had gone Harry Dupont and Bill Coyte, though they had no authority to do so, and the Colonel was hopping mad at what he called this 'disgraceful behaviour'. If they felt as useless as I did, I am not now surprised at their action. If I had had the opportunity, I would have done the same. We were all completely wasted for what we were doing and might as well have been lance corporals. Bill Coyte certainly got back but I don't know about Dupont.

Wednesday, 10 July 1940

Today, we received our first taste of Red Cross parcels – one nineth per man. So, I got the following:

    Two Squares of chocolate
    Six lumps of sugar
    Two Boiled sweets
    One tinned apricot
    A little diploma cheese
    Half a sausage
    A portion of chicken and ham roll
    A maconochie stew
    A spoonful of marmalade, margarine, cocoa, soup powder, milk powder and
        condensed milk

It seems an infinitesimal amount to make a fuss about but it is a luxury. How I have hoarded it and sparingly issued it out to myself. During all this time the outward optimism of the camp in the light of events was we know them was amazing. In spite of all the German papers said and in spite of what we knew, there was never a doubt that we should finally pull through and win as we had always done. German accounts of the bombing of England are flaunted daily before our eyes but, luckily for us, we don't believe a word.

Monday, 5 August 1940

Today, the new system of university lecture came into place. These take place in a number of locations around the camp and include Spanish, German, geography, insurance and a number of different histories covering modern, Roman, Greek and medieval periods. Gradually, as these classes were started, everybody was, of course, full of enthusiasm but like most things it gradually tailed off leaving a few staunch supporters or those who decided to stick to one subject.

Friday, 30 August 1940

Bells were ringing in the village at about 5.00 am this morning. We thought first that it might have something to do with the anniversary day of the Polish invasion, but it turned out to be a fire. Anti-aircraft fire was thought to be heard in the distance during the night but nothing definite. All day long I was thinking of what I was doing on this day last year. At the time I was sitting in the billiard room on the African pouffe cleaning my equipment in the specially dimmed light for the ARP. Mother was darning near the wireless, and Dick and father were reading. How vividly it all comes back, especially the voice of the announcer on the wireless, giving out the precautions to be taken.

The 'Laufen Six'. (Left to right) Harry Elliott, Rupert Barry, Pat Reid, Dick Howe, Peter Allen and Kenneth Lockwood. All had been held at Laufen with John Blomfield Dixon. This image was taken at Colditz Castle following their recapture. (*Courtesy of The J B Dixon Collection*)

Friday, 6 September 1940

News today that six British officers have escaped overnight. There are no real details but everyone is excited, and hopeful, that they will make it to safety.

This was the first breakout made a group of officers, who would become known as the 'Laufen Six'. It took seven weeks to complete a tunnel 24 feet in length, from the prison basement to a small shed adjoining a nearby house. The escapees, all disguised as women, made their getaway and made for Yugoslavia, 150 miles away across the mountains of the Austrian Tyrol, a difficult journey in which they were forced to use the roads due to the terrain. After five days on the run, and having only travelled 50 miles, they entered the village of Radstadt, Austria. With only one of them being able to speak German and carrying no identification papers, they were quickly arrested. They were returned to Laufen and kept in solitary confinement, on a diet of bread and water. They were then sent to the notorious Colditz Castle, designated Oflag IV-c, a special 'escape-proof' camp.

Sunday, 6 October 1940

Church service today. Congressional and I didn't enjoy it very much, so had a C of E natter afterwards. The afternoons are so boring but managed to make the evening pass very quickly by talking. I have spent the last two days laying in the garden, it being quite sunny and everything was so peaceful with the slight sound of music playing somewhere. My thoughts turned very much to home. How far away it seems now, but at times when daydreaming I have to stop myself from thinking of what I would normally be doing as I suddenly come back to earth with a bump and realise where I am. I think the reality that after the next issue of Red Cross parcels we shall have nothing more unless anything turns up anew is rather weighing on our minds. It's such a long time now since we had nothing but the German rations to eat.

Monday, 7 October 1940

I received my first letter from home and was so thankful. It's impossible to describe my feelings on so doing, they are beyond all imagination. It seemed at one time as if one would never come and with everybody else getting mail, it was slightly depressing. Mother has been simply wonderful, there was a letter from Mrs Toyne at the same time, which described how mother kept on working at the canteen and wool depot all the time, waiting for news to come through and she never lost hope all the time. They have not yet received any news from me. I hope by this time that something at least will have got through.

Tuesday, 8 October 1940

A very disturbed night – I dreamt a lot about all our battles and somehow or the other the nuns of yesterday were mixed up in it as well. From that I went on to dreaming about home and all the various people mentioned in mother's letter were there, and I was home on a holiday from this place! When I came back I cursed myself for not bringing any cigarettes! Felt browned off to hell in the afternoon, I think it was the after effects of the letter, and I felt very homesick. In the canteen afterwards I sat and talked to Norman and Vincent and this, combined with the music, made me feel slightly better.

Saturday, 12 October 1940

Another letter from home today. Apparently, the office knows I'm a PoW as well and want to send me something, but the most galling words of the whole letter were, 'all are back, except you!' These words kept on running through my head the whole time I was walking around the garden. What a life!

Saturday, 19 October 1940

The last few days have been terribly cold both in the morning and at night, but beautifully sunny in the afternoons. I went to a concert tonight with Norman Bonner, it was called *Laufen Calling* and was a mixture of songs and music that we all know and love. The new dance orchestra was in evidence and played along with the topical sketches to suit the place and occasion. One of the famous people held here is Victor Wood, the composer, who has written several tunes whilst in captivity and sang one of them accompanied by the orchestra, titled *Mooncloud*, the first time it has been heard.

Sunday, 27 October 1940

The first snow fell and the surrounding hills were coated with it on top, and all during the day it kept falling in spasms but failed to settle. I felt quite cheery during the day but in the evening got the same old browned off feeling. The news too was not too cheerful, talking about German domination in Europe and didn't add anything but gloom to my frame of mind.

Tuesday, 5 November 1940

A letter from Elinor today. Very cheery and containing great news about the children. Mary is walking and talking all the time and they are thinking of sending Colin to school as the two get into such mischief together. They must be great fun now. I'm so looking forward to the time when I get back and can take them out.

Thursday, 14 November 1940

A magnificent day, sun shining and quite warm. There are rumours of a lot more leaving the camp. I hope to God I don't go. Two letters today, one from Dick and one from Mr Rhodes. Both very cheery. Pantomime rehearsal in the afternoon and after my hot shower I put on my clean pants, vest and socks and also the marvellous roll neck sweater. The feeling was indescribably marvellous, new and clean clothes after five months. The regimental dinner tonight and we had a damn good time.

Monday, 18 November 1940

About fifty more people left the camp today, but only one from our room, and he was no loss. Quite a lot of fellows got tight on the strength of it and this led to Jerry shooting at some who were leaning out of the windows. He hit one chap in the arm, unfortunately the fellow was an innocent one.

Wednesday, 20 November 1940

Cambrai Day. We were rather disappointed that we weren't invited to the RTR dinner but made up for this by having a celebration on our own with Chris Witt (Lieutenant Christopher Tansley Witt), who was in the same position as Jock Jones. We fried some onions and potatoes and they brought some very good soup, and had a simply marvellous meal with wine and beer. I addition, as is my habit here, I ate too fast and got indigestion. I bought a thermos flask for 5 *Reichsmarks*, it will be useful to keep coffee in for after lunch.

Sunday, 1 December 1940

Went to the colonel's room at 10.15 am for a 'C' Squadron party. There was just the four of us and the colonel provided wine, cigarettes and a few sweetened almonds. It was very pleasant although I was rather out of it at times when they talked about their friends. He started calling me by my Christian name though, which I feel is rather an honour and makes one feel more part of the regiment than before.

Tuesday, 17 December 1940

Six months today we've been here and I can really hardly believe it. The thought that if only we'd managed to get back, we'd have most probably been in Egypt now and beating up the Wops, fills me with inconsolable rage. My God, what we are missing.

Wednesday, 18 December 1940

At last, a letter with 'write lightly to avoid delay' all over it. Jo was there when mother was writing. I wonder if she'll write to me? I remember I wrote a letter to her from France asking whether she would, but whether it arrived I don't know.

Thursday, 19 December 1940

Dreamt a lot last night, especially about Jo. It's enraging to think that I am shut up here and can't speak to her, and all the time someone else might be taking her out. Why the hell can't she write more. But still that wouldn't be much good as it takes months to get a letter through and back.

Tuesday, 24 December 1940

A better day today. Everything is marvellously decorated, Christmas trees in the canteen and recreation room. A sing-song carol service in the evening with orchestral items as well. A hell of a fracas in the evening, had my bags taken off in room 80, and then we all raided it and had a return raid from them. Got soaked with water and blancmange powder. A chap came round in the evening, whom we took for an American, to wish us a merry Christmas. He was very rude, however, as we were making a bit of a row and we learnt afterwards that he was wasn't an American at all but a chap from the German foreign office.

Christmas Pantomime at Oflag VIII-c/h, Laufen, 31 December 1940. (Back row): Raymond Grace, Tony Green, Bertie Harwood, John Pearson and Bill Rawlings. (Second row): Brian McIrvine, ?, ?, Peter Monico, ?, Major Anderson. (Third row): John Lightfoot, Paul Milne, Bobby Loder, Desmond Llewelyn, Sam Crouch, John Calthrop and Bill Surtees. (Front row): Tim Bailey, Victor Prestidge, Arthur Barradell-Smith, Bill Brewster, John Blomfield Dixon and David Read. (*Courtesy of The J B Dixon Collection*)

Wednesday, 25 December 1940

Surely, the weirdest Christmas Day ever. If anyone had suggested that I should be in Germany for this Christmas, how I should have laughed. Any thoughts were very much of home today, although it's very difficult to get a quiet moment to oneself to think these days. I wonder what they are doing now and whether they are thinking of me. Had quite a good lunch, better than expected. Last night, one of the sentries, carefully looking about to see that no one was looking, said to one of our chaps, 'the Italians? Kaput!', and went on to say I am not a German, but an Austrian.

Thursday, 26 December 1940

Didn't get to sleep till very late last night as there was a colossal amount of noise until the early hours. As a consequence, I felt sleepy all day. The official show of the pantomime today. It went off quite well.

Sunday, 29 December 1940

My birthday and what a place for one. We had my cake for tea, which I had iced with chocolate icing and put twenty-two little piles of jam on top. It was quite good but I wish I hadn't put any blancmange powder in it. I went to the carol festival in the evening, it was magnificent and brought back many memories.

Chapter 6

1941: Another Bloody Year –
A Killing in the Camp

As John Blomfield Dixon began his diary entries for 1941, he had been a PoW for a little over seven months. The mundane routine of daily life had really begun to impact upon his notes, comments often being not much more than 'another bloody day'.

Wednesday, 1 January 1941
Happy New Year! And I hope to Christ it's a damn sight happier for us than the last one's been! We saw it in with the usual revelry last night and kept the lights on until well past 12.00 am, singing *Auld Lang Syne* and *God Save the King*. The Hun was quite decent about it, though in one or two cases he lost his temper. A hell of a lot of new books in the library today, decently bound ones too. There was very good orchestral concert in the evening which included a German march *Greetings from the Rhine*, *Wine, Women and Song* by Strauss, *Tancredi Overture* by Rossini, *Intermezzo* from Cavalleria Rusticana, and a waltz from the Student Prince. Still no news of my boots from the cobbler. They seem to have completely disappeared, damn it!

Friday, 3 January 1941
Two letters arrived today, one from Mrs Kitto and another from Aunt Madge. This method of transit seems to be fairly settled now, I wish ours from here could go as quickly. A denial in the Frankfurter Zeitung of a report by the BBC that a commission had left Italy for the USA to try and make peace between Britain and Italy! Another commission is trying to patch up peace between Greece and Italy from the Italian side! The theatre photographs arrived today, but I haven't seen them yet, although I'm told I look very aggressive.

Saturday, 4 January 1941
The truth came out today about the mail, there are far too few censors, as we thought, and they have applied to Berlin for more, but at the present nothing has happened and for the moment they are struggling on as best as they can, with stacks of mail piled up in the room, as a standing witness for anybody

who comes to enquire into it. The German air force is now operating in the Mediterranean. It would appear the Italians are in a tight spot, I wonder how much more help the Jerries will give them?

Sunday, 5 January 1941

Loads of parcels came in during the afternoon. The Jerries must be wondering how to deal with them all. Rumour has it that the brigadier is applying for parcels to be issued without so much breaking up, and so speeding up the delivery. General Wavell has made a statement that under no circumstances will Germany get any colonies after the war. A new type of submarine catcher is at work and Bardia is being assaulted from all sides.

Tuesday, 7 January 1941

A German prison commission came round today, so we had to be out of our bed and on parade early. I hope they took note of the parcel and letter situation with regard to censoring. I wrote home to mother and received letters from Pete Kitto and Aunt Marie. News tonight that the Red Cross voluntary staff at home have been sacked and replaced by paid workers. Reorganisation is also going on, so let's hope something happens.

Wednesday, 8 January 1941

Bardia has fallen at last and large quantities of men and material taken. A rather fantastic account of life in the camp has been published in the Swiss press, emanating from German sources. In the evening somebody brought a gramophone into the room. It was marvellous to hear it after so long an absence from mechanical music.

Thursday, 9 January 1941

Red Cross parcels were issued the new way today, intact and no tins opened. We got Christmas ones, with cake and Christmas puddings in. I have discovered that Cyril Whitcombe is a PoW, but I don't know whether he is in this camp. Food here has become no question at all at the moment. Soup goes for anyone who wants it, I had third helpings, and potatoes are ad lib. What a contrast to two months ago when everyone used to jealously guard their extra soup ration and count for the days on which we got extra potatoes.

Friday, 10 January 1941

What a day! I received four letters, one from mother, two from Betty and one from Greta Bateman. My books arrived from the censor, I must try and fix up my shelves. The slats have arrived so work will commence, if I can find a substitute for string. There was another issue of Red Cross parcels, so we're literally wallowing in food!

Monday, 13 January 1941

Skating started today but I didn't do any as I had no boots. My stomach is out of order, I think it must be all the food. I had two letters today. One from Elinor dated 17 October [1940] and one from mother of 15 December [1940] with a photograph of Dick in it. It was very welcome to get it and I hope some more come soon. Mrs Jan Campbell has written to her husband saying, 'I know for a certainty that you will home in the spring or at the latest early summer.' I wonder? Got some boots at last from the cobblers. They're not a perfect fit but I hope they'll do with some socks in.

Thursday, 16 January 1941

Had my first skate today and enjoyed it tremendously. Although I say it myself, I did extraordinarily well, and went round swimmingly. Wore my new bags today, which have been dyed a terrible mustard colour, after a shower and felt marvellously clean after ten months of battledress. It seems that the Jerries have discovered some of our chaps are not returning their tins, which are being used for escape purposes.

Friday, 17 January 1941

According to a Swiss newspaper there are alternatives to the war.

1. Germany will attempt an invasion and succeed and the war will be over in three months.
2. Ditto and fail and the war will be over in six months.
3. No invasion and we shall win in twelve to eighteen months.

In the news too, Japan would appear to be getting deeper and deeper into the morass in China and finding it impossible to extract itself. Apparently, guerrilla warfare went on during 1940. We have lost the *Southampton* it's one of the newest types [of ship] and will be a bad loss.

Monday, 20 January 1941

Today passed very slowly, far more slowly than any other day recently and I don't really know why. It may be the browning off effect of [Prime Minister Winston] Churchill's speech yesterday in which he said that we had a stern time ahead of us and that one slip would be fatal.

Tuesday, 21 January 1941

The world brightened perpetually for us today around about noon. We received slips from Danish Red Cross parcels, a very welcome sight and hope to get them tomorrow. I attended my first German class under the new system tonight, the fellow instructing is quite decent.

Wednesday, 22 January 1941

A search this morning for the missing hammer, but fortunately only amongst those rooms on the floor concerned. I hope it's found as otherwise it may be our turn tomorrow. I drew my Danish parcel, it was the magnificent and contained fifty Ryvita, 0.5 kilo of sugar, 0.5 kilo of butter, two jams, a large sausage, small piece of soap and two cheeses. The best parcel yet. We have taken Cassola in East Africa, or rather the Italians say they have evacuated it for strategic reasons. British troops have surrounded Tobruk and there is news that we have entered the eastern part. A farewell party tonight for the whole of room 39 who are off to another camp, probably Tittmoning.

Saturday, 25 January 1941

The Bosche committed murder today. I don't know the full story yet but apparently from what I can piece together from eyewitnesses this is what happened. An officer named Dees was standing in the ablutions window next to our room making a sketch of the customs buildings. Whether he leaned out or not, we don't know but it seems unlikely from people who saw him doing it yesterday. The people in the garden heard a whistle blow and looked about for it. It was blown again, and they then saw the sentry in the box by the river raise his rifle and fore at one of the windows. He fired a second time though, why I can't make out, since the first shot hit Dees in the cheek and must have killed him almost immediately. The second shot almost hit one of our chaps who rushed in, and it landed above the door. There was a terrific to-do and a wiregram was sent to the American Embassy informing them of his death. A Court of Enquiry (British) is to be held and for the moment our position is reserved – we don't want to put ourselves in the wrong by being accused of rioting or such other. What I think about the case is unprintable and I only hope the true facts get home.

Official reports indicate there was a German order forbidding officers to lean out of windows. The motive for issuing this order was unclear but would not have been to prevent escape, because nowhere were the windows closer than 20 yards from the barbed wire. An eyewitness, Lieutenant John Alexander Elphinstone, claimed that at 3.00 pm on 25 January 1941, Lieutenant Dees

On Saturday 25 January 1941, Lieutenant Edward Lough Dees was in his room, sketching at Laufen. The window was open, but Dees was not leaning out of it. The German commandant, the monocle-wearing Prussian Oberst Dr von Frey, had given an order that any PoWs seen leaning out of windows would be shot. A witness saw a camp guard kneel down, rest his rifle on the rail of a watch tower box, and fire a shot. Dees was killed outright. He was buried at Laufen Civil cemetery on 28 January 1941 and a wreath offered by the Germans was refused. His body was reinterred at Durnbach British Military Cemetery on 17 July 1948. A series of photographs showing the funeral were found in the John Blomfield Dixon collection. The killing of Dees was investigated by the War Crimes Branch after the war but it was believed Oberst von Frey was, by that time, dead. A German soldier, Unteroffizier Xavier Kistler, was also investigated but it was found he had never served as a camp guard. The perpetrator was never to answer for their crime. (*All courtesy of The J B Dixon Collection*)

was sketching from a third storey window in the centre of the building, about 80 yards from the perimeter and near to a sentry box, a large hut with glass windows on stakes 12 foot above the ground. A sentry was seen to be watching the officer, who had been standing at the window for quite some time. He was not leaning out but standing close up to it, resting his drawing block on the window sill. The sentry was then heard and seen to shout and gesticulate towards Dees, who neither heard nor noticed. The sentry was then seen to kneel down in his box and, resting his rifle on the window sill, took aim. Officers in the exercise ground shouted to Dess but at 80 yards he did not hear. The sentry then fired, Dees remained motionless at the window, ten seconds later the sentry fired again and this time Dees disappeared. He was found by an officer from the neighbouring room, unconscious on the ground with a bullet wound in the head. Two minutes later he died in hospital. After this incident Brigadier Nicholson demanded that the order not to lean out of windows should be cancelled, if not, it should be enforced other than by the use of firearms. The German commandant, Dr [von] Frey, refused to consider these demands. A week later a representative of the American Embassy arrived and investigated the incident, which caused the German officers and NCOs to feel very ashamed of the behaviour of Dr [von] Frey, with whom they were in complete disagreement. On two previous occasions, shots had been fired at officers leaning out of the windows and in one case an officer standing on a table in the room concerned was hit in the leg. A post-war investigation determined that Dr von Frey had died before the cessation of hostilities. A German soldier, Unteroffizier Xavier Kistler, was investigated for the crime but it was determined that he was not the individual that was sought. No one was ever convicted for the murder of Lieutenant Edward Lough Dees.

Sunday, 26 January 1941

Absolute silence on parade this morning – you could have heard a feather drop. I think it affected the Hun too, as they seemed rather nervous. They are all out to get another shooting too, as we have been told not to look out of the windows at all, so as not to make our case weak by allowing the Huns to say we don't obey orders. It is requested also that we don't go into the canteen after 5.00 pm tomorrow. The commandant when asked to allow officers of Dees regiment to go to the funeral said no as he was afraid of a demonstration. The brigadier's reply to this was that British officers were not in the habit of demonstrating at a fellow comrades funeral. After this, the commandant said that his soldiers would have orders to shoot at the slightest sign of a demonstration. My God! They have got weird ideas of behaviour! Kreuzknacker seems to be the only decent one among them. He at least does behave like a soldier.

Tuesday, 28 January 1941

Dees was buried today, and we had a two-minute silence at 4.00 pm as the commandant refused to allow a memorial service. The Germans brought a wreath which, I believe, was refused. There are rumours that the village is in a rage about the shooting. 'A British officer shot by a peasant' they say. In the paper, the Italians deny the presence of German troops, except airmen, in Italy. On the other hand the *Völkischer Beobachter,* [a Nazi newspaper,] shows a picture of German troops marching through an Italian town.

Thursday, 30 January 1941

Had our cards returned today, as we are not allowed to make comments about the murder, only state its fact. British AFVs are attacking south of Derna. They seem to have shifted pretty quickly.

Friday, 14 February 1941

Things have now settled down to a definite routine, after the first few months of getting everything organised. People were settling into messes, and one found a general air of patient resignation, which was bad. After many rumours for some time and one or two false starts 500 of us, mainly subalterns, were to be moved to Posen. I am reading *News of England* by Beverley Nicholls, it is an extraordinarily good book. Although it was written before the war it has some remarkably sound suggestions and one feels so helpless that these things have not been attempted before now. If we win this war God send we have men of foresight who will be able not only to plan well for our future and that of the empire, but to put those plans into operation. In spite of all my protestations to the contrary about the female sex, Jo is my one obsession these days. I think about her during the day and dream about her at night. It makes me so mad to think that I can do nothing about it to let her really know what I feel. It's impossible to start straight away in a letter, although I intend to send my next one to her, and yet I must do something to let her know something of my heart. She's the only girl I ever had or liked and when this one chance arrives, I get no opportunity to carry out what I would wish. Not that I say I would marry her (if she would wait long enough for me, I feel I would though). She is so fresh and charming and to think that this one chance I ever had is to be wasted. By the time I get back (if ever in the next five years) she will be 22 or so and most probably engaged to some young chap like Jim Ripley. (The thought of the latter drives me to fury.) My feelings on all this are too strong and muddled to really be put on paper.

Tuesday, 4 March 1941

I didn't sleep too well in the night as most of our blankets and bedclothes were packed in preparation for the move. All my meagre belongings being packed in a tomato box and wrapped round with my blanket. We were roused at an unearthly hour, got up at 3.00 am and had a room check before being marched off to the recreation room, where we were left until 6.00 am when tea arrived. We were each dished out with a loaf of bread and chunk of sausage, and then taken to the parade ground and put in groups. The commandant made a speech before we left and said we were going to the 'fine old city of Posen'. Just after 8.00 am we left Laufen, and the journey began. Firstly, we were marched off to the station amidst cheers from those remaining, amongst whom was Norman Bonner, who had been ill. Each of us had to carry our own luggage, which was indescribably heavy, and for 1.5 miles and it was agony with my arms soon becoming numb. On arrival at the station, we found General Fortune waiting for us, and a very welcome sight it was indeed, and cheering to know that he was coming with us. On getting on the train our party of four were very lucky and got second class carriages, and, as far we could see, comparative comfort. The only thing was, we didn't know how long the rations were to last. The journey was, of course, the usual type of stopping and starting, and lasted two days and two nights. Several times during the journey I thought of jumping off but was deterred by the fact that no one would come with me. I had hardly any food, no maps or compass and the country was badly flooded practically the whole way up.

Major General Victor Fortune cheering on British troops as they left Laufen for the reprisal camp at Posen. (*Courtesy of The J B Dixon Collection*)

Chapter 7

Punishment at Posen and Thorn

Thursday, 6 March 1941

Finally, at 8.00 am we arrived at Posen station, cold and hungry. It was a dismal day, and the appearance of guards did nothing to reassure us. We were marched as fast as possible, with only one halt. Carrying all our belongings through the town and out the other side to the camp, only some 3km in all but a march that will always live in my memory. Harried and kicked by German mounted police, we struggled and sweated on, belongings were cast aside in despair by those who could carry them no more. We stumbled, gasping and struggling for breath through two iron gates down into what appeared like the mouth of a great black pit, and came to a halt on the drawbridge to the accompaniment off the crash of the gate behind us and the sound of shots outside. We really began to think that our last hours had come, and the shock was pretty terrific. Shortly after arrival, a proclamation was read out which stated that we were being put in this underground Fort, as it turned out to be, as a reprisal for the treatment of German officers in Canada. I was placed in a small dim lit room with twenty-nine others on a level with the moat. The tiny windows allowed hardly any light in, beds were in shelves of five, blankets were sopping wet, and we had a total of two stools and one small table. Rooms were locked at 9.00 pm and a bucket provided in the room as a latrine. One of the rooms had a stream of sewage running through it from the proper latrines, which apparently had been blocked for some considerable time. Our promenade into the moat, about 15 yards wide and 200 yards long. It is also very unpleasant as a cesspit runs the whole length and everywhere pervades the smell of sewerage and damp.

Food was slightly better, in quantity if not quality, and for some time we thought that we were on strict rations, until we realised the extent of the German cookhouses at Laufen. The whole place was a rabbit warren of echoing black corridors of and many were the expeditions and quarrying that went on while we were there to discover a way out. The general was a tower of strength and provided us all with the power of resistance to overcome every difficulty. Each company was provided with a German NCO in charge, who used to come round and talk. They were all supposed to carry rubber truncheons but none of them were in sympathy with the idea and openly expressed their disapproval. It was

British and Commonwealth officers entering Fort VIII at Posen. (*Courtesy of The J B Dixon Collection*)

here that we first got to know the 'goons'. When I say 'know', I don't mean it in a friendly sense. Having at least escaped from the iron jaws of Laufen, we did not at first realise what a blessing it was, but gradually, as with all similar camps up to Warburg, our condition blossomed, showing us that the goons were not persons to be feared or bowed down to, but ones to be flaunted and cheated (and how easy it is if only one puts a brave front on). If they shout, you shout back, and they soon [would be] eating out of your hands. At this time of course we were still in the position of being dependant on them for such essentials as food and cigarettes. The time was to come, not very far distant, when they would eat out of our hand for a few cigarettes, a piece of chocolate or soap. Lice and flees abounded in great numbers and the catch used to be totalled up at the end of each day. In some rooms the number reached astronomical figures. Washing facilities were nil and every morning one had to be content with a 'shower' under an old pump, paddling in icy water amidst filth and potato peelings. It was the only way of attempting to keep clean. Winter, of course, which had gone before we left Laufen, was still with us here and icicles 6 feet long used to hang from the roof. After a week or so, we were allowed exercise once a day, just outside the fort. Nothing much, but better than nothing.

Saturday, 22 March 1941

Things started to slacken off. No locking in rooms, only two 'appels' a day, letter writing etc. The day after, Red Cross parcels arrived amidst scenes of thankfulness and jubilation. During all this time there were rumours of trains full of troops going east through Posen and also skirmishes on the frontier. We did not really believe them, and the Germans always made out that Russia was friendly.

Thursday, 27 March 1941

News came today that 150 officers were to leave the camp. Ten from our room were to go and I immediately volunteered, as I felt that nothing could be worse than our present one. 'Tiny' Waters, Arthur Walker, Geoff Cowen and Robin Steele-Mortimer were among the others, and from this date on [it] really dates our connection together. The top of the fort was opened just before we left, which made a great change.

Monday, 31 March 1941

The Swiss Commission, who are acting as arbitration in the reprisal camp business, came round today and had a shock. They said that conditions here were ten times worse than Canada and that, in any case, the chap who complained was undergoing simple confinement for escaping twice. When told we had no hot water and were shown the flea bites, they had a second shock. They said that our conditions outside Germany were 'big news'. I only hope our people aren't too worried as, when one considers it fully, we are very fit and well. All we should wish is that the German PoWs should be treated as badly as ourselves. News comes of 20,000 deaths and 40,000 wounded in England, through air raids. God, I hope all my dear ones are safe.

Wednesday, 2 April 1941

We paraded at 12.15 pm after a farewell address by the General (Fortune), and then left Fort 8 Posen. Our journey was slightly different to the arrival, as luggage was taken down by lorry and most of us now had managed to obtain some kind of suitcase. After a longish wait at the station, we arrived at Thorn about 10.00 pm. With a lot of shouting and bustle we were marched off to our new home, which proved to be another fort of similar design to Posen, but which had been lived in by the Germans and consequently was moderately clean, light and spacious. Beds were separate and a hot meal awaited us on the table, with an orderly in attendance. We had all managed to stick together, and it was with a sigh of relief that we lay down to sleep. The gamble had come off. It was much better than Posen. Next day we settled in and looked about us. A hot shower, the first for over a month, was a great relief and we would get them twice a week. The members of the camp were not 'Laufenites' as we thought, but from Spangenberg, a mixture of army,

Brigadier Nigel Fitzroy Somerset CBE DSO MC, presenting boxing prizes to British PoWs at Thorn in spring 1941. (*Courtesy of The J B Dixon Collection*)

Left Behind. The officers of the East Riding Yeomanry who were not sent from Laufen to Posen as part of German reprisals. (Left to right): Norman Bonner, Bob Smith, Malan Wright, Colonel William Douglas Baird Thompson, John Hodgson, George Wade and Sidney Bearne. (*Courtesy of The J B Dixon Collection*)

navy and air force. None of them were very recent arrivals, but it was grand to meet some new faces. It was here that we were surprised and overwhelmed by meeting the cavalry. Trading was also quite rife, but nothing like the size to which it afterwards grew.

Thursday, 17 April 1941

An intensive search by the Gestapo and local police today, the worst we've had. They started on parade and continued until 3.00 pm, we getting our midday meal at 4.00 pm. Great fun was caused by officers tearing up blank pieces of paper and stuffing them in the ground, which were eagerly seized by the goons who tried to put them back together. It was very tiring and I had a splitting headache at the end. Jeff had his gold wristwatch stolen and they took five diaries of mine, and also my grey trousers, which I had dyed khaki, [and] which they would not believe.

Thursday, 24 April 1941

God I am depressed! I think I've reached about the lowest ebb ever since I was captured. Everything seems to go against us. Whenever we come up against the bloody Bosche on land everyone seems to be either laughing at us also have lost faith in us. As far as I can see the reputation of the army after the war will be as good as the Italian after the last one. We're still retreating in Greece and the Germans say in yesterday's paper that we are evacuating and they have sunk six of our transports full of fleeing troops. They have taken Larissa and the Pass of Thermopyles. Our reputation in the USA at the moment must be bad.

Friday, 25 April 1941

Another letter from mother today. Sally Toyne is engaged. It's amazing, she's not as old as I am. Still I suppose that's not old for a girl to get married, it rather pulled at the old heartstrings when I heard, as I believe I rather had designs on her myself once. Dreamed a lot last night thinking of Jo. It makes me feel wild again to be cooped up here. I must make an effort.

Sunday, 27 April 1941

I wasn't going to church at first, but was up there in the queue for the washing when the lights fused and the issue stopped, so I decided to go after all. I had no wash and it was very cold. Two more chaps tried to make a break for it today but were caught. They hid in the potato peeling cart and were grabbed outside the gates. The eight potato orderly's were also shoved into the jug, because Jerry thought that they had something to do with it. Went to a very good gramophone recital in the evening, where somebody came around with a rumour that a Russian reconnaissance aircraft had been over. However fantastic this rumour maybe, it is noticeable that during the last few days a steel sentry box has appeared next to the wooden one outside and also they are very hot on blackout. Tonight there are no lights in the corridors and the searchlights outside on not on. There's something about letters arriving again, it makes the weekends appear noticeable once more. They are the curse of my life.

Tuesday, 29 April 1941
A great to do about rising in the morning today. It has been pretty intense since we arrived here but came to a real head today. Lights out have gone back to 10.00 pm because people are not getting out of bed early enough. The brigadier has now made it an official order to be out of bed by 8.00 am. He seems to take the Germans side in this and not ours. Instead of our treatment being made better they seem to be taking a worse attitude. The commandant seems to have a personal grudge against us. Managed to get a new pair of boots today the first decent pair I've had for months.

Wednesday, 30 April 1941
This time last year I'd just finished dinner on the *Duke of Argyll* lying in Spithead and thought what a bloody awful meal it was. I'd seen my last of England for God knows how long. I get more and more browned off as the days go by. No parcels, no letters, only six in the whole camp today.

Saturday, 3 May 1941
The washing came back today, mine was alright but several of the others had bad results. Some pants were shrunk to the size of a handkerchief and some clothes looked as if they'd been washed in acid and came apart at the slightest pull. A very good show in the evening by the boys from Laufen and Posen. Most of the pieces were rehashes of stuff we'd seen at these places, but rehashed extraordinarily well and I enjoyed them better than before.

Sunday, 4 May 1941
God I am getting browned off. As every day goes by the more I have a fatalistic feeling that we are not going to win the war and that Germany will. I know it sounds pretty awful and unfaithful to my country, but I can't help it and I wish I could. Oh God! I wish I could really think the other way but in spite of everyone else's optimism this doubt gnaws at me the whole time and I can't stop it.

Friday, 9 May 1941
This day last year Germany marched into Belgium and Holland. I can remember as clearly as anything, listening to the wireless in 'B' Squadron mess before breakfast and Major Wade coming down the stairs very seriously. Very bad rations today. The soup consisted of just one cupful of barley and four potatoes. There were rumours open air raid alarm last night and I have just heard that the

camp commandant told the brigadier that there were British aircraft over Posen and last night. Nice work! I got my diaries back that were taken in the search.

Wednesday, 14 May 1941

Another attempted escape last night. An airman tried to scale the moat but failed and was caught. It was almost opposite our room, so we heard most of the fun. I was asleep unfortunately. Colonel Kennedy went down to Stalag today to enquire into the parcel situation. He satisfied himself as regards personal ones and then turned to the Red Cross. Here he met with a stern rebuff and was told that this was entirely to do with the Germans and they had the decisive say as to where and when they were issued. In fact, he was roughly handled and had a rifle dug in his back. There is no doubt in our own minds that there is something going on and that the Germans are hanky-pankying with these parcels. It's clearly a case for the American Embassy.

Thursday, 15 May 1941

At last my November [1940] closed parcel has arrived but some dirty bastard had pinched four of the seven packets of chocolate. It'll be marvellous to sleep in pyjamas again though. Two people were shifted out of the room and so we got rid of one bed, which makes quite a bit of room but unfortunately puts me in a bottom bed and in a very dark corner. Went to a recital of light opera in the evening. A jolly good programme and the best were a selection from *La Bohème* and from *The Mikado*. The former was exquisite and it made me think a lot, why is it that the best chaps always go?

Friday, 23 May 1941

Did a lot of sunbathing today and made myself two pairs of shorts by cutting off the legs of my long pants. Got a letter from Jo, how my heart jumped when I saw the writing, but there was very little in it. She had not had mine yet and, of course, there was no photograph in it.

Sunday, 25 May 1941

I went to holy communion at 8.00 am. This was a special service for those who lost their lives about this time last year. I talked to a Jerry in the afternoon, who was very browned off. He was very anxious to be assured that the war would be finished this year. Somebody told him that they thought it would, which I think was rather stupid. I decided to take my name off the move list, for what it's worth. The smell of the latrines outside is getting simply terrible, and comes to a head about supper time.

Tuesday, 27 May 1941

We're off again! Official intimation has it that we are going in a short while to an unknown destination. The *Hood* has been sunk by the *Bismarck*, I hope to Christ they get the blaggard. The drink question here is very acute. We can't drink the water unless it's been boiled, and that is rationed anyhow and there is no beer and very little mineral water. Went to a very good show in the evening, which saw the first appearance of a piano that had been bought by a British family who had one son killed in the war and another taken [as a] PoW and later killed.

Thursday, 29 May 1941

A day of rather note! My clothes and uniform parcels arrived. It was very disappointing that the buttons and badges had been taken off the tunic. I'm really almost getting to the point of being nauseated by the amount of food about, which is hardly what I ever expected. Two lots of escapes today. One chap was caught immediately, but the other five are still loose. We had a very long appel in the evening and lots of rushing about. There are rumours of another search, and that we are moving to Lingen on the Dutch border. This is a strong favourite, although Mecklenburg was also mentioned. Another strong rumour is that we are not going at all, which I shouldn't be a bit surprised at.

Friday, 30 May 1941

My anniversary of capture today and also of Bray's death. At a gramophone recital in the evening they played one of his favourites from *La Bohème* and, if he can see and hear me, I hope he knows that always will I remember him and follow his example if I can. It was marvellous to get letters from home today, mother's were full of courage and strength. I'm so ashamed of myself when I think of my writing and asking for everything so brazenly last year. The *Bismarck* has been sunk at last, thank God. It is, at least, some recompense for the loss of the *Hood*, although I would have rather welcomed her weight in submarines. Three chaps were caught today and they have put the Pole in the jug, believing that he is incriminated in the case of the chap who tried to walk out with his identity card yesterday. It's a damned shame as he is absolutely innocent.

Saturday, 31 May 1941

A terrific day! There were about 5,000 letters in the camp and I got 11. Two of these were from Vic, which are the cheeriest ones I've had yet! He is a grand chap and it's bloody bad luck that he's had such a tough time. There were four marvellous letters from mother, with two photographs in one of them. One of

Jo, in company with some others. She looks grand, but I do wish I could get one of her by herself. She's a wizard [marvellous] girl and I do hope she likes me a lot. I put on my Service Dress for the first time, but took it off after a short while as it was too hot. Another rumour has come about moving, apparently we are going to Laufen or Denmark. I hope to Christ it is the former.

Sunday, 1 June 1941
Tried to write a proposal letter to Jo today. Finished it but decided that I dare not sent it off yet. I shall wait till I get another letter from her. But my God the agony of waiting is awful. Very hot today and did some sunbathing. It was marvellous lying in the sun with the blue sky clear above, the breeze murmuring round, and a gramophone playing opera in the distance.

Tuesday, 3 June 1941
Packed my luggage very carefully and neatly in the morning and tied it all up, then had it torn to pieces in a search by the Jerries in the afternoon and have to pack it all again. Strong rumour again that we are going back to Laufen. Wrote a letter to mother [regarding] Jo and tried to get to find out whether there was anyone else.

Chapter 8

Biberach and Murder at the Railway Station

Wednesday, 4 June 1941

Today, 150 of us who had come from Posen, started out on 1 of the pleasantest journeys of our career. It began about 4.00 am when we marched down a very dusty road to the station where we were issued with a further Red Cross parcel. On passing a siding we saw what the Jerries use their ambulances for – loading petrol onto trucks all with very large red crosses on. The carriages were third class but moderately roomy and there was a guard in each one. With the abundance of food, life looked pretty rosy, and we settled down to a pleasant time. I found that sleeping in the luggage rack was the most comfortable, if you are small enough, as on the seats there is no grip, and the floor is too dusty. In any case the sentries' trip over you at night. The weather was terribly hot, and we wore as little as possible. The view as we arrived at Leipzig station was grand. People getting in and out of trains, lots of girls and women and all very interested in us. Very few of them, however, were anywhere approaching what one could call attractive.

Saturday, 7 June 1941

I spent another night in the luggage rack, whilst John Wallace and Bill Rushton made a break for it. I wished I'd been with them. The scenery had now changed completely from the long rolling plains of yesterday, we were now in the wooded slopes and hills of the Thuringen Wald, and a light rain was falling. By this time, we were drawn by an electric train and passing near Nürnberg, we saw the tops of the stadium towers and were then put into the goods yard there where we remained for the next five hours, arriving at Biberach around 7.00 am. We marched up a long hill to the camp (Oflag V-b), which consisted of long white stone buildings and looked very clean. Its occupants were thirteen British and Australian officers from Greece, otherwise the camp was completely empty, so we had a pretty good choice of rooms. Tiny, Robin, Arthur, Ronnie Eastman, Mark Carpenter, Nobby Clarke and myself managed to get an exceedingly nice room for eight after a bit of wrangling. At first the Germans tried to be very up stage with us, training us in German words of command and forbidding smoking in the rooms etc., but with our previous experience we soon tamed them of that. I settled down to quite an easy time.

Amongst the collection of photographs held by John Blomfield Dixon was this ariel image of Biberach Oflag V-b. (*Courtesy of The J B Dixon Collection*)

Wednesday, 11 June 1941

John Wallace and Bill Rushton were brought back today in the late afternoon. It was a great disappointment to us, as only this morning we had been told by the Jerries that they were still uncaught.

Thursday, 12 June 1941

Today, the remainder of the reprisal party arrived from Posen and filled out the camp a bit. We weren't frightfully pleased to see them. It's a damn nuisance all these people arriving, we were locked in all day while they are being searched and washed. In spite of the fact we know them, we aren't at all keen to see them. They seem to take it for granted that they are going to take over all the jobs, but they've got another think coming. I hope we can get rid of that fellow Timpson as adjutant and put Brush in instead. We only just managed to get iron beds for all our rooms before they arrived.

Major Theodore Livingstone Timpson, second-in-command, 1st Battalion, The Queen Victoria's Rifles. Captured on 26 May 1940, during the defence of Calais, Timpson was imprisoned at Laufen and Biberach, where he acted as the camp adjutant. John Blomfield Dixon had an intense dislike for Timpson and hoped he would be replaced by Major Edwin James Brush, but appears not to have explained his reasoning. (*Courtesy of authors collection*)

Monday, 16 June 1941

Some 250 officers arrived from Greece today. There was great excitement as this was the first batch of new *Kriegies* since we ourselves were caught and everybody hoped for news. As usual of course we were locked in but gave them a tremendous welcome as they came in the gate and some of us were afterwards allowed to go out and give them cigarettes and tea. They told us later that this was what cheered them more than anything, seeing blokes' heads poking out of windows and the great shout that went up when they entered the camp. There were quite a number of WOs amongst them and we all clubbed round and gave them food. Each room adopted their equivalent in another block and looked after them. We got some very nice New Zealanders amongst ours, though the English weren't much to tell about. About this time, I wrote home to mother about Jo. Afterwards I realised it was rather a foolish thing to do – it actually caused a bit of a stir at home – but I felt I had to have someone to confide in and ask advice from. At one time I very nearly wrote to Jo herself but luckily realised in time the absolute folly of doing that. Ever since I had met her, I had never thought about another girl, but the fact that we had seen too little of each other and also my prospects after the war had had a restraining upon me. Time alone however will show.

Sunday, 23 June 1941

After spraining my ankle on Saturday, I was in hospital when I heard the first rumours about the Russo-German war. I couldn't believe it at first and, in fact, did not fully credit it until the papers arrived and confirmed the fact. So often had we been bamboozled in the past that it was hard to credit, but now all the troop movements we had seen and heard about, all the minor clashes and stories were confirmed. Opinion in the camp was rather of the of mind that the Russians would not last long. 'If only they can last out for six weeks' was the most constant saying. 'It will give us time to land in the West and use up German men and material.'

Tuesday, 25 June 1941

I learnt that when we left Laufen, the Red Cross told our people that we were going from there to a modern camp to relieve overcrowding. Oh my God!, they've got something to pay for after this war. Afterwards, apparently, the story did come out the we'd gone to a reprisals camp and a good many people were worried. I hope mother was not affected. Alec has done a marvellous painting on the moon of a Clipper ship, it looks joy good and he's going to do some more. Learned that ninety-eight people are going shortly including most of the senior officers and the general, and also those who have been in jug for escaping including John Wallace and Bill Rushton, which is rather a blow.

Sunday, 29 June 1941

This place seems to brown me off for more than any other we've been at. There seems to be absolutely nothing to do and of course the ever presence of the barbed wire makes it worse. Our adoptees had a bit of dirty work done on them today and were chiselled out of their room and are now split up. Alan Tillick, a New Zealander, was telling us all about it and it seems that the company commander is a bit of a shyster and he seems to be the one most to blame

The Garden Kitchen and Theatre at Biberach. The gardeners are (left to right): Mike Farr, Basil Rought-Rought, John Parnell and Mike Lindley. (*Courtesy of The J B Dixon Collection*)

although the Rifle Brigade people who took the room over seem to have been just as much to do with it.

Wednesday, 2 July 1941

The Jerries discovered two chaps trying to get out in the refuse cart and after evening parade they found that two more had gone. It's very funny after all the time they've wasted putting up wire! We therefore had a four hour parade while they checked our names over in a most inefficient manner and searched the barracks. It was very tiring and the only thing they took from our room was a couple of steel helmets.

Thursday, 3 July 1941

A terrific day today. I got fourteen letters in the evening and two photographs, with Jo in a group in one of them, and also a letter from her, which I feel reciprocates my feelings. In a letter from Vic , it seems Eric Duncan has got a Bar to his MC for bravery. I didn't even know he'd got the first one! In the search yesterday the Huns pinched a hell of a lot of chocolate and about 3,000 cigarettes. When Todd informed the commandant this morning he said he didn't believe it. The dirty lot of thieving bastards!

Friday, 4 July 1941

Slept very badly in the night. It must have been the reaction after the letters. In Vic's letter he mentioned that mother had invited him to stay sometime. I hope Jo isn't there when he goes he might fall for her. In fact, I shall have to write and tell him I think.

Saturday, 12 July 1941

Blain has made it! Just heard that Martin has received a telegram saying, 'operation successful'. It's a bloody good effort but my God, it makes you envious. A very hot day again today, in fact almost unbearable, but it looks as if it's working up for a storm tonight. In the news tonight American planes have come over to Northern Ireland and air bases are supposed to be being built for them.

Sunday, 13 July 1941

Blain, Blain, Blain, nothing but Blain all through the night and day. Oh Christ! If only I could think of and carry out something original that would work. A rumour from the German doctor says that the Jerries have pierced the Stalin line. I hope to Christ the Russians can hold the Jerries. Another three months at least is what we need.

Thursday, 17 July 1941

Quite a day today. In letter from Jo she, at last, ends up 'all my love'. How I hope she really means it, no one but myself knows. Photographs started today and I think we shall get ours tomorrow. Quite a sensation was caused on parade by the photographer appearing with a girl helper of about 16 years of age. Its only about the second time we've had a woman inside the wire.

Saturday, 19 July 1941

The Swiss people were round today and were surprised we had not had the Red Cross, food and cigarette parcels. The commandant, when asked, said we'd had lots and stuck to this until shown the box of one, when he admitted we hadn't. He's going to get a big shock when he sees a full one. An officer from Berlin was here as well and said he would do what he could about quickening up mail when he got back. Actually, the speed of travel of the mail is alright, it's the censor staff at this end that the hold up comes and we need more censors.

Monday, 21 July 1941

The food was very bad today, only a sort of cabbage soup for lunch. Margerine is definitely off now as well, and since yesterday we have been having dripping, although a better sort than before. Somebody in the camp saw the Jerry midday meal yesterday. It consisted of a bowl of watery soup as we get, one potato and an egg between two. I wonder what the reaction would be if one of our Tommies at home had that put in front of them!

Wednesday, 23 July 1941

The Bosche are turning very nasty now. Lights out in future at 10.00 pm. They are locking the barracks at 8.00 pm. This they say is because of the noise made after 10.00 pm. They are also closing all latrines except for three blocks. My God these bastards have got to pay a lot for some things when we win the war. Got three letters, one from Betty Parry, and a composite one from Phil Brownley and Sylvia Parry who are unofficially engaged. I must say that I'd entirely forgotten about them. I bet there is some dirty work going on between them as they are staying at the same hotel on his seven days leave.

Thursday, 24 July 1941

The escape of three people, Hector Christie, Stewart Walker and Bernhard Dromgoole, was announced. All day there was terrific activity round the wire, the security officer and others looking for holes and poking about. Red Cross parcels arrived today, but according to reports the Bosche are going to open every tin, it's going to be a hell of a mess.

Saturday, 26 July 1941

Hector Christie has been caught near Lake Constance, about five minutes from the frontier. Quite a good show in the evening, where they did an action song on *Frankie and Johnnie*. One of the chaps dressed up as Frankie in a sort of cowgirl outfit. Gave me a bit of a shock when he came on, for the moment I thought it was Jo, and how my heart leapt. But what a deception! My life here is very slack. I must pull myself together and do some work. My brain is getting absolutely addled and God knows what I shall be like when I get back.

Monday, 28 July 1941

Heard today that Hector Christie had passed that last lot of German guards and was actually in no man's land between Germany and Switzerland when a patrol literally fell right over him. If that isn't tough luck, I don't know what is. I started my Spanish lessons again, and this time I really must keep it up. Colonel Everard had a dream last night. He was handed a copy of the *News Chronicle*, which he never reads, in which the headlines were 'Hostilities Cease', 'Germany Capitulates' and the date, very clear, was 28 October 1941. We shall see!

Sunday, 3 August 1941

Two good stories today. One is that the inhabitants of Biberach are getting a bit agitated about the amount of food coming in the camp. They say they've been told that England is starving and how can she send all this food if that's the case. The other one is that the guard, on having their soup put in front of them on Saturday, refused to eat it. Arranged for an audition with the gramophone in the theatre for the entertainments committee tomorrow.

Friday, 8 August 1941

Got the news tonight that Pete Douglas, who escaped from Posen, is now in England! Christ it does make me envious. Went for an audition for the *Ghost Train* in the evening with two other chaps. It was for the part of the young boy substituted for Julia and by luck I got it.

Tuesday, 12 August 1941

Had a letter from mother in reply to my one about Jo. Apparently, my proposal has been met with a bit of a shock. In fact, I'm rather dreading getting the first letter to see what's in it, as it was written before she had spoken with father. At any rate she says that I must not do anything till I get back as Jo is so sensitive and young that it would most probably hurt and shock her. Her own impression I gather as that my feelings have been brought on by the circumstances here, which is entirely wrong. In a way I feel that I have been rather pre-emptive and should not have mentioned it till I got home, but there it is, it's what I felt and still feel, and I thought I was doing right at the time. Thirty orderlies arrived today from Italy, and one of the more fantastic of their rumours was that a British army was outside Lille.

Saturday, 16 August 1941
Two letters today, both from mother and both had photographs in, one a very good one of Jo. Mother and Elinor both look rather weird though and it's not a good photograph of them. Went to a very good show in the evening by the 'Thornites'. It was a bit blue but very funny.

Monday, 18 August 1941
Went to the doctors early this morning as my left ear was bunged up all day yesterday, and funnily enough there were about three others for the same thing. Had them well syringed and feel much better now. A whole lot of battledresses came in today, enough for the whole camp, and I hope I shall get a bit. The French have arrived to build new buildings. They seem quite decent chaps although, of course, they are separated from us and not allowed to talk. They all seem to want to fight for [Charles] de Gaulle. Apparently, they say the inhabitants around this district have a very high regard for us and think us very good mannered and cheerful, especially the non-combatants, who, of course, they see more of when they go out for walks.

Wednesday, 20 August 1941
The people in Biberach sent up a note asking whether we had any spare chocolate or meat, as they can't get hold of any. There is also a Biberach Shakespeare reading society, which makes a collection of famous programmes of plays performed, and they have written to Colonel Everard to ask whether they can put the photographs of 'Leave it to Psmith' in their book and would he send them a programme as they want to record the historic event of the first performance by British players in the town. News from the French too is encouraging, they are all apparently itching to get back to fight Jerry and it is said that in a recent raid on Lille, thousands of Germans were killed. That's pretty good!

Friday, 22 August 1941
Two letters from mother. In the first one, about Jo, she is absolutely adamant that nothing can happen between us as we are first cousins and must remain nothing but that. Her opinion, after talking with father, seems to have altered a bit, but in the main I feel she is opposed to it. I thought that marriages between first cousins were quite frequent these days. In any case as long as there is no

The *Māori Review*. Performed by New Zealanders captured in Crete and North Africa. (Back left to right): Henry Hokianga, George Bennett and Jimmy Wiremu. (Front left to right): Tenga Rangi, Henry Ngata and Bill Herewine. (*Courtesy of The J B Dixon Collection*)

John Blomfield Dixon (Centre) plays a girl in the *Māori Review* next to Tom Jones. (*Courtesy of The J B Dixon Collection*)

real medical reason to prevent us marrying, and Jo is willing, I for one am adamant in my resolve.

Wednesday, 3 September 1941

The beginning of the third year of the war and feeling very browned off today. How much longer? It's nearly two weeks now since I've had a letter from home. A German in the camp has had a letter from friends and relations in Hamburg and Dortmund complaining of the severity of the air raids and imploring him to send them food as the situation is very serious. Another move is indicated in about two weeks, and I'm rather fed up about it. Asked to take the part of a girl in the *Māori* [*Review*] show. They'll be a bit of party afterwards I should think.

Saturday, 6 September 1941

Spent most of the morning writing out the part for the *Māori* [*Review*] show. In the afternoon we had a rehearsal, and it didn't go too well.

Tuesday, 9 September 1941

Went to the dentist in the evening and had my teeth scaled and cleaned. The former was rather a painful process and drew rather a lot of blood. During the night a Frenchie fell ill with a lot of shrieking and screaming and had to be taken away in an ambulance immediately. Today I celebrated eighteen months of commissioned rank and, therefore, should become an Oberleutnant!

Wednesday, 10 September 1941

A letter from my darling Jo of 15 August [1941]. It was so good to get it and she at last says 'dearest' and ends asking me 'to take care of myself'. My cup is almost full. An orderly came from Stuttgart and said that it has been bombed to hell. The hospital there was full of *Stuka* pilots suffering from wounds, young Germans who had been malingering on the Eastern Front and also a chap who had been slapped across the face with a knife by a woman as he was leading PoWs away.

Friday, 12 September 1941

First night of the show today and it went extraordinarily well. John Lightfoot said that he'd enjoyed producing it the most of any of his shows. It was announced tonight that we were leaving this camp between 23 and 28 September and that we should be getting a card with which to say where we are going. For a certainty its Nürnberg.

Sunday, 14 September 1941

Well, they have done it! Twenty-six got away by the tunnel during the night and Robin was amongst them. The Jerries took it very well and seemed quite amused. So far, we haven't been inconvenienced by a search but I'm afraid they'll be one tomorrow. The audience at the *Māori Review* was very, very rowdy at the show tonight, in fact, it was almost the worst one I've been in front of. Very cold today and the stone building makes it colder. In a way I hope we're going to wooden ones for the winter in the next camp. I've now shifted into Robin's bunk as I like a top one better.

War Office,
12th February, 1942.

The KING has been graciously pleased to approve the following awards in recognition of distinguished services in the field:—

The Military Cross.

Lieutenant (acting Captain) Hugh Barry O'Sullivan (62674), Royal Tank Regiment, Royal Armoured Corps.

Captain Henry Brian Burn (65362), The Royal Northumberland Fusiliers.

Lieutenant (temporary Captain) Hugh Austin Woollatt (71125), The Lancashire Fusiliers.

Lieutenant Angus David Rowan-Hamilton (95492), The Black Watch (Royal Highland Regiment).

Lieutenant Michael George Duncan (65656), The Oxfordshire and Buckinghamshire Light Infantry.

Lieutenant Henry Edward Stewart (154077), Intelligence Corps.

Photograph showing Military Cross recipients who had escaped from Biberach on 13 July 1941. (*Courtesy of The London Gazette*)

I can't make up my mind whether to write a letter to Jo this week or whether to write to Holland. I rather think it will have to be the latter.

(Left): The Grave of Major Hugh Austin Woollatt at Fontenay-Le-Pesnel War Cemetery, Tessel, Normandy. (Right): Major Hugh Austin Woollatt who had escaped from Biberach on 13 July 1941 and made a successful "run" to Switzerland, was killed in action on 17 July 1944 serving with the 2nd/5th Lancashire Fusiliers. (*Both courtesy of authors collection*)

The mass escape referred to took place on the night of Saturday, 13 July 1941. Twenty-six PoWs got out through a tunnel which had been started on 24 June [1941]. Four of the group managed to reach Switzerland, a journey of about 70 miles, the remainder would be recaptured. The successful escapees were Lieutenant Michael George Duncan MC, who, like John Blomfield Dixon had been captured at Watou, Lieutenant Hugh Barry O'Sullivan MC, Lieutenant Hugh Austin Woollatt MC and Lieutenant Angus David Rowan-Hamilton MC. Travelling separately, each man crossed the Swiss frontier at various points following a hazardous journey of anything from five to fourteen days. On 12 February 1942, the successful escapees were awarded the Military Cross in 'recognition of distinguished services in the field'.

Each officer returned to service with the army but tragedy would follow some of them. After a successful escape, Hugh Woollatt (pictured) found himself reaching the rank of major and was posted to 2nd/5th Lancashire Fusiliers. During the Normandy campaign he was commander of 'B' Company and on 16 July 1944 was killed by German mortar fire east of Tessel Wood near the village of Landet.

Lieutenant Hugh Barry O'Sullivan MC, would survive the war and go on to serve with the Royal Tank Regiment, achieving the rank of lieutenant colonel, would be lost in a tragic boating accident on 28 July 1956. He would be posthumously awarded the Royal Humane Society's Stanhope Gold Medal for his gallant lifesaving efforts.

Wednesday, 17 September 1941

Six of the escaped chaps were brought back on Monday, and another two more today making a total of eleven, but no bad news of Robin yet. The Jerries came round the block today turning out lockers and stores looking for holes. The *Māori Review* went very well and an extra one was put on, as it was liked so much. Got our personal photographs today and most of them are quite good, although mine looks as though I was scared stiff or about to burst into tears. Got offered another small part today in a couple of sketches coming off in a variety show next week. It should be quite good.

Saturday, 20 September 1941

An abortive escape attempt this morning but they were soon brought back. News also, Robin and Johnny King have been caught. It's a great disappointment. The German food has been more filthy than normal, soups with absolutely nothing in them but water. If it wasn't for our Red Cross parcels God knows what we'd do.

Monday, 22 September 1941

The German dentist NCO committed suicide during the night. Today the Germans started to collect all their issue blankets and also took some Red Cross personal ones. Jack Paul came back to the camp today and, apparently, according to what he says he was actually caught in Switzerland. Personally, I think his being caught was his own bloody fault for sitting down and smoking a cigarette when he thought he was just over the frontier. You'd have thought he would have made absolutely sure where he was first! Robin and Johnny are in the Bunker outside. They seem very cheery and apparently there are still five outside the wire.

Thursday, 25 September 1941

Well, it's on again, blast it! The latest news is that we leave next Wednesday. We're all fed up to the teeth and if it's anything like the description we've heard from the French it's going to be pretty awful. In the dress rehearsal today they cut out the typist sketch so I've only got one now. Robin came back to the room today and we were very glad to see him.

Friday, 26 September 1941

News today by a letter from Betty Parry that Eric Duncan is posted as missing. I hope to God from the bottom of my heart that nothing has happened to him. His poor wife.

Sunday, 28 September 1941

The first night of the show *Stop Gap* and it went very well. Felt very tired after it. A Nazi officer in the camp today said that they would finish off Russia in two or three months and then settle down to a seven year war with England.

Thursday, 2 October 1941

Company orderly officer today, which was very boring. Last night of the show and John Lightfoot was present with a packet of dripping at the end of the show with a large label inscribed, 'from the female members of the cast to lights, in remembrance of past services'. It was his twenty-fifth show behind wire!

Captain Eric Duncan MC and Bar. A great friend of John Blomfield Dixon. He was killed in action on 15 June 1941 while serving with the 3rd King's Own Hussars, Royal Armoured Corps. He has no known grave and is remembered on the Alamein Memorial, Egypt. (*Courtesy of The J B Dixon Collection*)

Sunday, 5 October 1941

We're off again. This is the third warning, but I somehow don't think it will be cancelled this time. We're moving next Friday and searching starts tomorrow at 8.00 am. It's awful, after all the work we've put in with the room. I wouldn't mind taking any odds that we never get another like it, at least with [the] same eight people.

Tuesday, 7 October 1941

Four months today we arrived here and now we are on the move again. Got our luggage searched and packed away today, and it's a great relief to get rid of it! Still no news as to where we are going, although Nürnberg seems a strong favourite again. It is said to be only a normal six hour journey away, so it seems a pretty bet. The news tonight was very cheery. There were some extracts from [Adolf] Hitler's speech and although it sounds pretty good and he says that Russia is smashed forever, it is not borne out by today's news. A German soldier who came back for sixteen days leave from the Kiev sector said that the Russians put in a very heavy counter attack against a portion held by Romanian troops, whom they drove back with enormous losses to the Romanians, and the situation was only restored by German troops.

Friday, 10 October 1941

After a 5.00 am appel, we were off again, and the Germans turned extraordinarily nasty all of a sudden. We were locked in our rooms until we had been searched

The grave of Lieutenant Jacob Michael Sturton, 88 Field Regiment, Royal Artillery, Mentioned in Despatches. After making a desperate break for freedom at Biberach railway station, he chose to surrender and was shot dead on the spot by his guards. Originally buried in Biberach Cemetery and re-interned on 13 August 1948 at Durnbach War Cemetery, Germany. He was 21 years old. (*Courtesy of The War Graves Project and The National Archives WO416/349/229*)

and at 12.00 pm we were marched off to the station. The guards were the biggest bastards we've had since Posen, shouting and cursing at the station. This went on and there was a hell of a lot of shooting and threating with their rifles. We were all very depressed. They then brought in the most terrible gang of thugs I have ever seen, who had been used to transport Russians. We were forcibly restrained from laughing, talking and smoking. Rather stupidly Mickey Sturton made a break for it at the station. He dashed under the train but almost immediately saw that it was hopeless, turned round and came out with his hands up. He was immediately shot dead by the guards, who also wounded one of their own chaps in the neck with a ricochet. He came running past the window with a bleeding throat and there was a big pool of blood. A more blatant case of murder there never and we were seething with rage all through the journey, which was appallingly uncomfortable. The carriages were the worst we've had, no windows are allowed open and, as usual, the latrine door has to be kept open for 'activities to be observed'. The guards were very much on the alert and during the night, and going through the tunnels, torches would be switched on and about four loaded rifles pointed at us. No sleeping on the floor was allowed. At 4.00 pm [we] arrived at Ulm and at 5.45 pm went through Aalen, then the night sets in and we could see no more. I shan't be able to stand this train much longer.

Chapter 9

The Move to Warburg – Oflag VI-b

Originally planned to be an airfield, the PoW camp at Dössel, on the outskirts of Warburg, was opened in September 1940 and became known as Warburg-Oflag VI-b. At first French officers were housed there, but in October 1941 these were replaced by the British officers moved from Laufen, amongst whom was John Blomfield Dixon. Here, for the first time, he would witness the flashes of anti-aircraft fire and the sound of falling British bombs, as the Royal Air Force attacked targets in the Ruhr Valley.

With the coming of winter, the camp became almost unliveable, with John describing it as:

> The mud everywhere was terrible and to travel down to the Laufen end, a good trip in any weather, took ages. Going to the wash house in the morning was absolute agony, as there was almost 200 yards to walk in all kinds of weather. Conditions in the hospital were just as bad as the rest of the camp. Overcrowding, orderlies mixed in with officers, no proper sanitary arrangements, no running water and indescribable chaos. Fortunately, all the camp cellars were below our block, coal, turnips, potatoes etc., so when we were a bit short, we paid a visit there. Our stove was improved by getting a smaller one which gave more heat, so that at last we were able to do other things than fries and stews.

However, at the beginning of December 1941, John and his comrades got their first view of Russian PoWs.

> They were sent to build some new huts just outside the wire in front of our room. We threw them cigarettes and food and it was a pitiful to see. The rush they made for them, scrambling on the ground and then too weak to get up afterwards. The guards lashed at them with their rifles and fists and treated them in a brutal fashion. Shouts and protests were made, and they looked a bit ashamed of their work. Occasionally, Russians came in for delousing and we then gave them as much extra food as we could, which they wolfed like animals, greatly to the amusement of the German guards.

They were absolutely starving and from notes, which we exchanged with them secretly, we learnt that hundreds of them died during the ensuing winter. The Germans would not allow us to help them in any way, but in spite of this we managed to send them what we could.

The initial concerns at the state of the camp and the future of the PoWs soon began to ease as they settled into another series of long drawn out days filled with little else than the laborious wait for news of the war, the fate of friends and family at home and overseas, and a desire to escape their surroundings. But for many, the thought and sight of a Red Cross food parcel was the highlight of the week, as it was often the difference between living and starving, in surroundings where a PoW had little else to look forward to. Those who maintained a diary, believing it would be a record of short term incarceration, now began to make entries that simply read, 'terminated due to boredom.' John Blomfield Dixon, however, continued to record his daily routine at Warburg describing the weather, the arrival of letters from home and the need to respond, the rumours that abounded the camp, the outpourings of the Nazi propaganda machine, and his daily consumption of food. He also began acting again, but this time connected with the professionals in the camp. Besides a role in the pantomime he would obtain a part in *The Black Eye* produced by Michael Goodliffe.

Saturday, 11 October 1941

A dreadful night, I slept for approximately half an hour and had to read and smoke the rest of the time, it was absolute agony. We reached Bebra at 7.30 am, Kassel at 10.00 am, finally arriving at Warburg, our destination, at 12.30 pm. Just before arriving we were told by the interpreter that we were going to a German officers training school, which consisted of a double story stone building, very comfortable. We were marched 5km in the rain and then had an awful shock. At first, we were put in some terrible huts, which we thought were our final destination, but luckily, they were only for searching, and at last we were led over the hill and down into Oflag VI-b. The camp was an enormous size with buildings of all descriptions, of which we picked a stone building rather like a garage. Unpainted brick walls, cement floors and very dusty. Luckily our eight managed to wrangle a room together and roped in Brian Rich, Johnny Mumford and Jimmy Fitch. There was no electric light and to begin with there was some difficulty in obtaining carbide lights. We found the Spangenberg and Crete boys, the only ones in residence, and so the next day was spent in exploring the camp and raiding the unoccupied portion for anything we could lay hands on, especially wood. I think a description of the room might be apt here. It's a pointed brick walled room, white washed, like a barn, 14 feet by 24 feet with two windows. All around are the wooden beds, and in the corner the stove, which gives out very little heat. The filth on the stone floor is awful. There are three tables and all are piled high with dirty crockery as it is after supper. Two carbide lamps, which hardly give any light at all. A line of washing hangs over the stove, and locker the doors stand wide open with clothes of all sorts hanging all over the place. Such is our abode in a German officer PoW camp.

Monday, 13 October 1941
British officers from Laufen and Tittmoning arrived to fill up the rest of the camp. They got even more of a shock when they saw the place, as they had been living in luxury since we left. Norman and all the rest were very well, but I didn't feel like going back to live with them as we'd both made different friends now. Friction immediately set in between us all, and it was some time before everybody cooled down. Our room is such a mess and now we've got our luggage there's less room than ever. The filth is dreadful too and everything is a complete shambles. I don't know quite what I am going to do with all my stuff. Still, the General is having a conference tomorrow, so things may start happening pretty shortly.

Tuesday, 14 October 1941
A big parade today where we were addressed by the commandant, who is only a major, with the normal sort of bullshit. According to a speech by [Prime Minister Winston] Churchill, the end of the war is in sight but he cannot promise a victory before Christmas.

Wednesday, 15 October 1941
Another bloody day. Rained most of the time, the Swiss Red Cross chap came round and nearly went up in smoke and the last escapees from Biberach turned up. We got Dennis Faulkner and Geoffrey Barr in our room, so we had to shift round our beds and mine is now under the window and I have much more room to move. The light was bloody again tonight and we could hardly see. It has just now got a bit better, so I can write. Apparently, according to the Jerries, this is a 'reconciliation' camp, though to reconciliate what, we don't know. They say we have been moved here so we can get better conditions of living! The funniest thing of all is that there is a notice forbidden PoWs to approach German women!

Saturday, 18 October 1941
The news is very depressing these days. The Bosche is almost at Moscow and advancing along the Sea of Azov. If Russia packs in, the only thing I can see is that we're sunk. What has brought on the reaction so much is all these

marvellous rumours that we heard on our arrival here proving to have no sort of foundation at all, when I really did believe that something good had been happening. Bitten all over by fleas in the night and itched all day.

Sunday, 19 October 1941

A terrific wind storm in the night and several huts had the roofs blown off, with the inhabitants left staring at the stars in the pouring rain. The news was much more cheery tonight, although they say the position round Moscow is serious. I got the negative of my personal photo today and as it is a small one I shall be able to send it home again. There were no letters today, as was rumoured yesterday and, apparently, the brigade postal officer has not contacted the Germans. My God, some people are slack.

Friday, 24 October 1941

Very cold again today. I felt rotten all day, a beastly headache and a bit of stomach trouble. A parade in the afternoon to change the battalions around and that didn't help much, standing about in the cold. Received a letter circulated through the regiment from Brigadier Somerset about the good work done by 145 Brigade. It was quite cheering although how much was bullshit I don't know. According to the Laufen war party, who arrived today, incredible scenes took place after the main party left. The civilian population raided the place, searching for food and clothes, and were even scraping the margarine off the paper. They were driven out by the guards. A letter arrived today for someone in the camp from an American donor of parcels and this is an extract from it:

> I was in Canada two weeks ago and saw the German prisoners of war. I assure you that they have everything they want and are treated like gentlemen. They themselves admit this and say they are sure we are being treated the same in Germany.

My God if they could see us! Living like pigs or even worse, the bastards. Ever since leaving Biberach I've never ceased to hate them. While we were there I did think we had found some of the decent type, but the show they put up on our leaving and the drumming they've given us here has lead me to Arthur's very old conclusion, that there's no good German but a dead one.

Saturday, 25 October 1941

For the first time in my life I heard British bombs last night. It began about 10.30 pm when the goons here got in a hell of a flap, shouting, 'Lichts aus [(lights out)]', etc. and then we heard the thunder of the anti-aircraft fire to the southeast in the direction of Kassel. I went to a window I saw the flashes in the sky, and the thud of bombs was terrific. About 11.30 pm there were four terrific thuds and I think they must have been the 'all is kaput' type. According to an airman who arrived in the camp today after spending the night in an ARP shelter on Kassel station, the bombing went on till 2.30 am ending up with a terrific crash, which shook everything. The junction was wrecked. Did the first performance of *Sir She Said* this afternoon and it went down very well.

Friday, 31 October 1941

This place gets worse and worse every day, mud everywhere. The hospital is a positive disgrace, overcrowding and no better sanitary accommodation then the rest of the camp, just boxes in the corridor. There are quite a number of cases of diphtheria and more occurred today. I think it's mostly amongst the Crete blokes. I went to see Geoffrey in hospital today. He is not much better and hasn't eaten well at all yet. I hope he gets back to normal again, but a special diet is the only help I'm afraid and he won't get a proper one here. I heard a story today of the brave new German '*kultur*', apparently when the three officers were caught in the tunnel the other day they were taken along in their dripping wet clothes made to stand in a draughty corridor with hands out of their pockets for six hours before being allowed to see a German officer.

Monday, 3 November 1941

Four chaps were caught today trying the gate stunt. Two of them got as far as the station but were caught there, the other two were caught at the gate. The Germans are absolutely scared stiff what we think about this camp, and every letter that has the smallest reference to conditions, even people asking for chocolate and porridge, get their letters slung back at them. Parade was an hour earlier today due to the film *The Three Codonas* being shown. We went at 3.30 pm and it was quite enjoyable, although we couldn't understand the language. It was more of a novelty than anything. Started writing a letter to Jo. It's very difficult to put anything through without wondering whether it will be slung back by the censors.

Wednesday, 10 November 1941

The Germans have broken into the parcel room again. On arrival outside the camp this morning people found the wrappers strewn all over the place and muddy footprints leading from a window. Colonel Todd was one of those whose parcel was pilfered, so fireworks can be expected. The general is purported to have said that there is every reason to hope that officers caught in France would be interned in a neutral country early in the new year. Those caught in Greece and Crete would not be moved. I wonder?

Thursday, 11 November 1941

Apparently, the general is calling a meeting to tell us to prepare our physical and mental fitness as he thinks the war might be on its last legs and we must prepare to be in the midst of a bit of chaos and perhaps revolution. I hope to Christ there is a spot of the latter. Nothing would suit me better than to get behind a machine gun and in action again. I managed to get in the cast of the pantomime at last. Bobby Loder came in when I wasn't here and asked if I'd take part in the chorus. I've been looking forward to it all year and I'm so glad I've managed to work it. [Prime Minister Winston] Churchill made a bloody marvellous speech at the Mansion House, that will teach Adolf [Hitler] where [the Nazis] can get off.

Wednesday, 19 November 1941

A letter arrived for me today, and God what stunning news! Dick is keen on Jo. A line says, 'so perhaps in a few years, or sooner, there might be more news from that quarter.' Christ, I can't express myself – my heart and bowels are like stone and water. It's a thing I've always in my heart of hearts feared, but God that it should happen. I feel so sick. Still, I shall never give up hope. Who knows what she herself thinks. I give myself into the hands of providence though by no means leaving all the work to her. God, how helpless one feels here though. He has all the advantage. I've decided to do nothing about it on his part, but intend writing to Jo in the same feelings and perhaps increase the terms of endearment. Why don't her letters come through? Has she stopped writing or has Dick had any effect on it? I'd give anything for a letter from her which gave me a bit of hope, but I can't really go anywhere near the whole way myself from here. It isn't fair on her. If there is anything that browns me off more than anything it's getting no letters. It's alright when you know there are no letters in the camp, as is usual at a new one, but when they are they're there and you've been in the camp over six weeks and had damn all, It gets beyond the joke!

Wednesday, 26 November 1941

Got a part in the *Black Eye* given to me to read, and it is not a girls one but that of a young boy. At the moment I can't make head nor tail of it. I went to the reading and I think I've got the part, although I wasn't very satisfied myself.

Sunday, 30 November 1941

The last day of November 1941 and may we never see another one in *Kriegiedom*. A very good soccer match in the afternoon between England and Scotland, which was won by the former 3–2. It was quite exciting with the crowds that were there, neatly marked pitch and the teams neatly turned out. England in white with blue and white stockings and Scotland in khaki shirts and shorts with red and white stockings. Almost one would imagine a game at home on a Sunday and the play I gathered from the people who know wouldn't have disgraced even a third division team. A private in the Gordons who arrived the other day from the German military prison, said there were 5,000 goons there most of them deserter's who were sentenced to 99 days imprisonment and then shot. There were a good many naval chaps amongst them.

Tuesday, 9 December 1941

Today, we got news about the declaration of war between US and Japan in which we also seemed to be involved. The first successes of the Japs were terribly depressing, but everyone, however, was firmly convinced that we could hold them in Malaya. I was told by an RAF pilot who was shot down on 8 November [1941] that we were much more cheerful here than they were at home. I received a letter today from mother in which she says Jo is writing. She's such a long time about it though. It's ages since I had one from her, if this is her only one since the last time I wrote, that makes a two-month interval between letters since the last one I had was dated 15 August [1941] and considering I'm writing such a lot and sacrificing my letters for her I think it's a pretty poor show.

Wednesday, 10 December 1941

Rumours from the goons today that there has been a very big naval battle in the Pacific, we losing two capital ships the 'King George V' and the 'Repulse', but Japs lost eight capital ships – the bastards! An Indian who went into a trance today and when he came out of it said we'd be out of Germany in twenty-four days, and laid bets on it. I was very browned off today, rain, rain, rain and mud, mud, mud. Towards the end of the evening the whole room felt like going berserk and breaking things up.

Saturday, 13 December 1941

A bloody awful day. Some chaps tried to get out in the morning and failed. The goons had a search in the afternoon. Tiny and some others are thinking of moving and I can't make up my mind whether to go or not. On the whole I think not. The Colonel wants a detailed account from each officer as to how he was captured. I ask you – after a whole year, I can't remember a damned thing. I managed to get something together but how far the facts are true as to the names of places visited I don't know but in the main it tries to follow them as far as I remember.

Thursday, 25 December 1941

My second Christmas Day as a *Kriegie* and what a day. Blizzards of rain, snow and sleet, the worst winter for some 120 years. In the morning I paid a visit to Doug Allison and was greeted with a present of some cigarettes and plied with tea, biscuits and raisins. Our first Christmas with enough food too, and we made a real banquet of it. We had our meal in the evening, the menu was an *hors d'oeuvres* of jellied eels, sardines and tomato, dried carrots and potatoes with mayonnaise, roast meat roll with peas and mashed potatoes. A fruit salad of cherries, crushed pineapple and raspberries with cream; biscuits and cheese; coffee, cigars and chocolates. The table was properly laid out with decorated paper, and we had Christmas napkins. We all helped cook. The Christmas cake was terrific as well, although the taste of the chocolate used was abysmal. In addition, we had our hooch, or what remained of it, and it was very good. Altogether not too bad a Christmas and very much different to last year. Our toast with the wine was, 'the folks at home, God bless them'. The sentries around the wire had a very bad time, and had to be forced out in the open by an officer with a drawn revolver.

Monday, 29 December 1941

My birthday, 23 today. The mess made me a cake. Geoff iced it and Brian wrote 'Dickie Dooley' on it in white icing. A present from Norman in the morning of forty cigarettes. Last night it was as bright as daylight and there was a raid in the direction of Dortmund. It was absolutely freezing in bed too, and when we woke up this morning all the water was froze.

Chapter 10

1942: A Year of Change

A year of change began and despite the weather, and the deprivations of captivity, the show *Black Eye* went ahead and was a great success. I also starred in a show called *Miss Easton Suggests*, written by John Lightfoot but I was not very good. I was supposed to be the lead, but felt ashamed of it the whole way through and couldn't put my back in it. I was also cast for the maid in *George and Margaret* but due to a 'tube' blowing in the theatre, all activities ceased for two months. The main trouble in the camp was Hauptman Radenacher and Major Sturzkopf, the security officer and second-in- command respectively. Besides being very efficient, they did all they could to make life as unpleasant as possible for us, acting in a typically German manner.

Thursday, 1 January 1942
For the second time, we begin a year of *Kriegedom* and I hope that this will see our freedom and victory, that all may come well for me and mine and that some of my blackest thoughts will not come to anything. Harold Hopper is dreadfully ill, I believe with pleurisy. I hope he gets well soon.

Saturday, 10 January 1942
A terrific day today. I received letters from home, including one from Jo and a photograph! What a relief and what rapture. She's 21 next summer and I must send her a present. I must get hold of the Mappin & Webb catalogue. I can't stop looking at the photograph, it's forever with me in my mind.

I've decided on a sapphire and diamond brooch at about £14. It's the best I can see and do in it. There's not a very good selection. I've sent Dick a cheque for £5 to open a Mappin & Webb account.

Wednesday, 14 January 1942
Had a farewell party today for the Colonel, as all the senior army and RAF officers are being moved to Spangenburg. I put on service dress, but it was rather cold around the legs and I don't think I shall do it again. Major Coussons took command of the battalion. On both parades we were kept frightfully late, as they now will not allow battalions to dismiss until everybody has been counted. It was

hellish cold and we got very browned off. Peter Kitto was reported wounded in November [1941] and no further news. I hope to God he is alright.

Monday, 19 January 1942
Queuing up half the morning to get water from a little pilot tap that took ten minutes to fill one jug. After waiting there for nearly an hour, I discovered that it was on the other end of the camp – so had to walk to there! The first performance in the evening of *Black Eye* and it went very well but I was far from satisfied with my part, although Michael Goodliffe thanked me and said it was very good, but I have my doubts about it.

Tuesday, 27 January 1942
I am feeling very depressed. During the night the temperature fell to -50°F. It was frightful, everything in our room was frozen twice as hard as usual. I was shaving before parade and put down my shaving brush, when I went to pick it up it was frozen to the table. Apparently, it is the coldest for thirty-five years. Last night there was an air raid and Squadron Leader Fielder says he heard our bombers go over at 9.00 pm and come back at 1.00 am. They were four engine Halifax's and this is the route they use for Prauge. Big problem with water today, as it was off most of the time both in the camp and the village. It was the final performance of *Black Eye* tonight, which went well in spite of one or two technical hitches, such as the curtain breaking!

Saturday, 7 February 1942
Eric (Duncan) has been killed! Norman brought me the news this morning. I must say it did not come as too great shock at once, as I feared somehow he was gone. Why is it that all those good lads have to go and I'm left here to rot in my cowardice and not able to do anything? God knows what will become of us when I come back, I shudder to think. Ever since the colonel went my constant fear of what he would do about my statement has subdued a bit, but every now and then I get that indirect or direct sensation that makes a shudder go down my back. My God the disgrace of it if it does happen. But why is it all self, self. I must think of someone but that. Everyone at the moment is carrying me in everything and I'm nothing but a woman. Christ, what a specimen!

Friday, 13 February 1942
Depressed as hell again and the news is bloody awful. A 'tube' burst in the theatre and it is closed until 18 March [1942], so that for the moment has put the kybosh on any shows or rehearsals, it would come just now when the show is ready to go on. Personally, I think it's an absolute scandal and the thing

should have never been allowed with all the various parades so close. Cock up after cock up. It's about time someone reorganised the whole thing otherwise we're well on the way to losing this war.

Friday, 20 February 1942

Orderlies taking Canadian Red Cross boxes down to Warburg upset the cart in the snow and the lid came off. Inside were four dead Russian. Three died from illness and one was killed by a big bullet wound right through his side.

Wednesday, 25 February 1942

A grand letter from Jo today, and in it she said that she danced the New Year in for the first time this year and hoped to do it with me next time. They are also getting the photograph done, so perhaps before long I shall gaze on her lovely face as it really is. An air force chap has come back from the hospital in Warburg and says that there are seventy Jerries in the place, all with legs, feet and toes off due to frost bite. One fellow told him that in one day the casualties in his company were two killed, twelve wounded and over fifty frostbitten. A letter in the *PoW News* starts off by saying 'of course you must realise that there is a war on!' Stone the bloody crows. It's about time some of the people at home began to realise it from the accounts one gets of what's going on, and did something about it.

Saturday, 28 February 1942

Mother's birthday. Had a letter from her and thank God at last they have had a big spate of my letters.

Feeling very depressed today. A rumour tonight that a British parachute detachment landed in France, knocked out a coastal battery and then pushed off. Thaw now in full progress and there is a mess and a bad smell all over the camp. A rumour today that the whole camp is to move on 14 March [1942] or shortly afterwards. I hope to God it's true and that the Biberach contingent separate from the others, or at least from Laufen.

Tuesday, 3 March 1942

Ronnie Symonds had a stand up fight with the senior British officer today. He asked him whether he had signed the order for the exchange of old battle dress for new and when Kennedy said 'yes' he replied that it was bloody stupid and that it was a pro German order. The SBO threatened him with a court martial, and Ronnie said he'd welcome it. There seems to be quite an acute feeling for Kennedy amongst the camp and I hope he gets the push. There were two rather funny incidents today. Firstly, two Germans were talking in the parcel hatch, within earshot of a German speaking English officer. One of them asked what the other one was going to do after the war? The second one replied that thought he would buy a bike and cycle around the German empire. Thereupon, the English chap piped up and said, 'well what are you going to do in the afternoon?' The second incident happened at the hospital. The mad orderly, Christie, was supposed to go to the looney bin, and Captain Lynn-Allan was going to Warburg for an X-ray. In the middle of the night Germans came in – doped Lynn-Allan and took him off to the looney bin, and Christie to Warburg. It was only after they arrived there that the mistake was found.

Thursday, 5 March 1942
The Jerry engineers got cracking today on the tunnel they discovered yesterday. They proceeded to blow it in with explosive and made quite a noise in the meanwhile blowing in the windows of the SBOs office and the German quarters, bits of rock and earth were flying 100s of feet into the air and falling all over the camp. Inoculated again for TAB and had a stiff arm and felt very depressed in the evening.

Tuesday, 10 March 1942
A very heavy raid last night in the direction of Dortmund or Hals. It started about 10.00 pm and I could see the searchlights in the sky and hear the heavy thud of anti-aircraft fire, some of the bomb explosions shook the building. I hope to Christ they killed a lot of the bastards.

Thursday, 12 March 1942
Spring seems to have come partly to this godforsaken country. For the last few days the sun has been quite warm, although it has frozen at night. For a little while it is quite pleasant to sit outside the building but after that it becomes chilly. An example of some of the propaganda being pumped into the Bosche soldiers is as follows; they would beat Russia in the spring and then having done that would make peace with England and the USA and settle accounts with Japan.

Monday, 23 March 1942
A big rehearsal in the afternoon for *Miss Eaton Suggests* and a dress rehearsal in the evening, which was really a performance as the house was half filled with the committee, ticket reps, and odds and sods. It went quite well too, but try as I might, I cannot get my part to my satisfaction. John Lightfoot was very annoyed too because I would cut in on my laughs, it's all very disappointing as at one time I did think I was getting it OK.

Wednesday, 25 March 1942

The show went very badly today. I don't know what was wrong with it, but it was just dead. A story from an orderly, that during his two hours down in Warburg loading parcels, twenty-four trains passed by absolutely jammed tight with civilians going south-east towards Kassel. Another story in the lager is that a goon has committed suicide because his wife and children have all been killed in an air raid, and he was not allowed leave to go and clean up his affairs.

Monday, 30 March 1942

A red hot rumour that we have landed in France, and an armoured division has taken Lille. Another armoured division has reached Merville, and the Free French have risen and taken Rouen. The room has gone mad now and everybody is talking at once. There must be some truth in it somewhere.

Tuesday, 31 March 1942

A big reaction today as the landings seen to have turned into more or less Commando raids. Still there are some who believe that this is the beginning of the Big Thing. The Jerries claim they took 100 PoWs in the raid on St Nazaire and that no damage was done. If some of them come here we may get the proper story.

Thursday, 2 April 1942

A card from Mappin & Webb at last. They haven't got the exact brooch I ordered but they are keeping one similar to it and unless they hear to the contrary they are sending that, which is good news. The only thing now is that they haven't received the cheque yet, and I hope that either that, or my letter to the bank will be honoured. But if everything goes well my darling Jo will get her twenty-first birthday present.

I went to make-up class and did myself as a woman, but very slowly as I had to wait for instructions and people kept on borrowing my mirror. Eventually, I made myself up entirely on my own. It was pretty patchy but I hope I can improve on it. Geoff, Ronnie and I got together on a 'tube'. It wasn't very original, and we weren't allowed to start for some time, but it helped to still the feeling of unrest, by making one at least think that we might get out of that awful life. I resigned from *George and Margaret* to take part in this, but they were so hard up for people to take my part, nobody was suitable, that I was asked to come back and did so provided that it wouldn't interfere with the job.

Monday, 6 April 1942

I started drafting my twenty-first birthday letter to Jo. I can't concentrate very well though. A big raid last night about 2.00 am, but we didn't hear it. Five RAF officers and an orderly got out of the cooler last night and are away. I hope they make it. The guard who is in charge of the cells is in a hell of a mess as, apparently, on the night of the escape he swapped places with another camp guard without obtaining permission and is now cooling his heels in a cell preparatory to some heavy sentence!

Thursday, 9 April 1942

A story today from a chap who arrived from hospital. On the way here he had to stay the night at a German barracks and the German officer showing him into some very decent quarters apologised because they were so bad. Our chap, in reply, said 'This is paradise to what we are used to.' On being told his camp was Warburg, the officer said, 'Oh yes, that is the worst camp in Germany, we send all our worst soldiers there.' Three more chaps got away in the night.

Sunday, 12 April 1942

Another two got out today, and the bastard Hun have started this business about no tins. All private parcels had the tins turned out. We all reckon in our room that we've just about had it with this *Kreigie* life, I wish to God something would happen.

Wednesday, 15 April 1942

The Swiss were here today and we hope they are able to do something. It's a rather forlorn one though. I started my German lessons with John Lightfoot. The laundryman has explained that his inability to cope with the laundry is that so many girls have been taken away for munitions work. God, how browned off I am getting with this life. Nothing happens anywhere and most of us reckon we've just about seen this life to its end. God knows how we're going to carry on for another year or so if it's necessary.

Monday, 20 April 1942

Talking tonight amongst ourselves, and in some ways it's amazing how our nature has changed in this life. Nothing is safe from us. Potatoes, coal, bed boards, anything to make life a bit easier. Everyone is constantly on the look out for something that will turn out to be 'useful'. When I look back to the raiding parties that took place when we first arrived it makes me laugh. Bed boards, shovels, lamps etc., all stuffed hurriedly under greatcoats and brought back to our lairs. When we get back to England I reckon there won't be much we shall of go short of once we set eyes on it!

Tuesday, 21 April 1942

A 'tube' broke last night but owing to a cock-up only six made it, and one of these is already back. Two renegade Indian officers turned up today to try and entice the Indian officers here to go over to the Nazi's by offering them freedom. The Indians wouldn't have anything to do with them and told them just where they could stuff the offers of their Nazi masters. I'm still waiting for a letter and Jo's photograph. How I ache in longing for it. God send I'm not disappointed when it arrives. Four more chaps got away during the night.

Tuesday, 5 May 1942

Two very interesting letters today. One from Dick, in which he says he has got my cheque OK and Mappin's have accepted it. His account of his various love affairs makes bloody funny reading, I hope to God that he is careful though. The other was from Vic, telling me the news that he is getting married to an ASO in the WAAF. He says that if I were home he would ask me to be best man, but as I'm not, the next best thing is to invite me to be a godfather, whenever that is needed. As the days go by I find it more and more difficult to find anything to say that is in anyway interesting.

Saturday, 16 May 1942

At last, a letter from Jo, dated 12 March [1942], but to my mind it seems a trifle more cold than before. That isn't the word I want, but something approaching it. The stench today was awful as the Germans persist in emptying the shit cart only 100 yards away amongst the new buildings. It quite turned my stomach up.

Monday, 25 May 1942

Quite a day today. I went back into *George and Margaret* and although I was expecting a rather 'you've caused a hell of a lot of trouble' attitude, it was quite the reverse and everyone said how pleased they were to see me. They sent out an urgent SOS for me, as the people they had been trying were no good at all, which was quite good for my pride. I only hope it will continue to impress and warrant the trust in me.

Saturday, 30 May 1942

My second anniversary today. Tomorrow starts my third year of captivity. Very brassed off and didn't enjoy rehearsal again. A rumour today that Italy has entered Tunis and that Victor Emanuel has abdicated. I hope to Christ that this brings in the French Moroccan army on our side. That would just about finish off [Erwin] Rommel.

Tuesday, 2 June 1942
My darling Jo's birthday today and she is 21. I hope my present arrived on time and that she likes it.

Friday, 5 June 1942
The first night of *George and Margaret* and it seemed to be a terrific success. As usual though, I myself was dissatisfied. We have had no letters for over a fortnight and it is very worrying, and annoying! There was quite a big air raid tonight in the direction of the Ruhr and a lot of flashes were visible and every now and then a burst of flak.

Sunday, 14 June 1942
Today we had our big search. We were roused at 4.00 am and the bastards routed us straight out and then proceeded not to search, but chucking everything out of the windows and doors. Sometimes they hauled the things out of the locker and piled them in a blanket, meat and jam in open tins just thrown in, but mostly they just up ended the lockers, placed them on the window seal and gave a push, with crockery etc. inside. Beds were pulled to pieces and furniture and belongings from other rooms carted half-way round the block and mixed up with other people's things. It was a typical example of a 'hate' for no real reason whatsoever except Radenacher's bad temper. The goons, of course, enjoyed themselves immensely and even more so when they saw it was going to rain, a typical example of Nazi culture. Geoff and I walked round the camp and then joined the others in the old canteen where Tiny made a brew of tea so strong that you could have stood a knife in it. Quite a lot of food and cigarettes were stolen, and we finally got back to our rooms about 9.00 am when, of course, the process of bringing everything back had to be begun.

Wednesday, 25 June 1942
The brooch arrived OK and Jo seemed extraordinarily pleased with it, but I shall hear more about it when she writes to me. At first she didn't know who it was from and couldn't believe it was from me. I curse myself that I didn't have a card put in it to make certain.

Saturday, 26 June 1942
Started our 'tube' under the orderlies' hut, quite a successful beginning in a week, however, the goons appeared one afternoon and tore everything to pieces and

found the one next door, so we had to stop for a bit. Then we started again and within three days everyone had had it so much that we didn't feel like carrying on, and so all our great plans fell to pieces. Actually, if one could have taken the top layer of earth off the camp the appearance underneath would have been rather like the London Underground system. Everywhere one went you could see the earth suddenly give underneath and quite a number of buildings were in danger of collapse. Nowhere, I think, had so many tunnels been dug before. About this time one of the best jobs was carried out twice through the wire and some seven chaps got away, but unfortunately didn't make the final get away. We provided a bit of a diversion. I got caught reading on parade by a German officer and sentenced to ten days in jug. He was very taken aback when he found it was a German book.

Wednesday, 1 July 1942

Yet another black day, I am getting so depressed these days that a bit more depressing news doesn't make much difference. If nothing much happens in the next few days I must seriously get down to German and Spanish again. I live now only for getting Jo's portrait or a letter with some real news in it about her and me from her. When I get that I shall be satisfied for a bit.

Thursday, 9 July 1942

A letter from mother today, in it she mentions that Jo is in the same room writing to me and finding it very difficult. She warns me not to raise my hopes as I gather I shall most probably have them dashed.

Saturday, 11 July 1942

At last – today – Jo's photograph arrived. I must candidly admit I was a bit disappointed as it wasn't as good as some of her snaps, it makes her look so very young. I am so very pleased to get it though. Her letter was a bit queer though as, although she was very sweet, she said nothing at all about the brooch and dealt the whole time in generalities. What she said about Dick made me a bit jealous too, although why I don't know, except that ever since the bit in Graeme's letter I've felt there might be something between them. I must say it has rather mystified me – the letter that is – and I am rather at a loss as how to reply. Some more chaps were missing from parade tonight, I hope they make it.

Monday, 13 July 1942

Wrote a very difficult letter to Jo and expressed myself very badly – but I hope it will clear up some misunderstandings without putting it too bluntly.

Friday, 31 July 1942
Got a letter from Jo today, dated 14 June [1942], which pre-dates the odd one I received. In this one she thanks me for the brooch, which explains the silence in the previous letter.

Saturday, 1 August 1942
We think there has been a number of air raids during the day as the air raid siren sounded in Warburg this afternoon, since then we have heard a series of bumps and explosions. I only hope it wasn't a practice or blasting. I got offered the part as Jacqueline in *French Without Tears* if it comes off. I've hoped to get that, as I've long ago given up hope of getting a male part again.

Sunday, 2 August 1942
A hell of a thunderstorm tonight and one of the buildings outside by the *Kommandantur* was struck – we don't know which yet. A terrific fire resulted, clouds of black smoke and flames shot up into the sky for a hell of a height and it looked very much like oil of fuel burning. The move rumour seems to be off and for that I'm really rather glad. We are now down to drinking out of jam jars in the room owning to the shortage of mugs. The war news seems bad these days and I wish to Christ the pendulum would start swinging our way.

Thursday, 6 August 1942
Lots of rumours today. The move is on again because the dentists had been told to pack up the false teeth side and to take no more orders. Rumours also of the invasion starting with a big air battle over the Somme, British fleet bombarding the channel ports and big troop movements on the South Coast. The Jerries seemed to be very jittery, all leave has been stopped in the Munster area and those in this camp are confined to barracks.

Wednesday, 12 August 1942
The weather has changed for the better the last few days, although there is still not enough sun and all my tan is gradually disappearing, which in view of the new show is a bloody nuisance. My sentence for reading on parade was published yesterday and I've got eight days instead of the five I expected! The ten officers from North Africa arrived some days ago but their information, while interesting, gives us nothing much more to go on then the German newspapers have already told us, in fact, they are just about as much in the dark [regarding] things at home as we were.

Sunday, 16 August 1942

The last few days the smell of shit has been all pervading again as they have been emptying on the fields just outside the camp. If ever I wish to be reminded of Germany again, all I shall have to do is to go to a sewage farm and stick my nose inside the septic tanks.

Thursday, 20 August 1942

The news given to us by the Germans on parade today says that we made a raid, a big one, at Dieppe yesterday, including tanks. We are supposed to have lost 1,500 PoWs and a lot of aircraft. That part is pretty good bullshit!

Saturday, 22 August 1942

Both today and yesterday the camp has been the literally buzzing with rumours about a move it started early yesterday morning and continued all day and the final call was there will be three parties, one lot of over thirty-six to go to Rottenburg near IX-a and the remainder to go to camps in Pomerania and Saxony. Today the first party was confirmed and names given out. They leave about next Thursday, the second and third lots have now been amalgamated into one camp at VII-b Eichstätt in Bavaria. Interspersed with all these rumours is the commandant saying the move is off and there is nothing to it. Personally, I think we shall have all left here by the middle of September.

Monday, 24 August 1942

A tragedy has occurred during the night. It seems Don Norris became trapped in a tube collapse and did not survive. Not sure exactly what happened but it stunned the whole camp.

Lieutenant Donald Lapage Norris. It seems he became trapped in a tunnel collapse and did not survive. He had been serving with 'D' Company, 5th Battalion, Gloucestershire Regiment and was wounded at Arneke, Belgium, on 27 May 1940. He could not be evacuated due to his wounds and was taken as a PoW. Originally buried in Dossel Civil Cemetery, his body was re-interred in the Hanover War Cemetery, Germany, on 7 May 1947, along with Lieutenant John Bourlon De Pree. (*Courtesy of The National Archives WO416/273/428 and The War Graves Photographic Project*)

Friday, 28 August 1942

On 28 August [1942], the big raid on Kassel took place and planes passed over the camp going to and from the target. It was very exciting as it was the first time that we'd actually had the planes so near and the drone was incessant. About fifteen minutes after the first planes passed over us the fireworks started in the direction of Kassel. The anti-aircraft fire was big and, occasionally, we heard fighters buzzing about. Several times a burst of MG fire could be heard, while star-shells and pamphlets were dropping all over the place. The block was in pandemonium and hardly anybody was back in bed before 1.30 am. Early in the morning the goons were busy in the camp searching for the pamphlets, they searched the fields and the villages all around, it was bloody good to see. As far as we could see, however, when we passed Kassel a few days later, there was little or no damage.

Sunday, 30 August 1942

The best escape effort, from the point of view of ingenuity and braveness, took place. Forty chaps planned to jump the wire at night and the secret was so well kept that only about three hours beforehand did we know what it was, although they'd been practicing for months. Zero hour was just after lock up and the whole of the perimeter lights were fused. Ladders were placed on the wire and the chaps scrambled over. One ladder, unfortunately, wouldn't fit, so that team couldn't get over. The whole business was finished in about five minutes and the Germans apart from firing one or two shots were completely helpless and didn't dare come into the camp for the rest of the night. There was only one casualty, Mike Hunt, who had his heel grazed by a bullet, but in spite of that did over 100km before he had to stop. Three chaps, Rupert Fuller, Berty Arkwright and Henry Coombe-Tennant got home from this job and a more unlikely trio one couldn't have imagined, but that's just how escaping goes. It's 99 per cent complete luck.

Captain Henry Coombe-Tennant. (*Courtesy of Bernard Lewis*)

Of the forty-one men who made their break in the escape, the eleven man team containing Captain Albert Seymour Bertram Arkwright, Lieutenant Robert Joseph Fuller and Captain Augustus Henry Serocold Coombe-Tennant successfully scaled the perimeter fence and made a dash across open country under a full moon. The three officers, wearing their uniforms and home-made tweed caps, travelled on foot by night, and hid during the day. Despite being seen on several occasions, they travelled across Germany reaching the Dutch border by 14 September [1942]. Here, they made contact with members of the Dutch underground who, although nervous, were keen to aid their escape. Eventually, they were put in touch with an organisation which arranged for their travel through Belgium and France, and they arrived in Gibraltar on 6 November [1942]. After a ten-week journey across Europe, the trio arrived in Bristol the following day.

After their successful 'home run', all three men were awarded the Military Cross on 7 January 1943. Major Henry Coombe-Tennant MC went to see action with the SOE and would be awarded the *Croix de Guerre*. Post-war he served with the Welsh Guards in Palestine, later becoming SIS chief of station in Baghdad. After leaving the army he then became a monk at Downside Abbey in Somerset.

Captain Albert Seymour Bertram Arkwright MC suffered from ill-health and was eventually retired from army service with the honorary rank of major. Lieutenant Robert Joseph Fuller is believed to have left the army at wars end.

On the night previous to the escape, Lieutenant John Bourlon De Pree, an officer in the 2nd Battalion, Seaforth Highlanders, who had been taken as a PoW at Le Trépost, met his death through the collapse of a 'tube' while he was attempting to escape from the camp. Originally buried in Dossel Civil Cemetery, his body was re-interred in the Hanover War Cemetery, Germany, on 7 May 1947. He was 24 years old. (*Courtesy of The War Graves Photographic Project and The National Archives WO416/94/427*)

Chapter 11

A Permanent Home in Eichstätt –
Oflag VII-b

Originally planned as barracks for German mountain troops, the site at Eichstätt, Bavaria, was transformed in September 1939 to accommodate PoWs from the invasion of Poland.

The camp was located in a valley with a rocky slope on the north side and, to the south a river; beyond the camp was a wooded hillside. The camp itself was surrounded by a double barbed-wire fence, running along the rocky slope. To increase the guards' view of the camp defences, guard houses were placed outside and well back from the outer fence.

The first Polish PoWs arrived on 18 October 1939 but these were all transferred to Murnau on 22 May 1940 and were replaced by British, French and Belgian officers taken [as] PoWs during battles in France and Belgium. The camp was then designated Oflag VII-b. In summer 1941, Australians and New Zealanders captured in Greece and Crete during the Balkans campaign arrived in the camp. [Erwin] Rommel's second offensive of Tobruk, in June 1942, led to the capture of many troops from the South African 2nd Division, many of whom were interned at Oflag VII-b. Canadian officers captured during the Dieppe Raid arrived on 31 August 1942.

British officers from Oflag VI-b Dossel were sent to Oflag VII-b after the mass escape in August 1942. On the night of 3/4 June 1943, 65 men escaped from the camp, but all were recaptured eventually but this occupied over 50,000 police, soldiers, home guard and Hitler Youth for a week. After two weeks detention at Willibaldsburg Castle, the escapees were sent to Oflag IV-c at Colditz Castle. American and British personnel captured in the Tunisia Campaign arrived in spring 1943. Today the site of the camp is occupied by the barracks and training school of the Bavarian State Police.

Tuesday, 1 September 1942

At 3.00 am our party left for the new camp. The goons had the wind up badly after Sunday's effort and after being personally searched we were made to sit in rows in silence and without smoking in the German dining room. The NCO in charge was a bastard and some fellows were there for nearly ten hours without being allowed to go to the ablutions. At 7.00 am we were marched out, where a cup of tea waited for us and shortly afterwards left for the station. There our party managed to get second class carriages and at 10.00 am we had lunch of porridge and macaroni. Being well supplied with Red Cross food for the trip, the time passed more or less completely and we left Warburg at 12.30 pm. There was a guard in the compartment with us who proved very amiable, after we'd plied him with food and chocolate and chatted away to me quite amiably. He was very bolshie in his outlook and was a bit difficult to understand at times, owing to the noise of the train. We travelled through Kassel and afterward put on such a good speed that we reached Würzburg just before midnight. Shortly before here three chaps got off but there didn't seem to be much fuss and early the next morning about 8.00 am we arrived at Eichstätt, the prettiest town I've ever seen. Before we left our guard, I asked him to take a note back to Tiny and Lo, which he did only too willingly, and we accordingly gave them all the dope about the trip. The camp was only about twenty minute walk from the town and consisted of some old German *Gebirgsjäger* barracks. These were four, two storey, brick buildings along a proper built-up road, and beyond these, but lower down, were five long brick bungalow type huts. The recreational and sporting facilities were extraordinarily good and there was room enough to play almost

View of Oflag VII-b, from the commandant's building at the west end of the camp, showing PoWs playing hockey. In the foreground PoWs cut and cart wood near cattle in a field. Hockey sticks were just one of the pieces of sports equipment supplied by the British. Their hollowed out handles sometimes contained important secret messages. (*Courtesy of Australian War Memorial – P01.308.002*)

as many games as one could think of besides a soccer pitch. Ronnie, Jimmy, Geoff and I had a bit of trouble to begin with but finally managed to install ourselves in an upstairs room. We hoped, when the others came, to move down to the lower half of the camp. For the two previous years the camp had been occupied by Belgian's and they had left many mementos of their stay, including stores of food for us and various other things such as coal etc. Besides ourselves, we found about 100 Canadian Commando boys who were captured at Dieppe. After the first few days, food began to run very short as we weren't able to get at any of our own stuff, and we were finally saved by the arrival of some bulk a few days before the others arrived. The Germans had no idea how to run a camp on the British method as when the Belgans were here, they left everything to the goons and wouldn't do a hands turn themselves. The camp also had a soccer pitch, two tennis courts, a basketball pitch and a lot of other space. At the bottom, beyond the wire, is the river and there are several avenues of trees, and quite a large vegetable garden.

Thursday, 3 September 1942
After a day and a half of intensive work and a lot of changes the four of us are upstairs and I only hope we can stay there. It was very hard work and by Christ I'm glad it's over, the people down below were a dreadful crowd. I had my baggage searched today and lost my maps, like a fool, which made me very angry. There are 100 Canadian, naval and Commando officers here from the Dieppe raid and it is very interesting to talk to them, although they are very brassed off. Rumours that they cannot fit the rest of VI-b in here and 400 of them aren't coming. If that is so, it will rather bugger things up as we shall lose Tiny, Arthur, Robin and perhaps Brian.

Monday, 7 September 1942
The situation is very black. We are now living entirely on German rations and our meals consist of bread and margarine only, except for the soup at midday. The potatoes the Jerries give us are 75 per cent bad and the remaining 25 per cent have bad bits. The last of our tea goes tonight and there are no parcels yet, the Jerries want to tip everything out of them. They also say that they would only do a 100 a day, which is absurd, obviously they have no conception of what we get and are basing their ideas on the Belgian parcels.

Thursday, 10 September 1942
We were all rather depressed as there were rumours that, as the camp was getting so crowded, the remainder would go elsewhere, but on 13 September [1942] they did arrive and it was grand seeing them all again. Immediately of course

there started the terrible business, as in every camp, of getting people together, people running round in every direction, filling up rooms, getting everything settled and then having to start all over again because some selfish bastard won't move or somebody falls out, but at last by 18 September [1942], with a little jiggery pokery, we installed the nine of us, Tiny, Arthur, Robin, Jimmy, Brian, Johnny, Geoff, Ron and myself in room 6, block 7 and more or less settled down here for the end of the war. Nobby and Mark have gone their own way, and I for one am very glad, as relations between us were very strained ever since our arrival here. We decided in future to pool all food and tin stores and feed as one mess, [first,] because it is more economical both for cooking and feeding, [second,] because it's much more natural and civilised. The commandant, one by the name of Blatterbauer, was the worst one we ever came across. He was very anti-British and went out of his way to make things as unpleasant as possible. One of the first things he did was to order compulsory PT every morning and as one could imagine to order the British to take exercise was one of the worst things he could do. Consequently, there were some pretty good scenes with him. Several times on parade he lost his temper and we roared with laughter at him which only made it worse. We hoped he might possibly bust a blood vessel and get apoplexy. The goons seized hold of about 140 'record holders' and shoved them all together into block 2. With them went a padre, doctor and dentist, so they might be going to move. I hope they don't take any more as we might lose quite a number of our two messes.

Wednesday, 23 September 1942

We are all getting more and more browned off with this camp. Yesterday afternoon it took the goons all their time to do 250 milk parcels, and trying to find containers to put the things in is very hard. The YMCA are coming tomorrow, but I don't think they can do much good. The people we want are the Swiss legation. The other evening on parade we had an up and down with the two Sonderfürhers. I hope that we shall shortly see the last of them. Most of the escaped boys are now back and this last do doesn't seem to have done them much good. All of them seem absolutely whacked and ill. Bill Ashton seemed in a very bad state not knowing whether he was coming or going.

Sunday, 27 September 1942

This, to my mind, is one of the worst camps we've been in. Having been here for a month everything is just as disorganised as when we got here. The commandant, the bugger, is very anti-British. Luckily, they say he suffers from his heart, so perhaps we shall lose him like the first one at Warburg. He continues to order compulsory physical training after morning parade, which he has no right to do, and at the time the SBO very foolishly acquiesced as he was pressing for more important things. Now, the latter can't go back on his word and we are not going to do PT on orders from the Germans. All day long at Warburg, we did it voluntarily and played games, but to be compelled and to take exercise when ordered we will not do. The fuel situation is very bad and I don't know if we should get much this winter. I wish to Christ we were back at Warburg.

Thursday, 1 October 1942

The bastards have now brought in a restriction on our mail during which period we can receive only four letters. Before they try and equalise positions between German and British PoWs as regards mail I might first of all pay off the large debit owing to us from their PoWs in Canada. Then perhaps little differences in mail might be able to be balanced with some degree of justice. We learn from a Canadian in the camp all about these *Kriegie* camps in Canada. The German officers are comfortably housed in medium sized rooms with single spring beds. They don't, however, have to live and eat in these rooms, but have a proper mess with a large anteroom, better furnished than an average English regimental anteroom. There is a bar open all day selling all kinds of drink. Meals are served three times a day by German orderlies, and consist of normal British Army rations, e.g. bacon and eggs breakfast, joint and vegetables for lunch and a decent dinner. On Sundays, chicken or other birds. If they get browned off with this very frugal food, there is a canteen in which can be bought all other types of food! Of course, we who are seated in the midst of German 'culture' can only be fed and housed like pigs and even our own private food, coming from home and guaranteed by the Red Cross, is turned out and churned about like pig swill, so that in hot weather nothing can be kept longer than one and a half days and in the winter perhaps a bit longer. Well, one of these days we will teach these bastards a lesson it will take longer than twenty years to forget, and maybe after that they won't be so bloody keen to start another war.

Tuesday, 6 October 1942

A notice came round about permanent commissions today and I'm going to see the brigade major tomorrow to arrange an interview with the SBO I started my conversation periods with John Lightfoot and I hope they manage to keep up. Also, I received a grand letter from Jo.

Thursday, 8 October 1942

The day started very mysteriously. No goons were allowed in the camp at all and during the morning some seventy slats of beds were taken out of the camp. At 11.00 am we were paraded, all Dieppe officers were called out and marched

Oberleutnant Blatterbauer, know as 'Blatts' (centre), a ridged Nazi with an intense dislike of British officers, the commandant of Oflag VIIb at the time John Blomfield Dixon arrived at the camp. (*Courtesy of The J B Dixon Collection*)

Sports were a very important part of the recreational facilities provided for PoWs. Here, a cricket match is played on the sports field at Eichstätt. (*Courtesy of The J B Dixon Collection*)

This series of images, all taken from the John Blomfield Dixon collection, have been coloured by Doug Banks of Colourising History. My deepest thanks to Doug for all his patience, hard work and effort in producing these enhanced and coloured images.

(Left): A soldier in the making. John Blomfield Dixon in the uniform of the Officer Training Corps at St Peter's School, York in 1933. (Right): The Cricket First XI – St Peter, School, York in 1936. (Back): S.M. Toyne (Headmaster), P.C. Campbell, E. Gossop, John Blomfield Dixon, K.J. Jarvis, G.W. Russell, R. Lynch and G.S. Stead. (Front): G.E.L. Graham, C.A. Smart (honourable secretary), N.A. Newman (captain), K. Lockwood and V.L.F. Davin

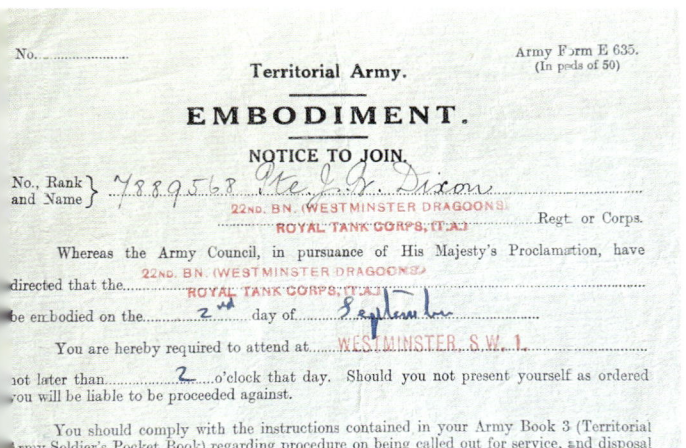

Call Up Papers. This notice was sent to Private John Blomfield Dixon on the embodiment of his regiment on war service. Within a few weeks the young cadet would be commissioned as an officer in the British Army, preparing to take men to war.

John Blomfield Dixon
at home in the garden of
High Oak Lodge, Ware,
Hertfordshire, with his
parents William and
Emily Dixon. His mother,
sarcastically, was often
referred to as the Duchess
of Ware.

Tank Training in 1939. John Dixon (second from the left), can be seen undertaking training at Bovington,
Dorset. He would bitterly complain that it was this type of equipment he was trained to use and not the
Bren gun carrier he was aboard at the time of his capture in May 1940.

A World Apart. Newly commissioned Second Lieutenant John Blomfield Dixon photographed in the garden of his home at High Oak Lodge, Ware, taken in October 1939. Compared with an official PoW photograph taken on 21 July 1941 at Biberach.

Second Lieutenant Norman Bonner.

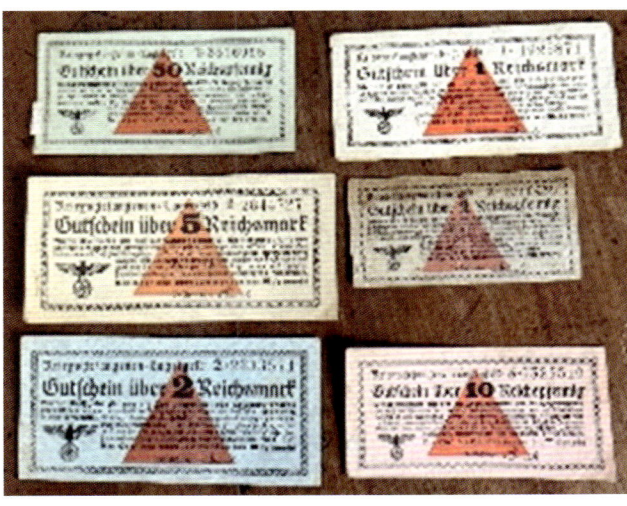

A series of PoW *Reichsmarks* contained within the John Blomfield Dixon collection of ephemera from his time as a captive of the German army.

Westminster Dragoons at Biberach, summer 1941.
(Back left to right): Ian Fisher (3 RTR), Brian Chick (3 RTR),
Ken Farquharson (3 RTR) and Vincent Hollom (RTR).
(Front left to right): Brian Bell (4 RTR), Doug Allison
(3 RTR) and John Blomfield Dixon (ERY).

'Tiny' Waters, Royal Sussex
Regiment Standing at 6 foot and
6 inches tall.

East Riding Yeomanry Subalterns at Biberach, summer 1941.(Back left to right): Jock Jones 'A', Harol
Hopper 'C', Brian Reid 'HQ', Mike Trevor 'A' and Roger Waterhouse 'C'.(Front left to right): Tom Carmichae
'HQ', Mike Lindley 'B', John Blomfield Dixon 'C', Sir Lindores Leslie 'A', Mike Longstaffe 'HQ'.

John Blomfield Dixon (second from left) plays Ailsa Crane in *The Case of the Frightened Lady*. John was regarded by Michael Goodliffe as an accomplished female impersonator. The play was deemed to be a huge success.

Dossing Dulchie. John Blomfield Dixon plays yet another female part, this time Princess Dulchibelle in the 1943 Christmas pantomime at Eichstätt. He came to hate the fact he was always cast as a female, despite the fact Michael Goodliffe recognised him as an accomplished female impersnator.

In early 1944, John Blomfield Dixon played the part of Louise Rogers in *I Killed The Count* a play by Alec Coppel, produced by Wallace Finlayson, who was a Canadian director and actor known as Wallace Douglas. Here he is seen opposite Don Ritchie who played Divisional Inspector Davidson.

Brigadier Nigel Fitzroy Somerset CBE DSO MC (Far Right) seated with German officers at a boxing match at Thorn in the Spring of 1941.

Josephine 'Jo' Blomfield (left) with John's mother, Emily, and his sister, Elinor Smith (née Dixon), and her daughter Mary, digging up the path with her toes! (*Image source: John Blomfield Dixon Collection*)

The grave of Josephine Blomfield.

Josephine 'Jo' Blomfield. The woman John Blomfield Dixon so desperately loved, but their lives were forced apart by their unfortunate family relationship.

(Left): John Blomfield Dixon and Leokadia Maria Dixon (née Mikolajczyk at the time of their marriage on 8 November 1947 at Hoddesdon Registrar Office, Hertfordshire. (Right): Their joint grave at Putney Vale Cemetery, London.

John Blomfield Dixon on a visit to the last resting place of his comrades at Hotton War Cemetery, Belgium. Their bodies were transferred here in January 1948, having been originally buried in a temporary cemetery in the Belgian village of Watou, close to where they fell during the Battle of Cassel.

This plaque is located at the point where roving US fighters attacked what they believed to be a column of Hungarian troops. In fact, it was the British officers from Oflag VIIb who had just begun their long march to Moosburg. Fourteen were killed in the attack and forty-six wounded. The German commandant blamed the disruption initiated by the prisoners in delaying their departure from the camp as the cause for the casualties.

Red Cross parcels. Often a lifeline for PoWs, the Red Cross sought to send one food parcel to each PoW per week, but logistical difficulties throughout the war meant that this was rarely achieved. The contents were often divided proportionally between the PoWs, as explained on many occasions within John Blomfield Dixon's diaries. The contents were also the target of theft by captors and captives alike.

Christmas fare 1942. The lavish meal that John Blomfield Dixon and his roommates missed due to stomach poisoning. The menu also demonstrates their continued anxiety as to when the war would come to end, with a question mark under 1943. Little did they know it would be more than two long years before they would see freedom, and for a small number it would never arrive. (*Image source: John Blomfield Dixon Collection*)

off including orderlies and then we were dismissed. Until the evening we were completely in the dark and then on evening Appel a senior British officer gave us the reason for the measures. Apparently the OKW said that on two occasions recently, when Germans had been taken [as] PoWs, they had been bound and handcuffed. The British government had returned unsatisfactory answers and therefore the OKW ordered that from 12 noon of this day all officers taken at Dieppe should be bound until action was taken by the British government. Reports from a Canadian who was taken there and then brought back, because he was wounded, they were put in the Schloss and had palliasses, but were bound with rope around both hands.

When the shackling of PoWs began at Eichstätt it was the only camp at the time using steel handcuffs, most other camps using cord as a means of securing each man's hands. The PoWs were kept in restrains from 8.00 am until 9.00 pm, only being removed at midday for an hour to allow the PoWs to eat a meal. In an effort to ensure the same number of men remained shackled at any one time, PoWs who were released due to illness would have their handcuffs removed, and they would quickly be slapped onto another poor unfortunate soul. The cuffs were separated by either a fixed bar or chain approximately 10cm long, which allowed the individual to still smoke or freely use their hands. Although lights out was at 9.00 pm for the majority of the camp, the manacled PoWs' lights were not switched off until 10.00 pm to provide them with the opportunity for a short period of relaxation and to complete their ablutions.

Saturday, 10 October 1942

Another parade today and the Germans took twenty-nine more officers from each block to go into chains as well. Apparently, the governments answer to the Germans was to bind a similar number of goons, so that the latter now ordered that three times the number should be bound or put into handcuffs. they put the whole lot, including the Canadian in block 1 and, unfortunately, Jimmy Fitch was one of those taken, the goons were evidently expecting some pretty drastic effects as they had all the guard boxes open with guns covering the parade ground and motors lined up in the *Kommandantur*. They were absolutely dumbfounded by our attitude, and I believe a little shocked. They could not understand why we treated the whole thing as a joke. No doubt because of their appalling inferiority complex. We understood later that the goons in England and Canada kicked up a terrible fuss and force had to be used. Those in block 1 had a baddish time of it for the first few days, but after that they managed to open all the cuffs and only put them on when the Germans came in. They were barred from the rest of the camp and had to have their food separately. Bit by bit people were got out and exchanged for others and, of course, in time, the whole thing became completely slack. Those Germans tied up in England were released before Christmas, but here the handcuffs did not disappear till over a year later, by that time the Germans were too ashamed to make an announcement and they just failed to turn up one morning. The Germans also kept up the reprisals on letters and it was only when the Swiss arrived that we learned that they had officially been stopped.

Sunday, 11 October 1942
Two rumours today, one is that the Germans have got into trouble around Stalingrad and are surrounded. Another is that the Japanese navy have had a beating in the Pacific and the remains are hiding in South American ports with our fleet waiting outside for them.

Monday, 12 October 1942
Big piece in the German papers today about the bad treatment of PoWs by the British. The tripe in the German papers is annoying and they seem to be trying to work up a hate against the British with this, and the terror air attacks. The only reasons we can think for this sudden outburst are that:

1. They're trying to cover up bad news from Russia or elsewhere.
2. The powers that be are aware over a growing feeling in Germany of patch up peace with Britain and let us both fight Russia.

They know that this is impossible and are trying to turn feeling against England.

Thursday, 15 October 1942
It's much colder now and winter seems to be approaching. The chain gang are still in existence and getting rather brassed off. Their hands get so cold and some who came out yesterday because they were sleeping on the landing had hands a bright red with continuous exposure to the cold. In the papers these days they seem to be throwing a lot of weight about concerning America's supposed increasing domination over England and the empire. The Germans seem to think America is about to take us over, lock, stock and barrel.

Thursday, 22 October 1942
Following up on all the previous bumf and following a 'successful attack by British bombers on a German dressing station in North Africa', the Germans now state that they now must come to the conclusion that the British intend to disregard the Geneva Convention. This might be what all the business was leading up to – so they can get out of it themselves. I've not received any letters

for a fortnight and the latest is dated 14 August [1942], while others have had five in October and the latest in the camp is 14 October [1942] – the mail is so slow, and the censoring even worse – the bastards!

Friday, 23 October 1942

An interesting piece of news came to light today. The time came to settle up with the goons for the razors and hairdressing equipment that we hire, and the officer in charge noticed the charges were double the usual amount. He told the goon officer that he would have to refer the matter to the SBO on account of this and they therefore went along to see him. The SBO agreed that the charges were doubled and asked why this was? 'Oh' glibly replied the goon officer, the extra is for the war widows' pension fund! Thereupon, the SBO told him he could stuff it and we'.d use our own instruments. The bloody cheek of them! It seems, based on a story today, that our line into North Africa has now been pushed forward to Mersa Matruh with the capture of numerous Bosche PoWs.

Friday, 30 October 1942

We have all come to the conclusion that this camp and all its points, combined with the length of our *Kriegiedom* is just about culminating in a 'high' of 'brassedness'. The parcel situation is very bad and unless we get Red Cross parcels come in by the weekend we've had it. Rumours are scarce these days but the ones we've had recently are that [Franz] von Papen had gone to Moscow, [Joachim] von Ribbentrop had done a bunk, and that large stores of gas will be laid in Germany. Very amusing story from yesterday. Upon opening a box of Argentinian cheese a German officer saw that it was rather damaged and asked whether we knew how it happened? We told him we didn't, and he stated that it was salt water that caused the damage and that it was obvious the boat on which this was being carried was sunk by a German submarine. 'Quite probably' we said, as it was a Red Cross ship!

Chapter 12

The Swiss Legation: An Initial Report

Sunday, 1 November 1942

Mary's birthday today and I wrote a letter to Elinor, but I don't know whether it will get through as it's supposed to be posted next week and have 'returned' put on it. We have had no letters for three weeks now, and it's been a month since I've had one from mother.

Monday, 2 November 1942

The first of a series of visits by the Swiss Legation was made to Eichstätt. The inspector, Rudolph Burckhartd, stated there was clear evidence of overcrowding, due mainly to the fact that PoWs were allowed to make their own messing arrangements, which resulted in rooms containing anything from ten to thirty-two men. It would seem that the camp commander, Lieutenant Colonel Blätterbauer, was deeply concerned that an infectious epidemic may occur if the facilities were not kept in a clean and orderly fashion, and begged the inspector to explain this to the PoWs. However, hot showers were only available twice a month, and the Swiss implored the German commander to change this to a weekly event. Whilst the latrines for officers were perfectly adequate, those in the orderlies quarters were described as 'primitive'. In fact, in the 'lower camp' where the other ranks were located, things were altogether a great deal worse than those the officers faced. The food for officers was described as excellent and the German rations had been reduced by a third, due to the fact the Red Cross parcels contained a plentiful supply of food and there was a high level of wastage amongst the PoWs. Oberstabsartz Dr Koglmeier was the German medical director in the camp at this time and he was assisted by three British doctors from a total of ten doctors who were held as PoWs. There were sixteen medical orderlies, out of which only two were medically trained. Most medical cases were treated in the camp hospital, which was sufficiently hygienic enough to meet requirements, whilst more serious infectious cases were sent to the hospital in Eichstätt. Dental treatment in the camp was provided by three British dentists but there were numerous complaints that they were desperately short of instruments. There was also an urgent need for dental material such as amalgam, rubber plates and artificial teeth.

The following is a list of doctors and dentists who were, at some point, imprisoned at Eichstätt in the period between September 1942 and April 1945, and who assisted in maintaining the health of the camp inmates, despite often having very little equipment or supplies to work with.

Doctors

The following officers were doctors:

Colonel David Proudfoot Levack (pictured below)
Major Thomas Patrick Howkins
Major Brooke Moore (Australian)
Major George Albert William Neill
Major F. Beaumont (USMC)
Captain John Edward Buck
Captain Arthur Raymond Dearlove
Captain G. Forest
Captain Maurice W. Harvey
Captain Joseph Henry
Captain John Russel Heslop
Captain John Goodworth Jamieson
Captain Samuel Lask
Captain C. Nongester (USMC)
Captain John Robert Odell
Captain Robert Pollock
Captain James Ross Sinclair Third
Captain J.F. Walmsley (Canadian)
Captain Samuel Thomas Williamson

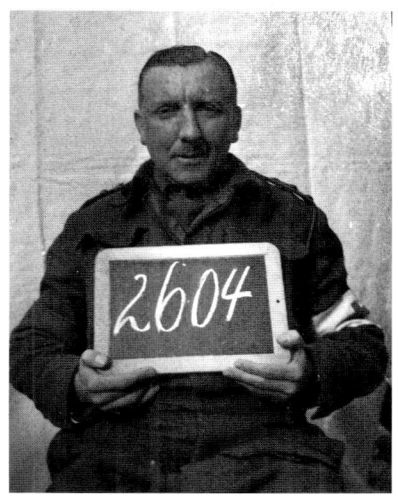

Colonel David Proudfoot Levack. (*Courtesy of The National Archives WO416222/159*)

Dentists

The following officers were dentists:

Captain Paul Menzies Calder
Captain Desmond Allen Greenslade (NZDC)
Captain Ralph Barker Neal
Captain P. Jacos (USDC)

One case described by the Swiss legation as being treated at Eichstätt Hospital was Captain Michael Anthony Biddulph of the Royal Engineers, who had been captured on the island of Crete in June 1941. He was found to be suffering from pulmonary tuberculosis. He was sent to Moosburg where a pneumothorax

Captain Michael Anthony Biddulph (left), Royal Engineers, who was captured on 2 June 1941 on the island of Crete. He died as a consequence of pulmonary tuberculosis on 22 April 1943. Originally buried in Thonstetten Civil Cemetery (right), his remains were moved to the Durnbach Military Cemetery in March 1948. (*Courtesy of The War Graves Photographic Projcet and The National Archives WO416/29/271*)

operation was carried out, but Biddulph died from the effects of the disease on 22 April 1943.

Laundry services for the PoWs were carried out by private enterprises in the towns of Eichstätt and Ingolstadt. Religious activity was deemed to be adequate, and it was felt the camp had by far the best exercise and recreation facilities the inspector had seen so far. There was a cricket field, volleyball field, basketball field and a football ground. Additionally, there was a large vegetable garden for PoWs to work in. There was a complaint that the cells for disciplinary punishment we're very bad and an inspection proved that there was one cell, which was very damp, but the German physician had already forbidden its use. A further complaint regarding the stable buildings, where the orderlies were located, was overcrowded. However, at least a third of the men were dispatched to another camp and the building was used to store Red Cross parcels.

The Swiss legation was to make a total of fifteen visits to Oflag VII-b between 2 November 1942 and 8 February 1945. Their reports continually raised concerns on the subject of food, accommodation, the ill treatment of PoWs, poor medical attention and the lack of hygiene facilities but, despite many recommendations, very little changed as a consequence of their presence.

Friday, 6 November 1942

At last, a letter, and it seems Jo has gone home for the moment owing to illness. Mother says she is run down. It must be what she mentioned in her last letter and I hope to God it's nothing serious. A parachutist in from one of the air force camps, 'Pissy' Edwards got so brassed off there that he walked to the wire in broad daylight and climbed over. Of course, he was shot and one can only think he was slightly mad. He was buried with military honours.

This entry refers to Flight Lieutenant Robert Howard Edwards who was shot down on 28 July 1940 when his Fairey Battle aircraft was on an operational mission from RAF Binbrook to bomb aerodromes in the Brussels region. He was shot while trying to escape from Stalag Luft 21-d on 26 September 1942 and is buried in the Poznan Old Garrison Cemetery, Poland.

Wednesday, 11 November 1942

Late last night I got six letters from mother, Dick, Aunt Marie and Jo, and I don't suppose I shall get anymore for some time now. For quite a while there have been double guards on the camp during the day, reinforced at night by patrols inside the wire. The other night we had the story that a large crowd of civilians had appeared outside the *Kommandantur* and that with this there was a great deal of activity in the lager, with goons rushing around the place. Today comes the story from a German officer, that the French, Belgian and British officers have been barricaded in there, barbed wire all over the windows, because the civilian population and threatened to rescue them!

Monday, 16 November 1942

Today, the first snow fell, and we were all finally reunited. Geoff came back from hospital where he had been with stomach trouble again for nearly six weeks, and Jimmy Fitch came out of chains at last. I have now become another godfather, to John and Barbara latest son George Victor, born on 28 September [1942]. I really don't want to do it especially as I've promised Vic that I'll take the job on for him, and that will make three, but one doesn't like to refuse for fear of offending them. I have started German again seriously with John Lightfoot. I have also started Spanish again, but somehow don't feel that I should get very far in spite of my good intentions. I haven't the same opportunities and inclination for reading and conversation as I have with German, but we shall see.

Wednesday, 18 November 1942

Two weeks supply of Red Cross parcels have come in over the last few days, including Christmas ones, and we hope another four weeks supply come in shortly to make us safe till the new year. A trainload of badly wounded Italian's have arrived in Eichstätt, complete with Italian Red Cross railway coaches, doctors, attendants and inspectors. Upon reading a letter from Elinor I nearly jumped off my chair, seeing a photograph of Colin and Mary, they've both grown so terrifically.

Monday, 23 November 1942

A big raid last night to the south-west, through which I slept solidly and only woke up at the end. Boy, was I annoyed. Other ranks left today for a new lager, said to be an Oflag. More are supposed to be leaving tomorrow and the general idea is they are an advanced party for a new camp – perhaps Laufen. I hope to Christ we aren't in the party.

Tuesday, 24 November 1942

With a great deal of time on their hands, the PoWs had the opportunity to observe any aspect of camp life that may provide the chance for escape. One such event was when it was discovered that French PoWs were brought to an English dentist in block 4, the hospital. A plan was soon deduced whereby one PoW would act as an interpreter, another as a camp guard and one as the Frenchman. First of all, uniforms were prepared and hidden in block 4 in readiness for the escape. On this night five officers, George Kane, Terrence Prittie, James McDonnell, Thomas Acton and Stuart Walker, all went into the hospital, dressed themselves in civilian clothes, over the top of which they placed their uniform. At 10.15 pm George Kane, acting as the interpreter along with Stuart Walker, dressed as a guard, escorted the three 'Frenchmen' from the hospital block to the south gate. An unsuspecting guard allowed the five men to pass. The group then went through the main gate, crossed over the bridge and walked along the road towards the railway line. On reaching a secluded spot the five men quickly removed and buried their uniforms and equipment. In an effort not to draw attention to themselves, the group then split into three parties. Terrence Prittie and James McDonnell caught a train and travelled to Munich, which they reached in the early afternoon. George Kane and Tom Acton arrived separately to Munich, and the four escapees eventually met up at the town of Tuttlingen, close to the Swiss border. Although they opted to then travel separately, it seems the men were followed, all four being arrested just 8km from the Swiss frontier. They were taken to the village of Talmühle where they were held overnight. The following morning they were escorted to a PoW camp at Villingen, where they met up with Stuart Walker. He had missed a train connection at Ingolstadt and opted to travel on foot to Engen where, exhausted, he was recaptured. The five men were returned to Eichstätt, where Blätterbauer took great delight in interviewing them. The were sentenced to thirty days' arrest, after which they were moved to Oflag IX-a Schloss Spangenberg.

Wednesday, 25 November 1942

We had one of our worst parades. As five chaps had got out, the Goons made a real hate day of it. There was snow on the ground, and it was bitterly cold. We were on parade at 8.00 am and were kept there till 10.00 am, when we were dismissed, only to be brought back at 11.00 am and kept there till about 4.00 pm, while the goons called the role of every single man in the camp, although they knew the names of those who had gone. There was a minus 22 degree frost in the night and we were hauled out on parade in the freezing cold at 11.30 pm and again at 5.00 am and neither time did they get the count right. This continued for some days, but really caused the goons more trouble than ourselves as it took them generally about three hours to count the camp once and even then, they didn't get it right as we foxed the count every time, and finally the commandant had to give it up.

Secret messages were often hidden inside sports equipment supplied to Eichstätt via MI9. Hockey sticks were a particular favourite and used to transport items such as radio equipment to help keep the PoWs supplied with up to date information on the progress of the war. (*Courtesy of The J B Dixon Collection*)

Friday, 27 November 1942

Another parade last night at 10.00 pm, just after we'd got into bed of course, and they bogged the count again. Thank God now though that it's finished, and we will be counted in our beds. More extra parades during the day though. News from the Red Cross today, that we will go onto half a Red Cross parcel a week as supplies will be difficult to get through. It's looking very ugly.

Wednesday, 2 December 1942

There has been lots of snow in the last few days, far more than in previous years. Today, however, it alternated between heavy snow and rain, which covered everywhere inches deep in water. Everywhere in the lager is an atmosphere of brassedness, which seems continually to exist and grow. I don't know why it should be as the news is very good. It must be the camp itself. I believe Jo, the darling, still keeps writing regularly and recently more. I feel it's very hard, I cannot write more and told her so in the last letter. I'm in the pantomime and started work yesterday, and I'm also expected to sing. I anxiously await the first test, as I am far from confident.

Monday, 7 December 1942

The pantomime, *Babes Up*, goes on slowly and I'm rather fed up with it. Last night the goons were up to their old tricks again having us out in the middle of the night. We got a bit of our own back though as they were at it from 5.00 am and didn't reach us until 8.10 am, a pretty long count.

Tuesday, 22 December 1942

It's father's birthday today and I've only just remembered it! There was a big raid in the direction of Munich last night. The goons say it was a general raid in which parachutists were dropped I bet the guards leave has been stopped in order to search for them. Ten Russians escaped from a camp near here recently. They killed their guards and on recapturing five of them more Goons, including one officer, were killed. Five are still at large and the Germans say that before they left they'd eaten seventeen of their number in the camp and that all that was found of the dead Deutsche was their hearts and livers! If the Russians were in the same state of starvation as those at Warzburg, I'm not surprised at it happening as they were pretty hard put to it for food. The pantomime is going quite well, but I still can't get my number right.

Friday, 25 December 1942

Christmas Day was a bit of a fiasco. we had planned a big meal, but the day before I went down with stomach poisoning, and I was quickly followed by

Tiny, Jimmy and Johnny, and actually quite a number in the camp were affected. Consequently, Christmas passed rather quietly, and we were unable to do much justice to the food. This year I came out of the chorus in the pantomime and took one of the leads, with Pat Sherrard. We had a very excellent number to sing, the best in the show most people reckoned, called *How wonderful You Are* and definitely made a big hit. This Christmas I ordered flowers to be sent to mother, Jo, Elinor and Aunt Maisie. It was rather a shot out of the blue, but from the letters I received later I was astonished by the immense surprise and enjoyment it had caused. The year ended with the usual hopes for 1943 and most of us did really think that this one would really be the last of our captivity. Events had started to turn in our favour at last. Russia, North Africa and the Far East and we all look forward confidently to the invasion, which we hope will come.

Thursday, 31 December 1942

The last day of the old year, and what have I to say. This year has certainly ended on a more promising note for us, and I can only hope it continues. Whether we shall see another New Year's Eve in captivity I can't say but here's hoping to God we don't. My birthday, two days ago, 24 and to my great disappointment nobody

'Our room'. (Back row): Brian Rich, Arthur Walker, Mike Kemp, John Dixon, Tiny Waters, Johnny Mumford, John Renton and Frank Pearce. (Front row): Ron Eastman, Geoff Cowan, Robin Steele-Mortimer, Dick Stafford and Jock Mackenzie (*Courtesy of The J B Dixon Collection*)

in the room remembered it, not as yet. Not that it's frightfully important, but one feels as if no one was particularly interested. I did hope that perhaps I had friends here and what is a friend if he can't even remember your birthday. The pantomime goes on and tonight and tomorrow we are giving performances for the chain gang who have been specially cut out to see it.

Our mess of eight, Geoff Cowen (Royal Warwicks), Ronnie Eastman (Royal Tanks), Johnny Mumford (Queens), Robin Steele-Mortimer (Royal Artillery), Brian Rich (Queens), Arthur Walker (Royal Engineers), Tiny Waters (Royal Sussex) and me (Royal Tanks – attached to East Riding Yeomanry) occupied one half of one side of a centre room on the western side of block 7. Many of us had been in the same room or messing together since Laufen and we got on well. In the other half on the same side lived another mess of five, so we were thirteen in all but not unusually unlucky.

Chapter 13

1943: Lost Comrades and
The Barbed Wire Theatre

I t is from this point that John Blomfield Dixon's diary entries begin to move from repetitive daily events to more occasional comments, or particularly important moments, concerning camp life, the war in general and his feelings about his captors, his fellow inmates, his loved ones, the desperate desire to be part of the war effort and the constant question of when will freedom come. In his eighth, and last, diary, John summarised much of what is contained in the others. What follows is lifted from that summary, much of which is centred around repatriation, his participation in theatre productions, the anticipation of an Allied invasion of Western Europe and the ever present 'black dog' of depression that spread across the camp.

1943

The beginning of the year started well. In spite of bad cold again it was nothing like the year before and we had comparatively plenty of food to help us remain alive. Towards the end of January [1943] the words 'defensive fighting' crept into the German military vocabulary. For the first time an incredible rumour started to fly about concerning the German forces in Russia around Stalingrad. Members of the guard company were continually being whipped away as fit for fighting and rumour had it that the Germans were aiming to form an additional army of 2 million men by April [1943]. A great wave of depression set in all over Germany at this time, and if they had known the real truth about their losses at Stalingrad it would no doubt have been much greater. On this date I think that the real turning point of the war can date, as from then on, the Allies never looked back. Although there were some sticky moments ahead, and some pauses for breath, the Germans from this time on continued to retreat till the end of the war on every single sector.

Both the British and the Germans regarded artistic activities at Eichstätt as a 'good thing'. In one part of the camp was the theatre, which included a full-sized stage and room for an audience of about 200 people. Many of the productions would boast lavish sets and costumes, mostly provided by Munich Opera, and would be performed by a number of professional actors who were imprisoned in Germany, amongst whom was Michael Goodliffe, who had been wounded in the leg during the retreat from Dunkirk and subsequently taken [as a] PoW. Initially, Goodliffe was held at Oflag VII-d in Tittmoning, Bavaria, but in 1942 he was transferred to Eichstätt. Here, where there were better facilities for theatre, he produced a series of plays and pantomimes along with fellow inmates such as, Dan Cunningham, Wallace Finlayson, Llewelyn, and Brian McIrvine, all of whom were professional actors prior to their service in the British Army. The performances were complimented by Leichner make-up, ordered from Berlin, programmes for each play were printed locally and orchestral accompaniment was often provided. Photographs of many scenes were taken by the camp guards. The Germans willingly co-operated, hoping to divert energies, which might otherwise be devoted to escape attempts. They also seem to have felt that the more serious productions benefited from the German cultural influence. A number of PoWs became accomplished as female impersonators. These included Brian McIrvine and John Blomfield Dixon: Michael Goodliffe is recorded as saying:

> A very interesting side of our prison theatre was the attitude of the audiences. At first, they would be easy to please, but we soon found that unless the presentation of female roles was intelligently tackled, any serious productions were impossible. Two or three clever actors solved this problem, so that our audiences accepted them exactly as the Elizabethans accepted their boy-actors.

Post-Mortem

One of the first Eichstätt productions, in January 1943, was *Post-Mortem*, written by Noël Coward in 1930, a bitter and gloomy anti-war play featuring a wounded soldier in the trenches, played by Michael Goodliffe, who is carried forward in time during his dying moments to visit England in the 1930s. The play, produced by Wallace Finlayson, had not previously been produced professionally and, given the audience consisted solely of British officers in captivity, brows were raised. In one of the scenes the lead character, John Cavan, remarks to his former comrades:

> Well, you'd better pray for another war for your sons that are not yet born, because it will be all just as you want. What happens to them out there will be entirely beyond your comprehension, then.

John Blomfield Dixon records his feelings about the performance:

Brian McIrvine (left) played a dual role as Lady Cavan and Monica Chellerton. Michael Goodliffe (right) played the leading role as John Cavan.(*Courtesy of The J B Dixon Collection*)

Went last night to see *Post-Mortem* by Noël Coward, a world premier incidentally and extremely well acted on the whole and well produced. Brian (McIrvine) and Michael Goodliffe shone above all others. The former particularly. The play has caused a good deal of controversy in the camp as to whether it was ever suitable for presentation and feelings were high in some quarters. Personally, I thought it was very good, though of course very bitter and cynical, but how true!

Thursday, 14 January 1943
A new chap arrived in the camp today. Caught near Matruh a week ago, he is in the Black Watch transferred to the Commandos. Yesterday, a big search in blocks 2 and 8, and we live in daily fear of one upon us. There seems to be a big flap on about repatriations and perhaps something will happen this time. We might even have a chance of going to a neutral country. According to letters from England the Germans there were let out of handcuffs sometime before Christmas, so there is some hope for us.

Saturday, 23 January 1943

A lot of interesting things have happened since I last wrote, not so much in the camp but in the war as a whole. The papers seem to be in a frenzy about Russia's bitter defensive fighting everywhere and the force enveloping Stalingrad is apparently surrounded. Today a goon came in to the lager with a tin of boot Polish. His payment of a bet that Tripoli would not fall before the end of the month. An interesting story from the *Kommandantur*, a week ago a German corporal arrived complete with credentials and made a doctor find the sixty-six fittest men, got their goods and chattels and march them off. Two days ago ten more men were dealt with in the same way. This, so they say, is happening all over Germany, ten here, six there, as the OKW must form an army of 2 million by April. I got a new part you know one act play being produced by John Calthorp, *Count Albany*, where I play Clemintina Walkinshaw.

Wednesday, 27 January 1943

The tone in the German papers these days is simply astounding. Summed up, it means literally I think 'backs to the wall'. We certainly have never seen anything like it before in our captivity. The only big thing they let out is the surrounding of one of their armies at Stalingrad. But this in itself, although an unusual catastrophe for them, doesn't seem to warrant the general depressing tone of the articles and one can't help feeling that in spite of their own advice it is not the time now to hide ones head in the sand the truth must stand they are defiantly holding back the degree of their catastrophe in the east. If we were to come in now in the West – the psychological effect on the German people apart from anything else would be terrific. The German doctor is reported to have said that we shall have won the war in two weeks.

Monday, 1 February 1943

With February [1943] came the beginning of the daylight American raids. Our first one came about the third week in February [1943] – a bright, sunny day and although we heard a lot passing over, I could see none at all because they were so high up. An abortive attempt at escape today, which caused a lot of bother but not as much as expected. Ronnie and I took over the PMC from Arthur who had got tired of it. The Germans did most of the work after a drink as I was away so often in the theatre. *Post-Mortem* was produced about this time too – a world prelude in fact and caused a good deal of controversy in the camp. I've started again by appearing in *Count Albany* as Clementina Walkinshaw, quite a good play but not very well produced by John Calthrop. I was completely at sea as he gave no idea as to how the part should be played.

Friday, 5 February 1943

The Jerries have taken the loss of Stalingrad very badly and some of them seemed to have heard the death knell of Germany quite definitely. The wave of optimism in the camp is simply terrific. A letter from my Jo has arrived with an adorable snap of her in riding costume. She looks much fitter than before and seems to have filled out a bit. The Garden City has been swimming in mud for the past two weeks, but this is clearing up now. Bad lights because we have run out of carbide and only through chance did we get a bit extra to tide us over. The night before last we had none at all and had to eat by fat light.

Wednesday, 17 February 1943

Hugh Davies died three days ago from peritonitis, poor chap. It was only a short while ago he was fit and well. Started rehearsals for *Count Albany* and I don't like it. I wish to Christ it was over and done with. When this is finished, I reckon I've had it.

Thursday, 18 February 1943

A visit was made by Frederick O. Auckenthaler of the Swiss delegation who reported that the heating facilities were far from adequate, the quantity of stoves being insufficient for the needs of the PoWs, and were of a model, which did

Lieutenant Hugh Abbinett Davies (left), Royal Horse Artillery, who died from the effects of peritonitis and his grave (right). Officially his death was recorded on 16 February 1943, but John Blomfield Dixon records his death as occurring on 14 February 1943. Originally buried in the Neuberg Civil Cemetery, he was reinterred on 17 March 1948 in the Durnbach War Cemetery. He was 25 years old. (*Courtesy of The War Graves Photographic Project and The National Archives WO416/89/400*)

not permit good radiation of heat, and there was not enough coal. Blatterbauer refused to allow the top floors of the concrete barracks to be used in an effort to reduce overcrowding, claiming it was a fire risk. In addition, the PoWs had removed some of the wooden flooring for fuel. A new order had since been issued, that only six bed boards per bed we're now allowed, which made them far less comfortable. The British senior officer had asked for a minimum of eight for each bed, but Lieutenant Colonel Blatterbauer claimed that he had taken this measure due to the fact that the PoWs had burnt their own bed boards, and were responsible for diminishing their own comfort. The inspectors insisted that had sufficient heating being provided the burning of bed boards would not be necessary. They also found that much of the bedding was damp, which Blatterbauer declared was probably due to some weakness of the bladder in the occupants of the beds. In blocks 4 to 8 it was found that only carbide lamps existed, which gave out insufficient light. This was made worse given that the ration of carbide was so small. Blatterbauer claimed electric lighting was planned to be installed in some of the blocks. The inspector was of the opinion that improvement of lighting should be carried out in all barracks so that the officers who have very little common rooms at their disposal can also read in their own lodging quarters if they wish to. There was no artificial light in the cells, as was required under the provisions of articles 56 and 57 of the Geneva Convention, Blatterbauer claimed he had never heard of it and that no one had complained in the past. However, he assured the inspector that he would do something about it – which he never did. Washing facilities had not improved and officers were still only taking a hot shower once a fortnight. Blatterbauer claimed he did not have enough coal to give them more hot baths and promised to raise the issue with the German High Command in an effort to improve bathing facilities. There were now only fifteen medical orderlies, and sixty-three of the eighty-three hospital beds were occupied. Four men were in hospital at Freising, three in Munich and another five in Neuberg. Several gastric ulcers, dorsal caries, pernicious anaemia, and chronic synovitis of the knee joint were all treated in the camp hospital.

Thursday, 25 February 1943

The first American officers arrived today, one infantry colonel and two tank lieutenant colonels, who were all captured in Tunisia only a week ago. They look just like the pictures of American officers in *Life*. The Germans also turned-out block 6 and a sort of general post let in, in which we luckily escaped. Quite a lot of air raids about this time, though all at night and the bombing at last seemed to be getting the Germans down. The papers were always full of accounts of terror attacks, although little did, they realise to what a pitch they would reach later.

Saturday, 6 March 1943

After over two weeks of superb weather, bright sunshine though cold in the morning, it broke today with snow sleet and rain. Two years ago today we arrived at Posen. What an age! If we'd known at the time what we had in front of us! A big search last Thursday in block 6 and they found something they didn't like in there and turned the whole lot out to dig up the hut. The inhabitants are spread all over the lager and I hope to Christ I don't go through the whole camp. *Count Albany* is going quite well. In my own humble way I feel I haven't done too badly, although I can't pretend that the part has got into me. I'm not good enough for that. Dress rehearsals tomorrow and we start on Monday. Lots of rumours flying about these days about the forthcoming revolutions in Germany and the old man of the lager himself it's reported to have said that Germany can't last more than two months more. This however, is stretching it a bit too far I think.

Wednesday, 10 March 1943

Sadly, there is a report that one of the British officers, Lieutenant Eric Charles Archibald Keen, has attempted suicide. I am not surprised, despite all the news about the war we have been here for a long time and our surroundings are very depressing, even though they're better than we had before.

Friday, 12 March 1943

A big week for mail for me. I got twelve letters in all, mainly all from home and Jo. I'm in a bit of a dilemma as in one of her letters Jo says that she is shortly going into the services. She's put down for the WRENs but is afraid it will be the ATS, and only one day before I asked Dick to send her flowers from me for her birthday, and I can just imagine her embarrassment if some arrived at an ATS depot. I shall have to think of something else, though what I don't know. They haven't heard from me at home for some time and mother is coincidently worried. She is also feeling it a bit, the amount I write to Jo I'm afraid, as one for her always arrives when mother has been waiting a long time.

Thursday, 18 March 1943

We had our first really big search since Lau>en. Luckily, the weather was fine and sunny. The troops, including SS and the Gestapo, arrived in a massive chain while we were on parade and were greeted with a burst of derisive cheering. From then on things went with quite a swing. In spite of an intensive search of the blocks and also a personal search they found practically nothing that couldn't be replaced, but on the other hand they had a hat and a coat taken from them. These were finally returned to them at the end of the search at about 3.30 pm amid more derisive hoots and cheers. Altogether, from our point of view, quite a successful affair. We understood from reports afterwards that the Germans were looking for (a) our trustworthy radio set, (b) our tunnel [and] (c) our printing press! Where on earth they got the ideas about the first and last I haven't the faintest idea. We reckoned they must have been reading too much Edgar Wallace.

Wednesday, 31 March 1943

I went into the 'bulk' jail for eight days, being my sentence received at Warzburg for reading a book on parade. The Germans were obviously intent upon cleaning up all the long-standing sentences for petty offences, which accumulated at Warzburg and by this means they cleared up about seventy of us in six weeks. It was quite a change for a bit living with other people, and in spite of locked doors one managed to get out a good deal. I personally was rather disappointed as I had hoped to go out to the proper jail outside. Shortly after this, more Americans arrived, and people were asked to adopt one per room. We got hold of a fellow named Toni Cipriani, who by his name and looks, was obviously of Italian extraction. He was a very decent fellow though and we had him into dinner quite often. Shortly afterwards about forty more arrived and we were asked to take one into the mess and did so. He was a captain by the name of Tony Lumpkin and came from Missouri. A more decent fellow you couldn't imagine, and we had some grand times with him.

Wednesday, 7 April 1943

Came out today after eight days in the 'bulk' jail, being my sentence, which I received at Warburg. It was a great change and very restful, but I was glad to get out from being confined. I met quite a number of chaps there I hadn't met before and made some new friends. While in there we missed some very dirty weather but came out just a bit too early as rain and snow continued for three days. I got a letter from Dick while there and was terrifyingly surprised to learn he was in Tunisia. It came as a bit of a shock to realise he was in the fighting. God keep him safe. I only wrote to him the other day too ask him to deal with the flowers for Jo's birthday. So that's gone for six and I had to tell her so in a letter yesterday.

Monday, 12 April 1943

A bumper mail today and six for me. Two from my darling Jo, and she is definitely going into the WRENS. I think, at last, she is beginning to long for me as much as I long for her.

Lieutenant Peter Allin Southan Dodd (left), aged 26, 6th Battalion, South Staffordshire Regiment. He was removed from Eichstätt Civil Cemetery and reburied in the Durnbach War Cemetery on 17 March 1948. (*Courtesy of The National Archives WO416/98/295 and The War Graves Photographic Project*)

Tuesday, 13 April 1943

A terrible tragedy occurred today. Peter Dodd was playing hockey and suddenly passed out. He was immediately taken to hospital but never recovered, having died from the effects of a cerebral haemorrhage.

Friday, 16 April 1943

Peter Dodd buried this afternoon. A Roman Catholic mass was held in the hospital and he was buried in Eichstätt. Some of his regiment attended the funeral and looked very smart with belts, etc. a turn out that would be deemed as very ordinary at home. Life is becoming terrible for me. If it goes on for much longer, I really don't know what will happen. I shall go crackers, I think.

At the end of April [1943], the Katyn business started, and the senior British officer was invited with other officers to go there on a tour of inspection by the Germans. He immediately got into touch with General Fortune, who said that he also had received an invitation and that he wasn't to go unless ordered to by the Germans. The order did eventually arrive and the senior British officer was due to go on the 10 May [1943]. On Sunday, however, he lodged a protest with the commandant, which was an absolute masterpiece of expression and having received this the commandant must have asked for further instructions from Berlin, because the visit was then cancelled and nothing further was heard of it.

While the Americans were still here, we did *The Case Of The Frightened Lady* in which one of the colonels took part as a footman. It was quite good fun while it lasted, but appallingly hot and I used to sweat gallons every night behind stage, which only added to my difficulties further. The first night drops of sweat dropped from my forehead onto the light grey skirt, the whole of the time that I was sitting on the settee.

The Case of the Frightened Lady

Friday, 14 May 1943
The Case of the Frightened Lady is due to come off stage tonight, and I am not looking forward to it. As far as I am concerned it is the most difficult part I have ever played, and I don't seem to get any further with it.

Thursday, 20 May 1943
We've learned that the RAF bombed some dams in north Germany. Nothing much was said in the papers and the whole matter made very light of, but reports from goons in the camp who had been on leave in the area, the damage

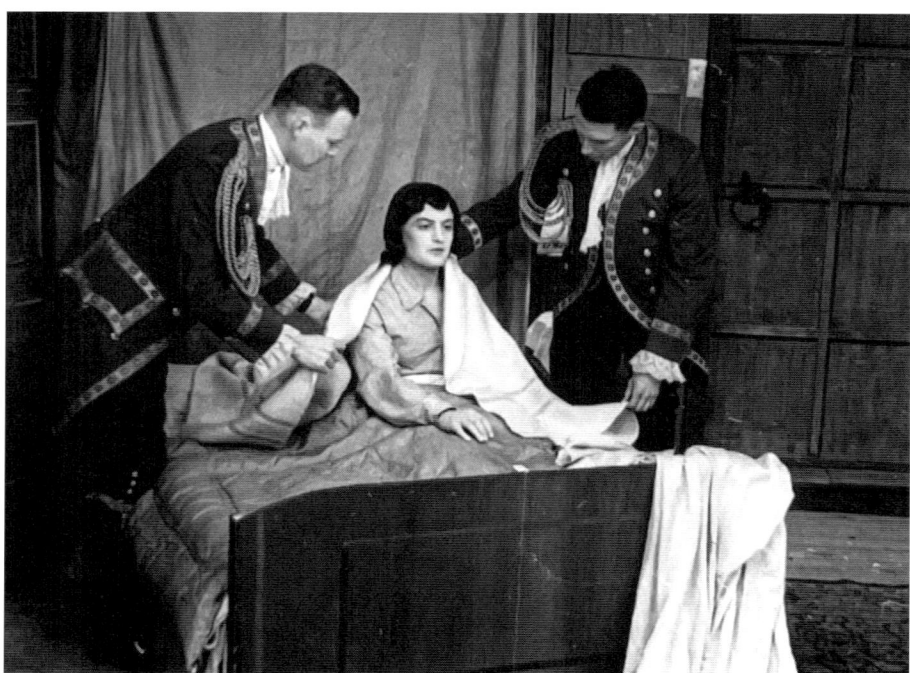

The Case of the Frightened Lady. John Blomfield Dixon, playing the part of Ailsa Crane, sits up in bed while he is tended to by Peter Ambery (left) and American officer J.D. Alger (right). (*Courtesy of The J B Dixon Collection*)

done was terrific, floods everywhere completely ruining the main potato area and devastating the Ruhr area even more since it left them without light power and water.

Sunday, 23 May 1943

The SBO didn't go to Katyn after all. Having received his letter of protest, which was a masterpiece, the commandant said a mistake had been made and the whole affair has been dropped. We now have an American living in the mess, Captain Tony Lumpkin. He's quite a decent fellow and comes out with some bloody funny cracks at times. A few days ago the Royal Air Force bombed some dams up in northern Germany. The papers don't say much about it but according to a goon who was up in their area the damage apparently has been terrific, floods everywhere, completely ruining the main potato crop area, stopping the power station and causing destruction everywhere.

Chapter 14

Escaping Eichstätt

More than 169,000 members of British and Commonwealth forces became PoWs of the Germans during the war. However, those involved in the planning and execution of escapes or in the production of equipment were in the minority. Many PoWs felt they had already risked their lives in the performance of their duty, and saw little value in the activities of the escapers. Escape attempts would see repercussions imposed upon the remaining PoWs, including the removal of privileges, such as receiving mail or Red Cross parcels. The business of escaping developed into an exact science and was strictly controlled. It was decided that all escaping would be concentrated in one compact organisation and that one team only would attempt to escape during a particular period. Records show that the following officers were part of the Escape Committee at Oflag VII-b:

Major Horace Maylin Vipan Wright, East Riding Yeomanry (chairman).
Major Robert George William Melsome, Northamptonshire Regiment (security).
Lieutenant Colonel Trendall (chairman – for a short period).
Lieutenant John William Morton Mansel (forging).
Captain Charles Hughlings Jackson (routes and stage manager of wire schemes).
Lieutenant Herbert Maxwell Graham.
Lieutenant Tom Preston (tunnel engineer).
Captain William Thompson (hides and construction work).
Lieutenant Charles Brydon Gilroy (special parcels).
Lieutenant Charles John Jervis Clay (special parcels).
Lieutenant Alfred Burke Thompson (escape 'I' and briefing).
Lieutenant Harry Shand (maps).
Captain Bryan Grosvenor Evers (tunnel look-out).
Captain Lennox Peter Divers Heery (Australian).

On the night of 3/4 June 1943, sixty-seven officers escaped from Oflag VII-b, through a tunnel in block 2. Plans for a mass breakout had begun in 1942 shortly after the arrival of two British officers, Lieutenant Jock Hamilton-Baillie (known as HB) and Captain Frank Weldon. They had been involved in an escape from their previous PoW camp at Warburg. The plan at Eichstätt was to dig a tunnel starting from under a latrine, passing under a rocky slope and up to a villager's chicken coop about 30m away. Tunnelling, featuring electric lighting and a trolley system, was difficult because of the rocky ground being excavated. However, the obvious difficulty of digging this terrain also meant that the Germans did not search this area of the camp for possible tunnels. Instead, they focussed their investigations on the other side of the camp, where they had discovered soil deposited by the tunnellers. The tunnel was completed by the end of

Photograph of the tunnel at Eichstätt. (*Courtesy of The J B Dixon Collection*)

May [1943] and the breakout took place a few nights later. By dawn, sixty-seven PoWs were out. Travelling either in pairs or small groups, most headed

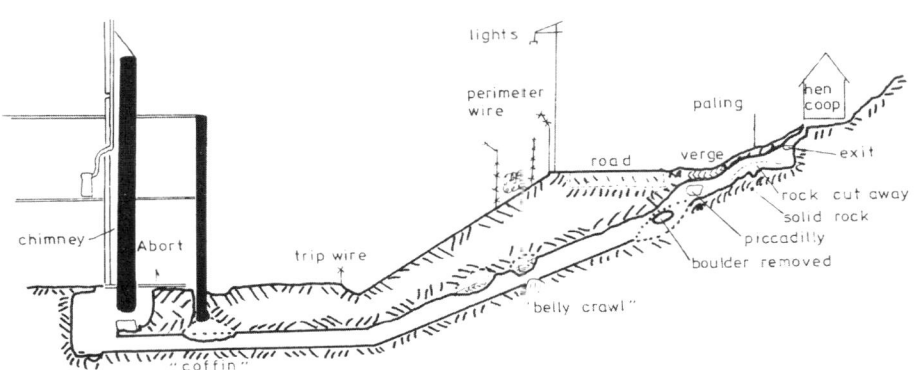

Map detailing route of tunnel. (*Courtesy of The J B Dixon Collection*)

for neutral Switzerland, but the Germans had mobilised the entire countryside and within three days fifty-four of the escapees had been recaptured. Eventually, every single escaper had been returned to Eichstätt and after two weeks in detention, all the men were sent to Colditz. Their time on the run had occupied over 50,000 German police, soldiers, home guard and Hitler Youth for a week.

The latrine showing the tunnel entrance. (*Courtesy of The J B Dixon Collection*)

Thursday, 4 June 1943

The king's birthday, Tony Lumpkin left us today, in company with the rest of the Americans. It was a great disappointment as we liked him immensely and got on very well together. I think he hated leaving almost as much as we did, and he very nearly broke down just before he went. We had a sports meeting at which the pipe band appeared for the first time. The commandant was present, a fact which troubled him greatly and which he considered a great insult afterwards, as during the night, while the Americans were moving out, sixty-seven chaps got out of a tunnel from in block 2. Unfortunately, combined with such large numbers, and the unfortunate coincidence that two other camps made large breaks on the same night, the Germans thought that a general uprising was in progress and called out the whole country on an emergency basis. None of the sixty-seven chaps got away, therefore, and the commandant who considered that he had been got into the camp under pretext so that final arrangements could be made, started to make a worse bastard of himself than before, if that's possible.

A sports meeting – triangular contest between England, Scotland, the Dominions and USA. This was proceeded by a performance of the pipe band playing Retreat. They put up a bloody good show. The commandant and his party attended, and it was this I think that put his back up, as unfortunately the 'tube' broke on the same night, and he thought the show was a blind for it. Of course, it wasn't, as the SBO told him, but you wouldn't expect a German to have either the mentality or the sense of fair play to believe that. On the following Sunday we had a spit and polish parade, and three cheers were given for his majesty, which fairly made the place ring. The sound of 2,000 voices raised a most inspiring sound and must have made the inhabitants of Eichstätt think the invasion had begun. His reasoning of course was utterly false, as it must be obvious to anybody who knows anything at all about it that the matter cannot be decided until night actually falls. The theatre was closed, and various other institutions shut as usual. This, I rather welcomed as it prevented the production of the *Mikado*, which I was beginning to loathe and also allowed me to do some work for my exams. Invasion rumours were rife at this time, and everybody expected things to happen at any moment.

Tuesday, 8 June 1943
A letter from mother with dreadful news. Aunt Nancy is dead after a very long illness. I am so very sorry, and I really don't know how I'm going to write to Jo. It is such a very difficult thing to do anyhow. Mother says she is being very brave about it, and I am proud of her for that.

Sunday, 20 June 1943
A year ago, today we started our one and only 'tube'. It didn't last long however, only seven days and I doubt we should have ever got anywhere with it anyhow. Things are terribly dull here now, everyone's nerves rather at breaking point and tempers frayed. Everybody expects things to happen any moment now and rumours of invasion fly around the camp daily. One can imagine what it must be like outside. A black day today, however, and we are more depressed than ever. The weather cleared finally after nearly a month's rain, and I spent a good afternoon sunbathing. No sign of the theatre being allowed open yet, though I expect now I have a chance to sunbathe it will open again.

The Pipe Band at Eichstätt, 1943. It was claimed the sound of the band practising was used to cover the noise made by tunnellers in the camp. (*Courtesy of The J B Dixon Collection*)

Thursday, 1 July 1943

The first exodus off the camp by the British took place and some 150, all with 'records' were sent away to Spangenberg. There was some frantic changing and substitution so that messes could stay together. They were all, with the exception of one case, detected by the goons and many sad faces observed the exit from behind cell bars. Many of the camp were suffering at this time from a disease class by the doctors as melancholia. Surprisingly enough, it wasn't so much amongst the France boys as amongst Greece and Crete and there were numerous cases taken to hospital. Freddie Gray attempted to climb the wire behind the hospital, but luckily the goon was prevented from shooting by Reid the interpreter. The latter, however, did almost exactly the same thing, that night, by going out of the hospital in the middle of the night and walking down Lagerstraße. The German doctor said that 50 per cent of the camp were already mad and that the remaining 50 per cent would go mad if they had to remain here another year. The number of melancholia cases was now eighty-nine.

Saturday, 17 July 1943

The camp seems steadily to get smaller, the naval people left a week ago, the warrant officers this morning and there is a possibility the marines may also leave. It's only dribs and drabs but it has quite an effect, and odd people here and there are also leaving. Work seems to be progressing quite favourably and my exam is a week next Tuesday. I hope to God I pass. It would be something achieved. Something seems to have gone wrong in the lager for me. Quite a number of people now refuse to recognise me. I don't know whether it's my imagination, but I don't think it is. I wish I knew what it was and am endeavouring, by careful means, to find out if I can. Continually, I am tortured by what may happen when I get home. The fact of a court martial looms over me like the nightmares I used to have as a kid. I know that if it comes off, I cannot escape and can only pray to God that at least I shall be given the chance to redeem my own cowardly conscience by putting up a real show against the Japanese. To meet, and actually fight them with the knowledge that I was redeeming myself, not only in my own sight, but in the sight of others, would be worth the fate of even being killed in the act. At least I should have died as a soldier and not wound my life on, tortured by memories of belated decisions and cowardly inaction. If I was sentenced, I wouldn't be so cowardly as to commit suicide, but I would never face going back home, branded as such. All thoughts of Jo would have to be banished from my mind. Anyone who reads this might think I was mad. I hope, perhaps in that sense, that I am and that these dull forebodings are merely the outcome of a three-year-old brooding mind. Whatever happens – God give me strength to overcome it – but above all let me first wipe the shame from my own mind by some really tangible act. Then, if they wish, they can deal with me. When I am satisfied that I in myself have, at last, a clear conscience.

Saturday, 31 July 1943

I myself went into hospital with an attack of the 'squitties' only a week before the exam was due to start. Actually, it was one of the best things that could have happened to me. I think I was suffering from delusions. Everyone I met seemed to avoid knowing me and my own mind was an absolute torment. Afterwards I realised it must have been entirely imagination but then it was very real. As a matter of fact, at the same time our trouble with Jimmy Fitch came to a head. For some time past he had been very queer and when he went into hospital he decided to move to another mess. He confided in me quite a lot, as I was confiding in him, and he seemed to have some idea that the rest of the mess had been telling stories about round the camp, which, of course, was untrue, as I later found out. The fact of the matter must have been an unintentional remark dropped by someone, which, in due course, was spread about and magnified, coming to Jimmy's ears at a bad moment. The upshot of it was however that he left us, and we were then down to eight. As the invasion of Sicily seems to be going great guns let's hope that this maybe the prelude to the big air bombardment and the final blow at the continent. The camp seems to get steadily smaller; the naval people left a week ago, the WOs this morning, and there is a possibility the marines may also leave. It's only dribs and drabs, but it has quite an effect and odd people here and there are also leaving.

The news of [Benito] Mussolini's arrest whipped into the camp in record time. The chattering and laughing that went on during appel was amazing and everyone expected a big allied strike now that would end the war in a very short while. The goons were obviously expecting it too, and showed so in their newspapers. Finding myself too fat at this time, so I've started to do PT in the mornings before parade and also did a lot of road work in the camp. Upon weighing myself, however, for the first time since captivity found that I only weighed 10 stone 8 pounds, so something was wrong somewhere as my pot and chest was simply oozing fat.

They decided now to make some more silence rooms in the camp and our room was one of those selected. There was, of course, a good deal of ladder pulling and the situation almost turned into a stand-up fight. Finally, they gave in, and we weren't split up, but sent to room 4 in block 6. Besides our eight, Jock Mackenzie, Mike Kemp, Johnny Renton, McWilliams and Frank Pearce came with us, and we left the whole side open this time, which the us gave much more room and was slightly better than before. Parole walks in limited numbers now started for those who worked about the camp, gardener's etc., and I went on one with Tiny. It was a wonderful experience to go out without guards, but on the first ones we still had to move about in a group and so didn't quite get the feeling of freedom that was prevalent later on. The first authentic rumours about repatriation also started about this time and in the case of old PoWs they were to go on fruitlessly for over a year gaining strength each time until the final release came.

Monday, 9 August 1943

Last week we had two more cases of attempted suicide. Freddie Gray climbed over the wire behind the hospital in broad daylight and Duggie Reid walked up and down Lagerstraße in the middle of the night. A search in our room today, which caused a bit of bother, but on the whole not too bad. We are moving from here on Thursday to block 5 room 4 as this room is being turned into a silence room. The whole move was a typical Bosche balls up and ladders were pulled up right, left and centre. It was only by great good luck that we were settled all in together.

Tuesday, 24 August 1943

A visit from the Swiss delegation, along with a German general, who made a most comprehensive trip around the camp that I have ever known. He seemed to be very pleasant, and we were all hauled out on parade and left, so that he could go round in peace. On complaining to the Swiss about the jam, he said it was the same all over Germany and that in Berlin they'd found a new use for it – house decorating!

In the report detailing his visit, Rudolph Denzler states,

the general impression of this camp is not quite satisfactory. However, it is much better than under the former Camp Commander Lt. Col. Blatterbauer, as much has been done to alleviate the conditions of those imprisoned officers.

The tension which still exists between the PoWs and the camp authorities has to be attributed to the constant affairs of escapes for which the present occupants of this camp have a quite genial aptitude.

The number of PoWs at the time of this visit was:

1,470 British officers
1 Free French officer
1 Greek naval officer

1 USA officer
256 British other ranks
2 USA other ranks

Camp Commander: Oberst Wellhausen
Assistant Camp Commander: Major Gehring
Abwehroffizior: Hauptman Klau
German High Command: Hauptman Schaade
Representative of the Auswrtigos Amt, Berlin: Herr von Fetter
British Man of Confidence: Major John Higgon

Religious Activity
Following chaplains are in the camp:

Major Robert Stuart Louden, Royal Army Chaplains Department (Church
   of Scotland)
Captain Anthony Antrobus, Royal Army Chaplains Department
Captain Eric Victor Cave, Royal Army Chaplains Department
Captain J.D.K. Hunter, NZYMCA

Wednesday, 25 August 1943
The war goes on but slowly, and every day we have rumours that Italy has been
invaded or packed in. Following the Swiss visit yesterday, a German general
made the most comprehensive trip round the camp that I have ever known.
He seemed to be very pleased, and we were all hauled out on parade and left
there so that he could go round in peace. On complaining to the Swiss about the jam, he said it was the same all over Germany I met in Berlin they found a new use for it – house decorating! I am playing a lot of games but my fat doesn't seem to go.

Relaxing in the summer sun. PoWs look out over part of Oflag VII-b. Note the wooden barrack huts in the background. (*Image source: The Paull Chick Collection, courtesy of Martin Mace*)

Wednesday, 1 September 1943

A year ago, today, we left Warburg, and this is the first camp I've ever been in for a whole year. I went out for my first parole walk. It was very enjoyable, but somehow not a performance I would wish to repeat often, unless we could go into town. We went over the Southern hills, down the other side, around the base of the castle and back just skirting the town. We had a couple of beers in a pub, but it was the same watery stuff that we get here. There was great excitement in the camp by letters from Denmark, Sweden and England about the repatriation of PoWs and the interning in a neutral country of long term *Kreigies*. As the war looks as if it is going on for at least another six months, if not a year or more, I don't think I could stand it. To go to Spain where one would learn the language or do something useful would be delightful. I must start work again next week, I'm not looking forward to it much. Rumours that Blatterbauer and Muller are bound for the *Ostfront*. I hope the bastards are captured by the Russians.

Wednesday, 8 September 1943

The news of the surrender of Italy and once again the information spread like wildfire, bringing with it wild hopes of the war ending soon, which, of course,

The officers John Dixon refers to are Captain Peter Rowdon Kitto, 8th Royal Tank Regiment, RAC, who died 8 December 1942, aged 22. He is buried at Gaza War Cemetery, Israel. (*Courtesy of The War Graves Photographic Collection*)

Captain Henry Arthur Hulton Beckwith, 7th Battalion, Rifle Brigade (1st Battalion, The London Rifle Brigade), who died 5 May 1943, aged 26. He is buried at Medjez-El-Bab Memorial, Tunisia. (*Courtesy of authors collection*)

were not fulfilled. To celebrate, the brass band played an impromptu concert in the evening. How I cursed the Italian *Kriegies*, and still do for that matter, although many of them too have had their chances spoiled. News came that Peter Kitto died after an accident, which aggravated his wounds. Henry Beckwith also had it and the band of friends got noticeably smaller. I wonder what they will think of me if I ever get convicted. Oh God! What a disgrace!

Thursday, 9 September 1943
Yesterday, four days after our landing on the mainland, Italy surrendered unconditionally. The news was brought into the camp early this morning by the goons and spread like wildfire. To celebrate, the band played in the evening and we are having a bash on Sunday. Those lucky, lucky *Kriegies* in Italy – practically the last to be captured and the first to be released – what must be their feelings be at the moment. Maybe one day – maybe one day sooner or later – we shall have those feelings. I pray to God that it happens this year. The repatriation of old *Kriegies* seems to be official and every day we receive news of more rumours regarding interning in a neutral country. The Swiss government is supposed to have intimated its willingness to receive us if the Germans agree.

Wednesday, 29 September 1943
Working for my exam in November [1943] is very trying these days and I hope the papers don't arrive till December [1943], at least to give me time enough. I get up at 7.30 am every day, have breakfast before parade and then work in the silence room till 12.00 pm. Afternoons, I work in the room, but the cold and my eyesight are great deterrents. It is nothing unusual to have a greatcoat on and a rug wrapped around my knees while working, but it is very dark, and it makes my eyes ache.

Thursday, 14 October 1943
The old *Kriegies* are on the move. The first lot left last Monday week and rumour has it that they have arrived home. Two more lots have left since and all that remains to go now are the doctors, padres and protected personnel. Great rumours are flying round about us going soon, but I can't bring myself to believe it. It made my blood boil to think that in 1940 the Germans refused to exchange any because we had not got equal numbers. Those poor chaps had to wait another three and a half years before they could get back, and then the Germans talk about their culture and their humanity. They haven't the first notion of either culture decency or fair play. From my long observations of them over four years the only thing one can say about them is that they are typical bullies and always will be cock of the hoop when they're winning and brutal

Gaslight, set in 1880s London, is a dark tale of a marriage based on deceit and trickery, and a husband committed to driving his wife insane in order to steal from her. John Blomfield Dixon was cast in another female role, as Nancy the maid. (Left to right) Michael Goodliffe as Mr Manningham, John Blomfield Dixon as Nancy and Brian McIrvine as Mrs Manningham. (*Courtesy of The J B Dixon Collection*)

as you can make them but when they are losing, weak, cowardly and clinging squeakily for mercy.

Have started work in the theatre again as Nancy in *Gaslight*. It's a very difficult part and I have many doubts as to whether I can do it. The pantomime is also being written and I've been asked to take part.

Last weekend about fourteen chaps arrived here from Salerno. They seemed quite cheery, but new *Kriegies* have lost their attraction for us.

Tuesday, 16 November 1943

We went for our first visit to the cinema. These parole walks, which were now a 100 a day, were only some of the official attempts to try and make us forget their brutality in the early days and to make us remember only the good points now that they realised, they could not win the war. Amongst the officials of the camp of course the feelings were even more apparent.

Saturday, 20 November 1943

We were all X-rayed for TB and unfortunately about four people were found to have traces of it. The rumours about repatriation once again came in great force, so much so that I stopped writing my diary as I thought it would be useless anyhow.

This caricature of John Blomfield Dixon was drawn by Frank Slater while they were imprisoned at Laufen and is titled 'Gladys'. It appears in Slater's book *As You Were*, produced in 1947, which contains images of many well-known PoWs. John came to hate playing the role of females to the point where, in January 1944, he recorded in his diary, 'I shall go on strike for a male part. I am getting so terribly fed up with females.' Despite this, he continued to appear on stage in a number of productions as a woman. (*Courtesy of The J B Dixon Collection*)

Early in December [1943] the colonel arrived and we were very glad to see him. He gave us new confidence and said that having brought us into captivity he had now come to see that we got out of it safely. He was very pleased to see how cheery and fit everybody was and glad that most were not just wasting their time. The pantomime, our last it was hoped, was rather a flop. I was supposed to be the heroine but had a very small part and made worse by my so-called singing. As a Christmas treat from the Germans, we were taken to see the coloured film *Baron Munchausen*. In our frame of mind, it was very exciting but as a jubilee film of life it compared very unfavourably with even a British film. For my birthday party I had the colonel as a guest and I'm afraid we rather stumped him with the food.

Chapter 15

The Murder of Poole and Duncan

1944

With the beginning of a new year our hopes again were really for the greatest of happenings and this time our hopes were not disappointed. Our fourth anniversary was rapidly approaching and we all of us felt that we couldn't stand very much more. I started the year with a new play, *I Killed the Count*, in which I played the count's wife, Louise Rogers. A very, very trying part and was promised a male part soon as a reward for my great patience, a promise which has not yet been kept and which now I don't think ever will be.

John made an entry in his diary that perhaps helped explain the sudden lack of momentum in his writing.

Sunday, 2 January 1944

A very large gap in this since I last wrote, which was caused by the big rumours about the repatriation of old *Kriegies*. When the senior PoWs went, they were not allowed to take any books with them and so I thought it was hardly worthwhile carrying on, but now all that has broken down I shall try and keep a small record of events. It is very hard though, and barely seems worth the trouble. The colonel is now with us in camp and is a great help, although I still cannot get over my feeling of awe with him. He came to dinner on the Sunday before my birthday. *Gaslight* was a great success and I have been congratulated many times for it. At the moment, the pantomime is on, and although I am supposedly the heroine, have a very small part, which I have managed very badly. At the moment, I am rehearsing in *I Killed the Count* and Michael Goodliffe has asked me to play Ophelia in *Hamlet* in future, but I am very diffident about. After that though, I shall go on strike for a male part. I am getting so terribly fed up with females.

The war seems to be going well at least, as well as can be expected. So far as we're concerned it doesn't seem any nearer to the end, although we hope and pray that it will end shortly. The old sayings, 'home by Christmas' or 'by this year' have become so worn out that no one dare use them again. How I long to be home again and with my darling Jo. I love her more and more as each day goes by and she is never far from my thoughts at all times. She sent me a small

Polyphoto the other day with a large one to follow. I was astounded with the change in her, the last portrait I had of her showed her more or less still as a girl in her teens, but this shows her as a woman. Obviously, the death of Aunt Nancy has had something to do with it and I am proud of her for bearing up so well under the strain. I long to tell her outright of any adoration for her, but I cannot bring myself to write the words. They are not to be written, but spoken, and in any case, it would not be fair to her. Reading through some of the things I have put in this book, I shudder at some of the kitchen maid drivel I have written, but then I suppose I'm incredibly romantic and sentimental. God grant I shall never disappoint Jo in that regard.

Monday, 28 February 1944

There was another big raid in the afternoon. This time they were much more visible, and we saw hundreds passing to the north and south of the camp. This day, however, remains to us memorable for the fact that the Germans once again committee cold-blooded murder. They published an order after the first raid that officers were to go inside their blocks. During this raid, as usual, everybody got very excited, pointing to the sky, and laughing and talking. There were quite a number outside block 4, and they were shouted at to go in by the sentry. One of them wasn't very quick and the sentry, egged on by the guard commander, took deliberate aim and shot him. One of his comrades, inside the block seeing

PoWs playing ice hockey during winter1943/44. The large barrack blocks in the background suggest that this is the Upper Camp. (*Image source: The Paull Chick Collection, courtesy of Martin Mace*)

him fall, shouted to the guard that he was coming out and came out with his hands up to help the chap inside. The sentry shot him deliberately as well. No doctor was allowed down for some considerable time afterwards and the two officers, Duncan and Poole, were dead by the evening. Enquiries were held and it was proved that the Germans were responsible. They, of course, acquitted the sentry and the guard commander, by the name of Unteroffizier Metz, and the latter was afterwards put on a security work inside the lager. We treated the Germans with the contempt they deserved. The officers were buried in Eichstätt Cemetery.

The weather had been very kind to us up to now but on 6 February [1944] the weather finally broke and winter arrived with snow in immense quantities. Cresta runs were made all over the camp and we made two sledges, which gave us a great deal of fun, but also some very heavy colds and a lot of bruises. The wood party too was going strong about this time and tulips were also flourishing. we used to get quite a lot of stuff in especially flour, saccharine and bread and during the cold weather this was an absolute godsend. Parole walks too were extended to the playing area we were allowed to wander more or less where we wanted. Fir cones brought in on every walk kept the fire going too very nearly June [1944] and it was a blow when no more wood walks were allowed. In March [1944] everybody got the knitting craze and people were seen appearing all over the camp in the weirdest of colours. Brian himself knitted about four including one for Tiny, which looked like a sack when it was being made. Geoff went into hospital again with tummy trouble for the third and longest time. he should have gone before the board, but owing to the inefficiency and slackness of the SMO He did not go. if he had gone, he would have passed almost certainly and a good many other officers as well.

Thursday, 16 March 1944

Today, we had our clearest daylight raid. Four columns of American planes passed directly over the camp, which they used as a turning point to go south. They were quite low and what easily distinguished by the enormous condensation streams, which remained behind them for some considerable time. What always amazed us about these raids was the complete lack of opposition. The planes used to sail through the sky in the hundreds, almost like a Hendon parade, and it must have given the goon civilian's something to think about too. The Germans insisted at this time that we should build air raid shelters, and these were begun about the beginning of April [1944], but they are still nowhere near completion. The wood party finished on 18 March [1944] and on 9 April [1944] we celebrated Easter by an enormous booze up. We had some fifteen bottles of wine between nine of us and I went through the party and felt fine until I got into bed, when I very nearly passed out and had to go outside and throw the lot up. Johnny Reuton was ill for the whole of the next day. We were all very invasion conscious at about this time and, as time went on, became more and more desperate in our efforts to force it by sheer will power.

Tuesday, 18 April 1944

On with the ban on the diplomatic services, tension rose to fever pitch, although no one really knew whether it was a bluff or not. A few more efforts by the Germans to worsen our last few months of captivity were made in May [1944] when they started a so-called 'luxury camp' to which officers were supposed to go for periods of about a month or six weeks. They started off in their foolish way of ordering people to go, whether they wanted to or not, but later they saw the light and the SBO and SBMO were allowed to nominate the candidates.

Saturday, May 20 1944

A show was given for our benefit by a small circus that had just arrived in the town. The actual show was a very third-rate wartime performance and no doubt they were suffering under difficulties, but the camp lapped it up right, left and centre. Never, I should imagine, had they received so much thunderous applause and the sight of young girls, only passably attractive from a distance, performing contortions in very scanty costumes proved almost too much for the majority, who had spent four years in celibacy.

Tuesday, 30 May 1944

The Italian campaign quickened in intensity about this time with the final breakthrough at Casino and on, with the fall of Rome, we were brought up to full pitch of expectation although nobody knew quiet what.

Tuesday, 6 June 1944 (D-Day)

The first news of the invasion was brought to us in the afternoon by Jimmy Fitch, who said that a very reliable rumour had just being brought in that we had landed near La Havre. Everybody went mad and then sobered up immediately, afraid to let their imaginations run riot in case they were only Commando raids or false alarms, but before evening the fact was confirmed and we knew then that our last months of captivity had really come.

Friday, 16 June 1944

Between 9 and 15 June [1944] the Americans and RAF made five raids on Munich, practically flattening the town and causing an untold number of deaths. Over 2,000 actually appeared in the VB and many more must have been unannounced. Amongst those killed was Hauptman Ditiner's son, who, at the age of 15, was on duty in a flak unit. The goons at this time, in spite of enormous efforts by the newspapers to impress them with the tremendous effects of V-1 [flying bombs], were no more impressed than ourselves and regarded it, as we did, as merely a piece of morale boosting. All who could, tried to ingratiate themselves into our good favour as they saw the final doom approaching.

Sunday, 18 June 1944

Last night saw the cracking of another 'tube', which proved a terrible flop. Only about six people got out, all of whom were brought back, except Thorneycroft, of whom there is no news to date. Shortly before this we received news of the massacre at Luft III. There, seventy-seven officers got out of a 'tube' and of these some fifty-one were shot dead in cold blood. The Germans official report was that officers were shot resisting arrest, but this was proved wrong by the statements of officers who did return to the camp. The case of one officer, which is almost typical of the whole lot, will give the clue to the complete case. He in company with two others got out in full RAF uniform. After being caught they were put in a cell by the Gestapo. Shortly afterwards two of them were called for questioning and were not seen again. On his return to camp, the third officer enquired after them and was told that they had been shot. From this it is clear to see that the Gestapo had taken everything out of the hands of the army and shot some fifty officers in cold blood for no reason whatsoever except the complete disregard of any principle whatsoever.

Tuesday, 8 August 1944

The last change of command at Oflag VII-b took place when Oberst Ried handed over to Oberst Bessinger, who had himself, been a PoW during WWI. With the breakthrough in France and the abortive attempt of 20 July [1944], the Germans seemed to lose any sort of control that they might previously have had. They were to be compared only with a wild animal brought to bay and making desperate efforts to prolong its life, although it knows that shortly it will be dispatched. There were some who reckoned that the whole of the 20 July [1944] job was 'put up'. At a time when it was necessary to keep the nation fighting the leaders thought it would be a great thing to try and unite the nation on one hand by calling forth a burst of patriotic fever, which would enable the Nazis to put into operation the severest restrictions in order to obtain really total war and on the other hand to get rid of all those undesirable characters and weaklings whom they knew were desirous of peace and yet whom they could not simply shoot in cold blood with no protest whatsoever. Myself, I believe that this was a very feasible solution as it was almost impossible to believe that the Führer could have escaped the scene of devastation almost unhurt and also that the leaders of the so-called revolt could have been so ham handed in their organisation, especially when one considers that their leaders were not just a small set of nincompoops but savvy leaders who had held responsible positions. Unfortunately, the papers describing the trial were not allowed to come into the camp and I was unable to obtain them for my collection.

Tuesday, 12 September 1944
With the advance of the Allies to the German frontier, activity has become more pronounced and we have had eight raids, day and night, over the last three nights, which drove the goons into a frenzy.

This time the guard completely had the wind up properly and all goon boxes were doubled, hatch's let down, armed patrols inside the camp and outside the wire, besides machine guns posted on the hill behind. With any continuation of the raids the guard company must have been completely worn out.

Thursday, 21 September 1944
With the setting in of stagnation on the [Western] Front and the failure (partial) of the Arnhem attempt, our hopes suffered a severe setback and a wave of depression settled upon the camp. All hopes of being home by Christmas vanished as if overnight and the terrible thought of another winter to pass in

East Riding Yeomanry Officers at Eichstätt, September 1944. (Back left to right): Nick Wilmot-Smith, Tommy Carmichael, Mike Trevor, Mike Lindley, Harold Hopper, Brian Reid, Roger Waterhouse, Sir Lindores Leslie Bart (9th Lancers). (Front left to right): Mike Longstaffe, Sidney Bearne (RTR), Lieutenant Colonel Douglas Thompson DSO MC TD, Bob Smith, John Blomfield Dixon (RTR). (*Courtesy of The J B Dixon Collection*)

Gefangenschaft proved too much for some. At times I myself felt the strain appallingly and wondered if it might not be too much. of course, I don't mean the ordinary strain, but that about which I should have not spoken. All day long and night the howls of what might and may be, gnawed at me and left me at times paralysed with apprehension. What do I do? but no answer came. The answer only can come when we get back on, I'm only too sure that I know the answer. A determination to carry on the war at all costs was the main theme of the German leaders and press in these days, and the formation of the *Volkstrum*, which followed on the 18 September [1944], seemed designed to get the people to carry on the war ostensibly as soldiers of the *Reich* with armbands to make them uniform and not liable to be called partisans by our people. At the time however I couldn't, and still can't, see our people wearing that one.

Sunday, 1 October 1944

Throughout October I am taking part in a one act play by Noël Coward, *Hands Across the Sea*, playing the part of Mrs Wadhurst. At first, I didn't think I was going to like it but ended up by being intensely interested and enjoying myself immensely. People seemed to think I made a great success of it.

After nearly three years of torturous thoughts, which recently had become so bad that I couldn't sleep, I summoned up the courage and confessed to Roger, asking him both for comfort and advice. He Pooh-poohed all my fears and told me that I was talking nonsense. He also told me of a lot of things, which the colonel had said, which put my mind at rest on a lot of points and made me realise what a fool I had been to keep it bottled up so long. The relief was so terrific that I felt I had started a new life altogether, although I must always bear the thought at the back of my mind and curb any overambitious thoughts I may have.

Sunday, 29 October 1944

In the afternoon we had a raid lasting two and a half hours where nothing was seen, but great excitement was caused at about 4.00 pm. I was at the top of the block, just below the married quarters when an Me 110 night fighter [aeroplane] came over the top of the hill behind, almost touching it. It was going quite fast, but I didn't pay very much attention to it except to look at the antennae. It disappeared from view behind the huts, when 'Woosh!', behind it appeared another and darker coloured plane. I did a double take as I thought I saw a circle on its side, but it was too fast and had gone, when there was another 'Woosh!', and low and behold there was a similar machine, this time no mistaking the circle on its side, red, white and blue! I dashed toward the abort to try and get a view of them over the valley, when a heavy machine gun or cannon opened

Pantomime rehearsal. (Left to right): Eric Arden, Bobbie Loder, Malcolm Fry, Tim Mundy and Frank Stewart. Eric Arden, a professional pianist, lost an arm on 14 April 1945 when the column of British PoWs left Eichstätt and were attacked by marauding US fighter aircraft. (*Courtesy of The J B Dixon Collection*)

up. It was terrific! People who were the other side said that the goon plane fired at the two British and was answered back by the second one, a long streak of smoke coming from the goon, then disappearing over the hill out of sight. It was said that the British were Mosquitoes, great excitement of course in the camp and we hope we shall see lots more.

Chapter 16

1945: The Allied Advance and the March to Moosburg – A War Crime

Monday, 15 January 1945

We expected a search for food and went fully prepared with picnic lunches onto parade. Sure enough, the gates opened and in marched a company of SS. The SBO then called us together and read an order from the Germans to the effect that since certain conditions had been existing in Camp 306 in Egypt for some two years, these conditions were to be brought into effect here. For this reason, all stools, chairs, tables and mattresses were taken away and at the moment we are living and eating off the backs of locker doors.

Saturday, 20 January 1945

The food situation is bad. We exist on 1/3 of an invalid parcel and this week there is nothing. With the bombing of the railways there is little hope of anymore coming in, and the only light that keeps us going is that of an end to the war in two or three months. I for one, however, have ceased thinking about the war and when it will end, it's still as big a mystery as ever.

Wednesday, 24 January 1945

My mind is right back to Laufen standards, guessing and thinking about food, the only consolation being that now everybody is in the same boat. What a bash I shall have when we get back. No news from home either, the last of my letters being early December [1944]. I'm very worried about Dick, as I have had very bad dreams recently of him. God keep him safe. I wonder when all the family will be together again. Bill away for ten years, myself five and Dick two. What a trial of endurance for our parents.

Thursday, 8 February 1945

The Swiss legation made what was to be its last visit to the camp. The British senior officers were:

Brigadier General William Wallace Southam DSO, Senior British Officer
Major John Higgon, British Man of Confidence
Captain Samuel Philip Symington MC, Brigade Major
Major Thomas Patrick Howkins, Senior British Medical Officer

The delegation found that there had been no real change in the general layout of the camp since their last visit, except that two new huts were nearly completed. There were now 1,577 officers and 269 other ranks held in the camp, but more officers were expected, in which case facilities for bathing, washing, and cooking were still deemed to be inadequate. A former quartermaster store was due to be converted into accommodation for the new arrivals, which the delegation felt was totally unacceptable. Hot showers were still only available twice a month, and the scale of rations had recently been cut and was now the same as that of non-working German civilians and not that of German depot troops.

Brigadier General William Wallace Southam DSO. He had been captured at Dieppe on 19 August 1942 and arrived at Eichstätt shortly afterwards. Although he was to survive captivity, his health was impacted upon and he suffered an early death on 1 April 1950 at the age of 48. Captain Samuel Philip Symington MC, the brigade major, also suffered an early death, and died on 28 November 1954 aged 45. (*Courtesy of The J B Dixon Collection*)

The SBMO, Major Thomas Patrick Howkins, informed the delegation that Lieutenant Frederick Gilmour, The Queen's Own Cameron Highlanders, was suffering from psychoneurosis and had been transferred to Kaufbeuren, where he remained. Gilmour, who came from Alloa, Scotland, had been captured at Abbeville on 6 June 1940, just a few days before his twenty-first birthday.

Four British medical officers were in charge of the camp hospital. The general health was reported to still be good. No improvement had been made in the lighting conditions, and the PoWs' eyesight was suffering as a consequence. Mail had taken longer of late to arrive and many letters arriving by airmail were posted at dates varying between July [1944] and November 1944. During January 1945, the Germans gave orders that all PoWs should be deprived of their mattresses. Almost all tables, chairs and benches were removed, and all public rooms were closed, except the Catholic chapel. The excuse given for this was alleged bad conditions at a German PoW camp in Egypt. Similar reprisals were put into force at Stalag 357. Strong protests were made to the German authorities by His Majesty's government.

Thursday, 15 February 1945

February [1945] was one of unparalleled air activity. Every day, there was a raid lasting at least three hours and generally going on for four. They seem to have been spread out all over Germany, but this area came in for more than its fair share. Targets seem to be Nürnberg, Munich and all the railways. In magnificent weather, squadron after squadron was seen passing overhead quite unmolested. Today we had a visit from low flying Mustangs, which came right down the valley at only about 100 feet, machine gunned the town and also the junction nearby. We then saw smoke target signals drop and immediately afterwards squadrons of bombers flying overhead wheeled to the area and let loose their load. They flattened the Treuchtlingen junction, only about 18 miles away.

Swiss Legation member Dr Roland Marti (left) with a member of the Red Cross Committee. (*Courtesy of IRC*)

Sunday, 25 March 1945

Although one almost fears to mouth the word even now, it seems that the war is really on its last legs and even the most pessimistic in the camp do not expect it to last more than a month. We are across the Rhine [river] in force not counting numerous other small bridgeheads, so it cannot be long now before they arrive here – always providing we are not moved.

Tuesday, 27 March 1945

Once again, the tension rose, and rumours were wild. Parachutists were supposed to have been dropped at Nürnberg. Very great activity on the main road, trucks and foot traffic passing all day long, some of the vehicles piled with troops. Everybody is packing feverishly, and I completed mine after having made one or two false starts. It is very difficult to settle down to anything at all and one is continually on the outlook for new events.

Wednesday, 28 March 1945

Confirmed this morning that American armoured cars were within 40 miles of the camp the day before yesterday but that they were only on patrol and of course turned back. Nine hundred and fifty officers and one hundred and fifty other ranks are expected today, so it looks as if this camp might be permanent. The weather has changed with a vengeance, and it is pouring with rain, somewhat dampening our enthusiasm and everybody is rather feeling an anti-climax.

Sunday, 1 April 1945

Once more that day started with news of parcels, a truck load of bulk at the station. On opening up, however, the loading party discovered that of the 300 crates supposed to be inside only 13 were left, the reminder having been rifled. Odd bits of crates were scattered about and from a few empty tins, which appeared quite fresh, it was apparent that the theft took place close to this facility and suspicion rests on either the SS or the Hungarians. The German papers give an impression of utter chaos, in spite of attempts to prove the contrary. They warn against rumours and panic, which they say are all caused by enemy agents.

Monday, 2 April 1945

Air raid warnings all day long and fighters were over machine-gunning troops on the roads. Lots of traffic on the road going west, including guns, mostly 88s. The commandant made a speech to his troops saying the war was nearly over and he did not want them to aid the German war effort – such as it was – but on the other hand they shouldn't obstruct the effort. Above all they must behave in a correct manner towards the British officers and treat them as they would wish to be treated themselves adhering strictly to the German constitution. Late tonight he is reported to have changed into mufti [civilian clothes] and pushed off!

Tuesday, 3 April 1945

An anxious day for us all. Rumours of a move to Moosburg were in the air all day long and we are still very much in suspense. On the wood party, Tiny and Mike spoke to some women refugees from Rottenburg who said that American tanks entered there at 6.00 pm last night. The *Kommandantur* is in a terrible flap and one of the first stories was that we were to move tomorrow. Later in the evening, the *Kommandantur* were undecided what to do. It is reported that three of the guard company have deserted already. If we can survive the next four or five days I think we shall be alright, but the question is can we do it.

Wednesday, 4 April 1945

In spite of numerous rumours that we are moving, or that we are not moving, nothing is really yet known. One story is the Jerries are trying to rustle up fifty cattle trucks to move us next week. It said the American's are on the Nurenburg-

Augdostadt – Munich *autobahn*, which, if true, is just what we want as it is to the east. The heavy bang we heard was two trucks of ammo [ammunition] blown up by fighters on the railway line near Weissenberg. They made a crater about 40 yards square and caused devastation over a wide area.

Thursday, 5 April 1945

A tiring day, but very good from the staff point of view. Air raid in the morning and they knocked the hell out of what looked like Ingoldstadt and Treuchtlingen. More stories about moving and the most reliable is that we are under orders to move but that the Kreigies are doing all they can to dilly dally. They have asked for seventy trucks to take us, and that is almost an impossibility. Apparently, standing orders are that we move out on foot if the Americans came within 15 miles, but I reckon in that case we can most probably waste time. In addition, many of the staff have their wives and children in the town so they wouldn't be very keen to move anyhow.

Saturday, 7 April 1945

I took my exam this morning in Spanish, but couldn't concentrate at all and the work was rather slap dash. More and more traffic today and in the evening, column after column of *Kriegies* passed along the road. They looked like Russians, and it caused great palpitations amongst us, in fact, it is said, even now, that we are moving tonight. If we can hold on for three more days, I reckon we should be alright. The sound of gunfire all day to the west and north and numerous air alarms. This area has now been included in the *Akute Luftalarm* area, that's for areas just behind the front, but so far, we have not yet had one.

Sunday, 8 April 1945

Mustangs went over all day long and a load of something was dropped in the Ingolstadt direction. The story is that we are going to VII-D, [a PoW camp], which is near Tittmoning. A rumour also that American AFVs entered Eichstätt last night, and then pushed off again. Some more American PoWs came in tonight, absolutely whacked, having marched from Frankfurt via Nürnberg at the rate of about 30 to 35 miles a day. They were attacked in the marshalling yards there by Thunderbolts and their blankets were full of bullet holes!

Monday, 9 April 1945

A big day of air raids once again, in the evening hundreds of bombers came over and dropped stuff on Ingolstadt and nearby airfields. They were a wonderful sight in the almost clear blue, sailing along as if in an air pageant, with the fighters zipping about in between and dropping smoke signals. There was one

Photograph of a bombed area of Ingolstadt. (*Courtesy of Traces of Evil.com*)

dogfight that we saw where three German fighters dived on four Americans, but they wheeled away to the South, and we saw no more. Bombers seemed to be concentrating in the Ingolstadt area, as a great column of smoke came from that direction.

What John Blomfield Dixon had actually witnessed on 9 April 1945, was an unplanned attack on the town of Ingolstadt, and undoubtedly the most fateful day in the history of the city. That afternoon, 212 USAAF B-17 bombers were on a mission to assault the Neuburg Air Base, the WIFO [Nazi solid fuel] tank farm near Unterhausen and the Munich-Riem Airport. On the return leg of their journey, ten aircraft from the 390th Bomb Group, still with their bombload aboard, established that they would not reach their home base unless they disposed of their deadly payload. Dropping from a formation height of around 7,000m to just 2,500m, one of the aircraft placed a smoke marker over the old town area. An air raid alarm caused many civilians in the town to flee to the nearest shelter. Bombs soon began to drop, with a focus around Adolf-Hitler-Platz, as the Rathausplatz was called at the time, turning it into a landscape of rubble. Direct hits on the Augustinian Church, built by Johann Michael Fischer in 1736, and the adjoining Franciscan monastery on Schutterstraße were particularly devastating for the population. Seventy-three people seeking shelter, mostly refugees from Pomerania, died in the basement

Photograph of a bombed area of Ingolstadt. (*Courtesy of Traces of Evil.com*)

of the rococo church. Only one young woman, who was rescued from the damaged monastery cellar after ten hours, survived. The destruction of the Heilig-Geist-Spital retirement home was also to see lives lost as many of the elderly residents stayed in their rooms, or in the stairwell, during the bombing rather than take shelter. Of almost 100 elderly people, 16 were killed and many injured. Other bombs destroyed the historic Salzstadel, the city theatre on Rathausplatz, the new municipal administration building on Schäffbräustraße, the newly built Danube Hall on Tränktorstraße, the Roli cinema, as well as numerous residential and commercial buildings in the area of Rathausplatz, Donaustraße, Münzbergstraße and Schäffbräustraße. Around 100 people were seriously injured when they were buried, and more than 1,000 civilians became homeless as a result of the enormous damage to the buildings.

Tuesday, 10 April 1945

The head doctor from Moosburg was here yesterday and today. He said that Typhus had broken out there and if the *Kommandant* moved us it was on his own head. Reports that American tanks broke through the German line at Bad Mergenthurn and pushed through to Crails Lein, which accounts for the *Kommandantur* standing to on Sunday night and for the flap the next morning. The move activity seems to have died away again, but I think that possibly that is a more dangerous state of affairs than before. Things seem to be stiffening up a bit on the fronts. Still, another day has passed, and we are still here – long may it last.

Wednesday, 11 April 1945

This morning squadron after squadron of Liberators and Fortresses came over and knocked hell out of the countryside all round us. Ingolstadt, Donauworth and Treuchtlingen were just a few in the local area and columns of smoke spewed up. By 6.00 pm the whole horizon from east right round to north was one mass of smoke and for all we know the whole region may have been the same. The detonations were terrific and at night there was a fine glow in the sky. A goon said that it was impossible to move more than 10 miles from Eichstätt by rail. American tanks were reported on the Augsberg-Munich Road and that refugees from Ulm had arrived in the town saying the Americans entered it last night. A Frenchman in the jug, asked whether it was likely if the camp would move? The goons said, 'move – of course not, don't you know that you are surrounded!'

Thursday, 12 April 1945

A day of constant packing and re-packing and great bustling about. The strain gets more and more and every day the cry goes up from 1,000 throats, 'for Christ's sake, put a sock in it!' The commandant has warned us to stand by for 5.00 am on Saturday, so it looks as though we are really off at last. The destination is said to be Meran, about 300km just west of south. The town is practically frantic at our leaving, and I only hope that they get a thorough pasting when we have left.

Friday, 13 April 1945

The last evening in the camp and we are sitting in the midst of an enormous rubbish heap. Everywhere around the room are piles of empty Red Cross boxes, packing, string and old clothes. God help anybody who has to clean it up! We have been issued with an enormous amount of food, a parcel, some bulk not counting the stuff we had in the locker anyway. My pack and kit bag weigh a ton and all of us will be staggering after the first 100 yards. I only hope that my supports at least hold together. Lots of people have made little trollies and the sight tomorrow will be ridiculous. All this makes one hate the Germans more and more. Our destination is Moosburg and what they hope to gain by shifting us 50 miles, God only knows! Let's hope the Americans come over and blow Eichstätt to smithereens after we have left. The most shattering news today is that [President Franklin D.] Roosevelt died yesterday. We had a minute's silence on parade in honour of him. The latest news is that bloody fool Patch has turned north.

Saturday, 14 April 1945

Reveille at 5.00 am and paraded at 7.00 am. We were supposed to move off at 7.30 am but people got fed up waiting and pushed back to the room. Finally, we moved off about 9.00 am. By this time, I had jettisoned a lot of stuff as very nearly creased me. It was a crying shame to see the food left behind and we ought not to have been issued with a Red X parcel. The bulk would have been sufficient. The goons gave up trying to count us on parade and did it as we went through the gate. There was a woman crying in the pub. Carts were breaking down everywhere and were left on the side of the road. We are trying to buy a pram or bicycle. Just outside the camp we halted and were inspected for some time by two Allied fighters. Traffic on the other road kept on moving by about 200 yards at a time and then stopping and bailing out when the fighters came back.

The most terrifying half hour of my life. No sooner had I put the book back, than four more fighters appeared followed by another four. They circled round and then dived down the valley shooting up the trucks that were there and dropping bombs on them! Then they turned their attention to us. Salvo after salvo came from them as they dived and dived. I ran down over the ditch into the field after about a minute and lay spreadeagled in a ploughed field paralysed with fear, alternately cursing and praying under my breath! We were all scattered, and time seemed to stop. Eventually, they went, thanks be to God and, after several false starts when we heard them coming back, we all streamed back to the camp and got into the blocks in Lagerstraße. The number of casualties is not yet known but I have heard of several wounded. Johnny Logan is supposed to have lost a leg and Ben Jickling killed. One goon lay smashed to bits outside the married quarters gate, and they say what caused the trouble was a goon in the box shooting. Certainly, the box was smashed a bit. In the camp, big 'PoWs' have been painted on the roofs and dug into the ground. At one time we thought we might stay in the camp but, however, we move out tomorrow night, by dark thank God. The commandant says we cannot stay because this camp is a 'special' area, so obviously they are going to fight here. Casualties were eight killed and forty-one wounded. Most of the latter have had to have limbs amputated owing to the size of the wounds caused by the explosive and .50 bullets. Block 3 was the worst hit with five killed and thirty-one wounded. The dead are being buried tomorrow. Later in the evening twelve more (fighters) came back, but they shot up some stuff well west of the camp. I only hope they check up on the photos the blokes took today. A radio (message) has been sent to the IRC about it so they may get it both ways. There is a rumour of a big breakthrough on the Bavarian front. Helmar is supposed to have said that shortly a government will take over which will stop all this.

Sunday, 15 April 1945

The death toll has now risen to ten. Very quiet today and took it very easy, resting in the afternoon to prepare for tonight. Rather nervous as to what will happen when we move from here and lie up during the day. Heard that Oflag 79 at Brunswick was released yesterday. News wasn't so good today as resistance is stiffening considerably on all fronts. It locks however as if the Russians are just due to start which I hope to God is tonight – I've just about had it. After five years this is almost too much for my nerves. We are supposed to parade at 7.00 am if the weather remains clear and I'm all set now. It's just like going into battle again.

Monday, 16 April 1945

We set out at dark and went by the main road. The journey was very bad and there were continual stops and starts. Practically all the town turned out to wish us farewell and the girls called '*auf wiedersehen*' and 'goodbye' as if we were German troops going to the front. It was a dark and cloudy night but later the stars came out. My feet got worse and worse and by the time we finally arrived at our destination, which was Gaimersheim, about 5km from the Danube [river], we'd very nearly all had it. We were put in a big barn with plenty of straw and never have I been so wonderfully relieved to take off my boots and lie down to sleep like a log. At about 7.00 am I woke rather cold but soon dropped off again. Brian and I scoffed a tin of bully [beef] and some biscuits. Washing is a bit difficult, and one has to be continually be on one's guard against aircraft. All day long aircraft have been thundering over, bombers and fighters and they give one a very queasy feeling in the stomach. No longer are there people leaning out of windows, laughing and pointing them out, but rather furtively listening and hoping for the best. There are several families here, evacuees and one boy who comes from Würzburg says that the goons put up a resistance here, the Americans sent over bombers for half an hour and 20,000 people were left dead in the streets. The news was excellent. Russians started on the main fronts, sweeping into Bavaria from the south. Americans nearly reached Berlin and also turning south from Bayreuth. There are also reports of a breakthrough on the Helibron front. It looks as if we shall be lucky if we reach Moosburg at all. I hope to Christ that the fighting does not involve us.

Tuesday, 17 April 1945

A dreadful march last night. Opinions vary as to its length between 27 to 30km, but it was certainly the worst yet. We started at 9.00 pm and didn't stop till 5.00 am. We were expecting to cross the Danube [river] pretty soon, but time went on and we were still marching, and the first thing we did cross was the

Nürnberg-Munich *autobahn*. On our right flank for about 5 or 6km was the flashing lights of an aerodrome and it never seemed to get further away or come any nearer. At about 3.00 am we did finally cross the river at Großmehring and struggled on. From here on the march was a terrible shambles. We had been told that our destination was a village 5km from the bridge but we passed this village, and then another, and marched on and on, people cursing the goons, the bastards, and everybody they could think of, most of them, myself included, just managing to stagger along and cursing the frequent stops, when it was so hard to get going again. On the last portion of the march, the RAF came over and bombed the Regensburg area, dropping an awful lot of stuff and we could quite plainly see the anti-aircraft fire, both light and heavy. We also saw tracers of a night fighter and a bomber. At last, we arrived, to very bad, cramped quarters and nothing seemed to have been prepared. Everybody was in an appalling temper, and it was some time before we could settle down. There were very little washing facilities and people had to stay inside because as the village, Ernsgaden, was full of Luftwaffe it was expected that it might be attacked at any moment. The rear party of slow walkers say that the bombs that fell last night were some of them very close to the bridge and that American patrols were on the *autobahn*. It is said that tonight we march only 12km and then lie up for two nights. News bloody good today, Germany is nearly cut in half. A Russian girl in the village said that until fourteen days ago she had been working in a munitions factory in Munich, when she was sent to work here as there was no more explosive powder. A RSM of the Luftwaffe was over Nürnberg last night, his hometown, machine gunning the Americans there. He said that on the aerodrome here there plenty of machines and pilots, but very little petrol. One of the last bits of news we had was that the bastard goons had opened the floodgates of the Zuyder Zee.

Wednesday, 18 April 1945

Not at all a bad march last night. It was only about 15km and although some of the stretches were pretty long, I didn't manage too badly. Passed through Geisenfeld a very clean, attractive town as far as we could see about 11.00 pm and finally arrived at Rohrbach about 1.00 am, where our billets were an enormous barn, the biggest I have ever seen and quite recently built. Just after we arrived there was a raid and, of course, the lights went out. The bombs fell only a few kiometeres away and nearly brought our roof down with the blast. The first rumour of the morning was that Model had shot himself.

A most incredible day. We bought three pigs in the morning and made them into a stew in the evening. People started spreading out too and billeted themselves in private houses! Johnny Renton, Robin Steele-Mortimer and Jock

Mackenzie were in one little house, and we went down to visit them. We were plied with tea, *bauernwurst* and liver and they were being looked after by the woman and old man like lost friends. Then Tiny Waters took Brian Reid and I across to buy some eggs.

Thursday, 19 April 1945

Still at Rottenegg, thank goodness, and feeling all the better for the rest. Parade today and we were able to wander about the village as we liked, subject to our own precautions for air raids. Bought quite a lot of stuff, bread and eggs and there was also a quarter parcel issued, we shall have to get rid of otherwise there will be too much to carry. So far, all we have heard today is one or two planes and none have been near. God, send it keeps like that. Last night a new crowd of guards arrived from Munich – all of them over 50 at least I should think, and they had only been in the army for fourteen days.

Friday, 20 April 1945

Colin's birthday today for which I hoped I might be home. It's also that bastard Hitler's, and he certainly seems to have had a nice birthday present. Left Rottenegg last night and came via Mainburg, crossing under the Regensburg-Munich *autobahn*. A Red Cross lorry turned up again, just as we were leaving, to take away more sick. It was a beautiful moonlit night with a sky full of stars and, apart from the sore feet and the weight of one's pack, could not have been more delightful. The country was typically Bavarian, rolling hills and large forests and masses of maypoles about. Passed through one village before Mainburg with some very nice houses and some simply enormous farm buildings. We were given a tremendous send off from the village and everybody in the column was in wonderful form after the rest. All along the route, when we saw civilians, we told them the Americans were coming soon and only a few kilometres away – some companies were even singing and whistling. It's amazing how people stay up in the country. Wherever we have been, at whatever hour of the night, there is always somebody at windows or in the street fully dressed. We were in a barn here again – quite big, but in the afternoon when news came that we were staying for a few days we moved up to a house on the hill where we could get cooking done and live in the barn. Then calamity – we had got all our kit up there and were making the barn ship-shape when the sentry turned up and said that the commandant had commandeered the barn for ten men. So, back we had to go again – but hope to continue to eat there. Had a wonderful meal in the evening, cold bacon, eggs and bully and some biscuits and cheese and tea.

Saturday, 21 April 1945

Very cold in the night and didn't sleep too well but had a very good breakfast in the morning. The people we are living with occupy one half of a house belonging to a villager. They are evacuees from Lugnitz and have one child, one other having died on the way here. They are only too anxious to help and won't allow us to do anything. They are very anxious to get back to their home too, as soon as possible. The other couple, who own the house, are quite old, the woman very decent, but the old boy is a bit grumpy, and I don't think he likes us much. News that the Americans are about 25 miles away. Made friends with the old woman and got a *bauersloaf* and ten eggs out of her, but relations deteriorated a bit later. Sat about in the barn during the afternoon by myself. A heavy storm in the evening and rain came through the roof of the barn and some things got a bit wet.

Sunday, 22 April 1945

A bloody good breakfast again. It's amazing to see the twenty of us gathered round the small kitchen with the family, all chatting away. Quite a lot of visitors this morning, goon or otherwise and cups of tea were going all the time. Ronnie had a bit of luck last night getting forty eggs just outside the implement shed. Rumour this morning that the Yanks have crossed the Danube [river] at Ingoldstadt. Hundreds of PoWs passing through today, mostly British and US other ranks from Hammelberg. They have been on the march for a month and have very little food and have been smoking German tea as cigarettes. We gave them a brew and as many cigarettes as we could. We hear that Moosburg is an absolute shambles with PoWs streaming in from all directions, and no accommodation. Some of them are sleeping out in the open. We move out tomorrow at 6.00 am with white flags. Jack Hawkes made a pastry pie with some flour I got and also an enormous bread pudding. We left them with quite a lot of food too as they were very short. Seeing these people like this makes me very sympathetic.

Monday, 23 April 1945

I was up early and made us a brew of tea at 4.30 am and we had some bread as well. Jack Hawkes also made us up some egg and bacon sandwiches for the trip. We marched out this morning at 6.00 am. It was very cloudy, and we didn't see a single aircraft, although this time we carried recognition signals. Passed through Mainburg and arrived outside Moosburg about 11.00 am. Here we had a very long wait in the cold and the wet until finally our company was marched to the camp which was simply enormous. Absolute chaos reigned and there were all nationalities including a Russian woman pilot dressed in battledress. We had a perfunctory search, then particulars taken and finally a bath – our last I expect. Then we were led off to find billets and, after much wandering, were put in a long bungalow, some sleeping in the bottom of three tiered beds no bed boards, but most of us on the floor in the centre. Met Peter Dix almost opposite to where I was sleeping. We had no food left but luckily the cookhouse made an issue of a tin of stew, tea, potatoes, biscuits and cheese so we had something.

Tuesday, 24 April 1945

A bit of time to look round today. The first job was to find wood, and this we did from the slit trenches and also took some of the poles supporting the barbed wire separating the compounds. Washing facilities are awful. There is one tap, a small test tap actually, to supply the whole hut of between 500 – 700 people. Consequently, one had to queue up and washing and shaving occurs any time between 7.00 am and 4.00 pm. The camp is an amazing sight all day long. In between huts there are little fires without number of all kinds and description with people cooking up every incredible kind of dish and brew, Brian and I took a walk in the afternoon and had words with some American pilots. News tonight that the German government has agreed not to move any more PoWs so I guess we just sit here and wait and by the tone of the dope that won't be very long. Some very interesting chats with American chaps.

Wednesday, 25 April 1945

A beautiful sunny day with quite a hard frost in the morning. Lots of air activity and explosions going on all around us. Told this morning that Eichstätt has been flattened. I hope the boys got away with it alright. Awful flap in the afternoon when there was an announcement and we were all called out to march away, but it was a false alarm, and we all came back again. Personally, I don't think we shall ever get down there, bombing all around the camp today, Fortresses in the morning, and Marauders and Bostons in the afternoon and evening, so the spearheads can't be very far away. German fighters were skimming over the camp, running for home.

Thursday, 26 April 1945

There is really so much to write about here that my brain can't cope with it all, and it is especially difficult to find anywhere comfortable to write. It is difficult to estimate the number of people in the camp now but counting the Russians and Serbs and Commandos just outside, it should run very close to the 100,000 mark. It is amazing to think that our people must be expecting us home almost nearly and it must be a very anxious time for them all not knowing where we are. Sounds like gunfire quite close today and it may be the German artillery. One of the pilots who shot us up on 14th is in the camp, he was shot down on the same day. He told Richard Didham that they were informed by the recce plane there was a column of Hungarians to attack, but they were too close to the Oflag to bomb, so he had picked on some lorries on the road opposite. When they had done that there was still some doubt as to whether we were Hungarians or not, so they put a burst into the river, and when we ran for it that finally settled all doubts and they let us have it. Another thing that misled them was that the carts covered with tarpaulins looked like light tanks. He said one of the worst things we could have done was march by night, as Mosquitoes were sent out to bomb columns and they would have even less chance of recognising us. On five minutes stand by all day and couldn't use the compound, so that successfully foxed my having a bath. A rumour tonight that the Americans are only 12 miles away and as Patton has crossed at Regensburg that should be quite possible.

Friday, 27 April 1945

Very quiet today on the battle front and the only aircraft we saw were a couple of recce fighters that came over the camp and circled round, which looks as if they were keeping an eye on us. The death roll at Eichstätt is reported to have risen to fifteen. Rumours this afternoon that an armistice was made pm for forty-eight hours to allow terms to be made. Bavaria and Austria have refused to fight anymore – also Moosburg is supposed to have declared itself an open town. Bread is very scarce these days and every day the ration gets less and less. I hope the parcels hold out. No sight of the Yanks yet although we expect them hourly, and the Seventh [United States] Army are 25 miles from Munich. I expect it will be [George S.] Patton that relieves after all. A Frenchman came in today who said he had met a tank 10 miles away, which said it couldn't come any further as this is a neutral zone.

Sunday, 29 April 1945

This looks like being our day of liberation. The British authorities took over the camp last night and all during the hours of darkness one could hear scattered artillery fire or tanks. This morning at about 10.00 am quite a battle started outside the camp, mostly over towards the west amongst the woods. Tanks could be seen moving about there and the flashes of the guns were visible. Small arms fire went on quite close, and many ricochets were whistling about. There were four casualties on the soccer pitch and one near our hut. Shells from the tanks are whistling overhead and the story goes that there is a small group of SS holding out on the river and in the cheese factory. In spite of strays, people were standing on the roofs of the ablutions viewing the fighting. It's amazing to think that while outside people are fighting, inside we are just sitting down making brews. We have just been told that last night the commandant summoned the senior Allied officer to go and meet the American forces on the bridge. They waited till 1.00 am and no one arrived so they came back. At 3.00 am they were sent for again and this time went by car through the lines and met the American commander and also the SS general. The latter wished to declare the zone neutral until all PoWs were evacuated, but the Americans would not agree to this as it would deny them the use of the bridge. It is not thought that there are many German troops in the area and the Americans are very strong. At 12.40 am the stars and stripes were hoisted on the town flagstaff and shortly afterwards the union jack and stars and stripes on the *Kommandantur*. The Americans went absolutely wild but most of the British were rather quiet. I myself was busting with excitement inside and had that feeling of not knowing what to do next. Two fighters kept on zooming over the camp and two artillery planes also came to have a look. So far, there is no news of anything entering the camp although the tanks are outside – just before 2.00 pm there was a tremendous cheer and a rush. A tank came into the camp followed by a jeep, both absolutely covered with *Kriegies* so that it was impossible to see anything. It was surrounded as well by an enormous crowd which moved with it down the street and back again. The crew were throwing out bullets as souvenirs, but I couldn't get one. The excitement seems to have died down a bit now and people are wandering about aimlessly. I wish they'd issue some more scoff in celebration. It's amazing to think that by this time next week we may all be sitting at home. How sad it is to think of those poor fellows who bought it at Eichstätt and after all that time in the '*schaft*' there is no home coming for them.

Took a stroll round the camp this evening. Flags hung everywhere, British, American, French, Russian, Dutch, Polish and over the wire flying goon hats, boots and equipment being exchanged for food from the Other ranks. Yank photographers were in the camp taking photographs all over the place. Explosions still going on around the place and also desultory MG fire but it seems to be mainly to the South. [At] 10.00 pm just going to bed very tired with a bad headache. People still milling round and firing still going on in the distance. Radio reports 27,000 PoWs released in a camp north-east of Munich but gave no names or details. Expect to be in for a lot of bullshit in the next few days.

Monday, 30 April 1945
A hell of a lot of traffic along the road and tanks and jeeps parked outside the main gate. No news yet of going home although the usual bumph war is on. It is said that the Recce group is here, and the evacuation conference is at 3.00 pm. Three US generals arrived this morning and inspected the camp. This

evening an attack was launched across the river about 2,000 yards to the east of the camp. It was directed at a small pocket of resistance on whom leaflets were dropped this morning. An American battery was just behind the camp, very close and firing over the camp. It was lucky Jerry had no guns. The plans for the evacuation are out. A Captain Selinsky came in this afternoon and took over completely with a very firm hand displacing all the goons. It is hoped to start tomorrow but that is not certain, and an airfield is being built about 500 yards from the camp. Wirelesses are now sounding all over the camp and there is a loudspeaker at the end of the block, where we just trot up to listen to the news. Got my goon identity card today, for which I was very glad. The goon guards here were very glad to go in the bag, their main fear being of the SS Some chaps hid up in the camp until we were liberated and then came out and gave themselves up.

Tuesday, 1 May 1945

Guns firing all the night and when I went out to the latrine one could hear the shells passing overhead. It is hard to realise that we are really free. Apart from being unable to realise it, there is nothing except the absence of goons to give us that impression. We are still behind barbed wire in uncomfortable conditions. Not much extra food and although we have been divided into plane crews, the

General George S. Patton, commander of Third United States Army, arrives at the gates of Moosburg PoW camp on 1 May 1945. John Blomfield Dixon witnessed this historic event and described the American commander as, 'a fine tall looking chap with strings of gongs and carrying a silver plated six shooter with a string of bullets in the small of his back'. (*Courtesy of NARA*)

thought of flying is almost as fantastic as going home. General [George S.] Patton arrived in the camp this afternoon, and Brian and I were lucky enough to be at the gate when he came. He is a fine tall looking chap with strings of gongs and carrying a silver plated six shooter with a string of bullets in the small of his back. He inspected some of the huts, and then made a small speech in which he said he was glad to see us so cheery and so well disciplined. He hoped to evacuate us as soon as possible. Then, wishing us goodbye and good luck he rode off in his jeep to tremendous cheering. There were also some American Red Cross girls in the camp. They weren't particularly pretty, but it was wonderful to hear their voices soft and low after the hoarse screeching goon women. Scoff is more plentiful today and I couldn't eat all mine. Besides an issue of Argentine biscuits and flour, there was one of American bread, which we unfortunately didn't get, but had to be satisfied with commandeered goon civil bread. There must be one or two hungry stomachs amongst the civil population in Moosburg.

A doughnut factory has also arrived and hopes to start operations at a rate of 1,600 an hour as soon as they can get some flour. With regard to evacuation there is no real news except that a Squadron Leader has arrived from evacuation HQ at Mainburg and that an airstrip is being prepared about 5 miles from the camp. Conditions in the town are pretty low. Padre [Harlow] was down this morning and said the streets were full of broken goon rifles and drunken Russians. One woman has been raped four times and looting is rife. This afternoon we saw three separate columns of black smoke coming from the direction of the town and one of them was the brewery set fire to by drunken Russians who were still dancing amongst the flaming building.

Chapter 17

The Return Home and a Forbidden Love

Wednesday, 2 May 1945

Snowed quite hard in the night, thawing in the morning, so there was a bloody mess everywhere. Filled in our tickets this morning and at midday got news that we are the second British battalion to move. It is possible that the first may leave today staying the night at Landshut from where we take off. The first plane should leave tomorrow at 9.00 am. Masses of scoff to eat and nobody hungry. It's the same everywhere. Hitler is dead, but [Karl] Dönitz as his successor is carrying on the struggle. Much good may it do them. A Red Cross nurse was shot by a Hitler Jugend yesterday. They got the boy too. We are now standing by to be deloused. A great disappointment later in the day; at first, we were warned to be ready to leave at 7.00 am tomorrow. Felt absolutely bloody in the morning and had no supper. Sick once or twice, a touch of the squitties, and a chill, glad in a way we were not going yet, although I reckon, I could make that plane if both my legs were paralysed. A message from SHAEF saying that they are doing everything to get us back to a decent life after all our hardships.

Thursday, 3 May 1945

Stayed in bed all day and as the others left at 9.30 am, I was able to get a proper bunk. Felt a little better in the evening though still rather queasy and got up. [Douglas] Dakotas and C-47s were seen over the camp this afternoon, so there is hope that the first chaps have gone. No definite news yet, but we hope that we may go tomorrow. The weather has cleared a bit – we wait, and wait, and there is no news of anything, it is so exasperating, and we are not allowed out of the compound and there is nothing to do. The longest day I have ever known. The rumour here is an all-American day tomorrow and all British on Saturday, but the talk in the Yank compound it is the other way round. If only we could get some information. Two goons were sighted in civilian clothes in the town by Doug Channell. They asked him how he liked their new uniforms, he replied by handing them over to the Yanks.

Friday, 4 May 1945

Still no information expect that nobody seems to be moving today. No one knows whether the 3,000 went yesterday or not. Some say yes and others say only 600.

There certainly has been no aerial activity today yet. The only consolation is that we are more free to move about a bit. Allied HQ went to Landshut this afternoon and found that only 550 of the 3,000 that left yesterday actually flew away from the aerodrome. The evacuation people didn't know anything either. They say that there is a hitch somewhere, but what it is they either don't know or won't say. Willets and Goode are now going to the Third [United States] Army HQ, though what good that will do I'm damned if I know. On the wireless tonight it said that 3,500 *Kriegies* arrived back by air yesterday, it looks as though they've started on someone else and forgotten us. Colonel Goode spoke to the Americans tonight on the subject and it was a real upbeat Yankee speech, making no bones. He swore he was going to do all he could and if nothing happened, they would call him a son of a bitch! It looks as though we shan't be back in England for V[E] Day after all worse luck as the only positions left fighting now are a small part of Austria, Czechoslovakia and Norway. I reckon we shall be lucky if we're away a week today.

Saturday, 5 May 1945

Still no news this morning and things are becoming intolerable. Shortly, unless something definite happens, there is going to be a big explosion of some sort. Already the American battalions are over 1,000 short and more seem to be going every hour. The weather has turned bloody again too, and it is raining again with the camp getting muddier and muddier every minute, for the moment at least our worries about food seem to be over. As we had an ample Argentine issue yesterday also bread and hope to get more today. Nothing to do except mooch around and wait. Not even books to read and even if we had them it's too dark to read. The only news tonight is that Colonel Earpe has been to Army HQ, and they say that everything is being done to expedite the evacuation subject to operational requirements.

Sunday, 6 May 1945

A delegation from SHAEF were here this morning and got it hot and strong. They were so impressed by the filthy conditions here that one of them hurried back to HQ almost immediately. They said that one of the difficulties was lack of transport, and another the vast number of PoWs. Personally, I don't think they really know anything at all but are just making excuses. Some 20,000 fresh eggs in the camp today to be issued tomorrow, also some other food taken from the goons. Wrote a V-mail home. Hope I get there before it. Long queues for doughnuts and chewing gum this afternoon. I only got the latter. Went to the flicks in the evening in Moosburg and saw a wild west show. Very amusing but the town was more interesting. Hardly any civilians about and white flags still flying. The high street has been fairly well peppered but not much damage. Got back about 10.00 am to hear the glorious news that we are off at 5.00 am in the morning. Lots of bustling about and washing.

Monday, 7 May 1945

Couldn't sleep all night and got up at 3.15 am and shaved. We marched off at 5.00 am in the dark and reached the lorries about 5.30 am. There were rows and rows of them, and we finally moved off forty to a truck at about 7.30 am. It was a wonderful drive through the countryside with the blossom out and we arrived at Landshut about 8.30 am and on the airfield at 9.00 am. We were very downhearted to see no planes and thought it was another washout. But at about 10.00 am four planes did arrive and then nothing more. But at 12.45 pm they came in droves, and it was wonderful to see them far off on the horizon, then near, finally, to our relief dropping their wheels and landing. There were still some 1,000s to get rid of before we went, so we sat on the trucks and watched, at first very optimistic and then increasingly more pessimistic as the queue of Yanks got no smaller. By 3.30 pm seventy planes had arrived and by 4.00 pm they had all left. At the moment it is very doubtful if we shall go today, or even tomorrow for that matter. There are rumours of 100 more planes arriving today, but I doubt it. All round the aerodrome are the burnt-out wrecks of German planes and I hope to get a bit as a souvenir. No more planes arrived, and we were sent after a lot of palaver very downhearted into the village to find billets. Five of us spent the night in a farmhouse, where the occupants gave us a lovely stew, for which we paid them in cigarettes as usual.

Tuesday, 8 May 1945 (VE Day)

This morning we all gathered at the airfield, where more planes arrived. One hit another during take-off and fell into flames, we believe some poor buggers were killed. Eventually, our turn came and we filed onto the Dakota sitting in seats alongside each side. With some trepidation, we took off, and were soon heading west, flying quite low. At last, we left Germany and as we were flying over France could see the old line of trenches from the First World War. Eventually, we landed at an airfield near Rheims and were taken to an American army camp at Bar-le-Duc where we were allocated tents, then had some marvellous food.

Wednesday, 9 May 1945

I slept very well and, after a fantastic breakfast, we were taken by truck to an airfield near Rheims where met up again with Tiny, Robin and co. but they were miles ahead of us in the queue. Here, some Lancasters did come in but not enough to take us off though. Towards the evening, we saw Tiny and co.

walk away amid much gnashing of teeth and so, depressed and frustrated, we were loaded into trucks and taken back to the US camp.

Thursday, 10 May 1945

After breakfast we were once again loaded into trucks and taken to the airfield. This time the Lancasters were coming in in droves and about mid-morning we actually got onboard. There were only about five or six of us in each plane and Ron, Brian, Arthur and I were together. Just as we were taking off, Ron was seized with terrible diarrhoea. He was told that he had to wait until we were airborne, which he did, though how he managed I'll never know. He was then sent to the loo on the back of the plane and literally exploded. The stench in the aircraft was appalling and poor old Ron was terribly apologetic. As we flew towards the UK we were allowed, one by one, up in the mid-turret to look out. My turn came just as we were hitting the coast and I have never seen something so wonderful. A land so green, so green, just waiting to welcome us. We landed at an airfield near Beaconsfield (RAF Wing) where we had DDT squirted under our battledress. There was also a marquee with tea and cakes and we gorged ourselves. We were asked if we were all well and Ron and I both said yes, although at the time I was not feeling too well. Then we were put in trucks and eventually ended up at a home in Chalfont St Giles, where all the local ladies were kitting us out with new battledress and sewing on our badges and medal ribbons. We were told that we could either telephone home, or send

British PoWs desperately awaiting a flight back to Blighty, and hoping to escape the privations of Moosburg PoW camp. (*Courtesy of The J B Dixon Collection*)

a telegram, to say we had arrived and would hope to be home tomorrow. I chose the latter, but either it was never sent or it never arrived.

The final entry in John Blomfield Dixon's diary reads, 'released into the community'.

Friday, 11 May 1945

We spent the night in Chalfont St Giles and in the morning we were taken by truck to Uxbridge station. There, Ron caught a bus home, so it was only Arthur, Brian, Johnny Mumford and me. We had previously been given travel warrants and double sets of ration cards, then told to go on leave for six weeks. Upon arrival in London we wandered round, but then said our goodbyes and split up. I caught the train from Liverpool Street, arriving in Ware in the early afternoon. There was no taxi at the station but there was a woman with a private car who offered to give me a lift. She dropped me outside High Oak Lodge and I went in through the gate feeling very nervous. The front door was open, it was a glorious day and the sun blind was down. I called out and no one came at first, but then mother came rushing to the door. She had had no telegram, so did not know I was even in the UK. It was one of the most wonderful moments of my entire life. She telephoned father to let him know the good news. It all sounds very dry and dusty years later, and I wish I had then there written down my thoughts and feelings, but it really was one of the most wonderful feelings in the world to be home again – safe and well.

Having returned home to High Oak Lodge and begun the process of rehabilitation to ordinary life, there is little doubt John's thoughts now turned to the woman who he had written to and dreamt of so much, Jo. In June 1939, a most important event had occurred in his life. His mothers' youngest brother, Uncle Tommy, who lived in Colchester, came to visit High Oak Lodge. John recalled the visit vividly:

> He brought with him his three daughters, Peggy, Josephine and Mary. Jo, as I knew her, was so beautiful and I fell in love with her immediately, although I did not say anything at the time. But for the next five and half years or so, she was the one whom I was determined to marry and make my wife and during all that time I corresponded with her whenever it was possible and tried to show my love. Jo would be my first and only girlfriend.

Josephine 'Jo' Blomfield was born on Thursday, 2 June 1921; her father, Thomas Walford Blomfield, had served as an officer in the army during the First World War, seeing action with 4th Battalion, Suffolk Regiment. Her mother, Annie Ellen Blomfield (née Fookes), was known as Nancy and was the daughter of George Oscar Fookes, a master of merchant shipping, and Ellen Keeble. In her early years Jo trained to play both the cello and piano and would eventually play in a local orchestra in her hometown of Colchester. Following the outbreak of the Second World War, she joined the Women's Royal Naval Service in 1943, where she was involved in secretarial work, being stationed at HMS *Northney* on Hayling Island, on the south coast of England. Throughout his captivity John wrote of his love for her, particularly in the early days of his incarceration, yet on occasions he dismissed her letters or the opportunity to correspond with her, a sneak reflection perhaps of his state of mind in an environment where the end of his confinement was unknown.

His diaries are filled with loving and adoring comments, but regardless of the feelings John had for Jo, their love was never to come to fruition.

Josephine 'Jo' Blomfield. The young girl John Blomfield Dixon met in June 1939, who became his obsession and true love while in captivity. The fact they were first cousins was to prevent a relationship from ever developing upon his release. Whilst John married another woman, Jo would remain unmarried for the remainder of her life. (*Courtesy of The J B Dixon Collection*)

They were first cousins, and, in an unwritten law, a relationship could not, and would not, be allowed to develop. It appears his parents ensured that any prospect of a liaison between the couple was completely stifled. Having completed her service with the WRNS, Jo Blomfield studied nursing at both the Braintree and Colchester general hospitals, where she qualified as a midwife. After working in several different hospitals in both England and the Netherlands, she decided to immigrate to Canada in 1962, joining her sister, Nancy, at Vancouver General Hospital. A very religious person, Jo left Vancouver and moved to Toronto with the view, it seems, of joining the Anglican Convent at Willowdale, most likely as a nun but, for her own reasons, returned to Vancouver and joined the Catholic church. A keen gardener and cyclist, she worked at the Vancouver Children's Hospital for many years, until her retirement. Throughout her life in the Canadian city, she would give piano lessons from her home and was a popular member of the church choir. Jo Blomfield, unmarried, died on Sunday,

1 August 2010 and is buried in the Gardens of Gethsemani Cemetery and Mausoleum, Vancouver, Canada.

After his release from captivity, John Blomfield Dixon continued to serve with the British Army for another three years. Firstly, serving in Germany with 7th Battalion, Royal Tank Regiment but later moving to service with the Intelligence Corps. He left Dover on 8 October 1946 aboard the SS *Victoria* and arrived in Trieste, Italy, a few weeks later to become part of the Allied Information Service. It was during this period that he met Leokadia 'Lola' Maria Mikolajczyk, a Polish woman, who was born in Kamienicza on the outskirts of Częstochowa, Poland, on Tuesday, 22 October 1918, the daughter of Stefan Janczek. Leokadia was a widow, who had been subjected to forced labour. She found herself in one of the German factories outside her home town of Kielce, where she worked as a machine operator. In late 1944, as the Eastern Front was approaching, the Germans transported the machines and the Polish forced labourers to Germany. Eventually, Leokadia found herself in an area that was finally liberated by British troops and, it seems, began working in a convalescent home for injured officers, troops and PoWs. She spoke German fluently, and the circumstances in which she met John Blomfield Dixon are a little hazy but, following their courtship, the couple returned to the UK and moved into the family home at High Oak Lodge. They were married at the Hoddesdon Registrar Office on Saturday, 8 November 1947. Sadly, Lola appears to have been a woman with poor health and the couple were never to have children of their own. After fifty-two years together, Lola passed away on 6 August 2000.

Following his marriage to Lola, John returned to southern Austria in January 1948, where he served for a period of time with No. 62 Field Security Section. The work was particularly important during the de-Nazification of Germany in the aftermath of the Second World War, and led to the successful arrest of leading Nazis officials. He was admitted to No. 31 British General Hospital on 2 June 1948 and, after two weeks in their care, returned to the UK where was discharged from the service with the honorary rank of captain. After leaving military service he settled into civilian life and, having completed his degree at Eichstätt, eventually took up a position with British Steel. Following the death of his wife, he saw out the remainder of his life at his home in South London, connecting with old comrades, attending regimental events and recalling his time as a PoW in Germany. He died on Friday, 24 May 2013, leaving behind a detailed account of his life, military service and captivity, which his family now desire to share with the world in perpetuity. Remember him.

Appendix I

Nominal Roll: Members of 'C' Squadron, East Riding Yeomanry, 1940

A list of officers and other ranks of 'C' Squadron, East Riding Yeomanry for May 1940:

Major Geoffrey Minto Radcliffe (OC), KIA.
Captain Thomas Edward Beswick Sissons (2nd IC), KIA.
Second Lieutenant Charles Nicholas Wilmot-Smith (No. 1 Troop), PoW.
Second Lieutenant Roger Waterhouse (No. 3 Troop), PoW.
Second Lieutenant Harold Hopper (No. 4 Troop), PoW.
Second Lieutenant Richard Lawrence Hudson (No. 2 Troop), KIA.
Second Lieutenant John Furley Cockin (No. 5 Troop), KIA.
Second Lieutenant John Blomfield Dixon (No. 5 Troop – attached from RTR as May 1940), PoW.
Second Lieutenant Leonard Thomas Bradbrook (No. 6 Troop), KIA.
Agent De Liaison – B. LeMaitre

Other ranks of 'C' Squadron, East Riding Yeomanry for May 1940:

Squadron Sergeant Major Holborn	Troop Sergeant Major Megginson (Troop No. 6)	Squadron Quartermaster Sergeant Charlton
Sergeant Albert Clare (Troop No. 3), PoW	Sergeant S. Clare (Troop No. 5)	Sergeant Page (Troop No. 2)
Sergeant Urry (Troop No. 1)	Lance Sergeant Cyril Bennett (Troop No. 4), PoW	Lance Sergeant Robert J. Pople (Troop No. 4), PoW
Lance Seregant Taylor	Corporal Addinsell (HQ)	Corporal Brogden (Troop No. 4)
Corporal Campling (HQ)	Corporal Danville (Troop No. 5)	Corporal Charles Garner (HQ), KIA
Corporal Harris (HQ)	Corporal Heath (Troop No. 3)	Corporal Peter Neesham (Troop No. 6), KIA
Corporal Richard (Troop No. 2)	Lance Corporal Basil Ball (Troop No. 4), KIA	Lance Corporal Albert J Brown (HQ), PoW
Lance Corporal Chapman	Lance Corporal Davis (Troop No. 5)	Lance Corporal Dransfield

Lance Corporal Dry	Lance Corporal Harvey (Troop No. 4)	Lance Corporal Major
Lance Corporal Nicolay	Lance Corporal Herbert Ostler, KIA	Lance Corporal Frank Overton, KIA
Lance Corporal W. Smith	Trooper D Adams (HQ)	Trooper Akeman
Trooper Aminsay (Troop No. 3)	Trooper B. Baker	Trooper Charles Baker (Troop No. 3), PoW
Trooper Cyril Bales (Troop No. 3), PoW	Trooper Bernard Banyard (HQ), PoW	Trooper Barker (HQ)
Trooper Batts (Troop No. 6)	Trooper Booker (Troop No. 4)	Trooper Buck (HQ)
Trooper George Burns (Troop No. 3), PoW	Trooper Burton	Trooper Chambers
Trooper Chapman	Trooper Chorley	Trooper Coates
Trooper Danville	Trooper Dent	Trooper Dickens (HQ)
Trooper Dixon	Trooper Dutton (HQ)	Signalman Eggington
Trooper Leslie Elsey, PoW	Trooper Green	Trooper Hendren (HQ)
Trooper Holborn (HQ)	Trooper Hoare	Trooper Harry Jackson (HQ), KIA
Trooper Kemp	Trooper Kirk (HQ)	Trooper Knight
Trooper Lambert	Trooper Livesey	Trooper Mainprize
Trooper Malam (Troop No. 1)	Trooper Martin	Trooper McCord (HQ)
Trooper Minter	Trooper Moss (Troop No. 3)	Trooper Moore
Trooper Moses	Trooper Jonathan Mouser, KIA	Trooper Gordon J Penney (Troop No. 5), PoW
Trooper Piper	Trooper Ronald C.B. Pople (Troop No. 5), PoW	Trooper Power
Trooper Redhead	Trooper Reis	Trooper Robinson
Trooper Charles W. Scotter, PoW	Trooper Scrivens	Trooper Scrivener (Troop No. 3)
Trooper Selfridge	Trooper Short (Troop No. 5)	Trooper Thomas M. Shortt, DoW
Trooper Simpson (HQ)	Trooper Ernest Smith, PoW	Trooper Smitherman (HQ)
Trooper Walter Stead, KIA	Trooper Swain (HQ)	Trooper Albert G. Taylor (HQ), PoW
Trooper Ronald Thompson, PoW	Trooper John Vass, PoW	Trooper Vass
Trooper William Welton (Troop No. 6), KIA	Trooper Edward Wiseman (Troop No. 4), KIA	Trooper John Wolfe, KIA
Trooper Henry Whiting (Troop No. 3), PoW	Tpr. Yeomans (Troop No. 3)	

Appendix II

Officers and Men of the East Riding Yeomanry KIA or DoW with the BEF

18 May 1940		
Officer	**Age**	**Cemetery or Memorial**
Second Lieutenant Philip Maitland Cockin	22	Dunkirk Memorial, France
Lance Corporal Frederick William John Arnold	20	Cement House Cemetery, Belgium
Lance Corporal Kenneth Albert Bellamy	26	Leopoldsburg War Cemetery, Belgium
Trooper John Reginald Gibbs	20	Dunkirk Memorial, France
Trooper Raymond Hill	22	Dunkirk Memorial, France
Trooper James Gilbert Macdonald	21	Graty Communal Cemetery, Belgium
23 May 1940		
Trooper Harry Jackson	37	Dunkirk Town Cemetery, France
24 May 1940		
Trooper Marshall Finnegan (DoW in Barnet Hospital, UK)	21	Dundee Eastern Necropolis, UK
26 May 1940		
Warrant Officer Class III Thomas Wyatt Arbon	28	St Sylvestre-Cappel New Cemetery, France
Corporal Thomas Michael Le Butt Brogden	20	Renescure Churchyard, France
Corporal Charles Garner	20	Dunkirk Memorial, France
Trooper Roy Beautement	24	Dunkirk Memorial, France
Trooper Joseph Park	20	Dunkirk Memorial, France
Trooper Edward Benjamin Wiseman	21	Renescure Churchyard, France
Trooper John Frederick Wolfe	26	Renescure Churchyard, France
27 May 1940		
Lance Corporal Herbert Ostler	21	St Sylvestre-Cappel New Cemetery, France
Trooper Jonathan Eggleton Mouser	22	Dunkirk Town Cemetery, France
28 May 1940		
Second Lieutenant Richard Lawrence Hudson	22	Horton War Cemetery, Belgium

Corporal John Edward Pickard	20	Hotton War Cemetery, Belgium
Trooper Douglas Bird	21	Oudezeele Churchyard, France
Trooper William Albert Grant	20	Terdeghem Churchyard, France
Trooper William Ostler	23	Hotton War Cemetery, Belgium
29 May 1940		
Major Geoffrey Minto Radcliffe TD MID	39	Hotton War Cemetery, Belgium
Corporal Robert Smith	23	Hotton War Cemetery, Belgium
Lance Corporal Basil Geoffrey Dennis Ball	22	Hotton War Cemetery, Belgium
Lance Corporal Alfred Cox	37	Dunkirk Town Cemetery, France
Lance Corporal Frank Overton	27	Dunkirk Memorial, France
Trooper Kenneth Baker	21	Dunkirk Memorial, France
Trooper Walter Alan Stead	20	Winnezeele Churchyard, France
Trooper Charles Edward Wales	25	Dunkirk Memorial, France
Trooper William Alfred Welton	20	Dunkirk Memorial, France
Trooper Albert Wilson	22	Dozinghem Military Cemetery, Belgium
Trooper Kenneth Wingate	20	Oye-Plage Communal Cemetery, France
30 May 1940		
Captain Donald Hall	29	Hotton War Cemetery, Belgium
Captain Thomas Edward Beswick Sissons TD	30	Hotton War Cemetery, Belgium
Second Lieutenant Leonard Thomas Brabrook	32	Hotton War Cemetery, Belgium
Second Lieutenant John Furley Cockin	20	Hotton War Cemetery, Belgium
Corporal Peter Dennis Neesham	22	Dunkirk Memorial, France
Trooper Stanley Foden	29	Dunkirk Memorial, France
Trooper Ernest Geoffrey Pocklington	19	Dunkirk Memorial, France
Trooper Arthur Todd	20	Hotton War Cemetery, Belgium
1 June 1940		
Trooper William Bailey	23	Dunkirk Town Cemetery, France
5 June 1940		
Trooper George Edward Clarke	23	Dunkirk Memorial, France
23 December 1940		
Trooper Thomas McCeag Shortt (PoW/DoW)	21	Berlin 1939–1945 War Cemetery, Germany

Appendix III

Senior British Medical Officers' Report on the Attack of 14 April 1945

Major Thomas Patrick Howkins was the SBMO at Eichstätt, and it would be his damming report that would so vividly describe the events of 14 April 1945 as the imprisoned officers of the British and Commonwealth forces prepared to leave their place of confinement:

In April 1945 it became common knowledge that as the front was rapidly approaching the personnel of the camp were to be moved to an unknown destination South of the Danube. On or about 12 April [1945] I saw the German orders for the march. These were in the usual form, written in German with the English translation underneath, and were signed by the commandant Oberst Bessenger. It was ordered that the march should commence on 14 April [1945] in the morning, and it was forbidden to exhibit recognition signals should allied aircraft approach the column.

The column moved off about 8.30 am on Saturday, 14 April [1945]. In my capacity as senior British medical officer I formed part of the British headquarters staff and remained in the camp with the senior British officer, Lieutenant Colonel W.D.B. Thompson DSO MC who was in command until the column had cleared the camp. The column halted outside the camp in order that our party might reach the head of it which by this time was about a mile down the road towards a village called Pfunz. I estimate that it was about 9.30 am when our party reached the head of the column, which consisted of some 1,600 British officer prisoners [of war] together with some 200 British other ranks. The German officer in charge of the column, Oberleutant Raum, delayed the march for a few moments and, just as we were about to move, single engined aircraft started bombing the railway which ran parallel to the road we were on and the road Eichstätt-Ingoldstadt, which was on the far side of it from us. I estimate that the bombs were falling about 3/4 mile away. A German officer, Leutnant Helmar, was in charge of this part of the column, but he gave no orders as to what we were to do, and we sat on the side of the road watching what we imagined was a demonstration for our benefit. After about ten minutes the planes came to our side of the valley and strafed the column with cannon and machine guns for about twenty minutes. There was very little cover and the column dispersed both sides of the road seeking what cover it could. At this time an Unteroffizier called Schmidt arrived at the head of the column and told Leutnant Helmar that some of the prisoners [of war] were escaping. Subsequently, I heard single rifle shots, though I did not see who was firing or what they were firing at. Leutnant Helmar still gave no orders and took cover with the rest of us. At this time an LMG on the hill above us started to open fire on the planes. Colonel Thompson immediately asked for it to be stopped as he did not wish it to appear to the aircraft that we were a combatant unit, but Leutnant Helmar still gave no orders. Eventually after being pressed, Leutnant Helmar allowed a very small Union Jack, which, as a result of the commandants' orders, was the only thing we had to be put on the road. Immediately the strafing stopped, Colonel Thompson asked Leutnant Helmar to allow us either to disperse to the woods or return to the camp, but he said he had no orders. In the meantime, I took Leutnant Helmar's bicycle and cycled back down the road to attend to the casualties. I gave emergency treatment to those that I found. On my way back I met Oberst Bessenger also on a bicycle and told him we were returning to camp. He said we were to do no such thing but to continue the march, and became very excited. However, it had become obvious that he had completely lost control of the prisoners [of war] who were streaming back towards Eichstätt. Further down the road I met the camp officer, Hauptman Ditmar, who had always been a co-operative type, and he immediately arranged for transport to come and collect the dead and wounded. These were evacuated to the camp hospital and eventually the serious cases were taken to the military hospital in Eichstätt. In this connection I received adequate co-operation from the German authorities.

Subsequently the camp was evacuated by March [1945] route to Stalag VII-a Moosburg. The march commenced on the night of Sunday, 15 April [1945]. This march took place in the hours of darkness and during the day we lay up in barns and villages, which were constantly patrolled by allied fighters hunting for targets. When we arrived at Moosburg I met several prisoners [of war] from other camps who had been evacuated by daylight marches and there had also been sick British and American prisoners [of war] through the camp hospital at Eichstätt evacuated from such marches. From these I learned that the Germans had allowed recognition signals of various kinds to be employed when allied aircraft approached columns of prisoners [of war] and that these recognition signals had been successful.

Sworn by the said Thomas Patrick Howkins at 6 Spring Gardens in the City of Westminster this thirty-first day of January 1946.

Appendix IV

Roll of Honour: Officers Killed and Wounded at Eichstätt, 14 April 1945

The following officers were killed or wounded as they left Eichstätt PoW camp on 14 April 1945 in an attack by US fighter aircraft. The dead are all buried in the Durnbach War Cemetery, Germany.

Killed

The following officers were tragically killed:

Captain Roland Davies, New Zealand Infantry, aged 31 – DoW on 21 April 1945.

Lieutenant Philip Henry Charles Denison, King's Royal Rifle Corps, aged 25 – DoW on 15 April 1945.

Lieutenant Arthur Michael Hart, 1st Fife and Forfar Yeomanry, aged 30.

Lieutenant James Patrick Heenan, Royal Corps of Signals, aged 39.

Captain Charles Benjamin Kemp Jickling, Royal Norfolk Regiment, aged 29.

Lieutenant Leslie Tom Lowe, Royal Army Pay Corps, aged 41.

Lieutenant Humphrey Richard Hickson Marriott, The Buffs (Royal East Kent Regiment), aged 25.

Lieutenant Andrew Mcnulty, Black Watch (Royal Highlanders), aged 26.

Lieutenant Richard Lacey Owen-Holdsworth, Pioneer Corps, aged 32.

Lieutenant Donald Chamberlain Price, The Queen's Royal Regiment (West Surrey), aged 34.

Lieutenant Cyril Sowden, King's Own Royal Regiment (Lancaster), aged 31.

Lieutenant William Templeton Steel, Royal Army Service Corps, aged 28.

Wounded

The following officers were wounded, but survived:

Major E.H. Arden, West Yorkshire Regiment – GSW to right arm (later amputated).

Lieutenant S.J.F. Barry, RAOC – wound to right knee.

Lieutenant W. Birtwistle, Royal Artillery – GSW to left shoulder.

Captain P.C. Catchlove (Australian) – GSW to right leg.

Major J.R. Cousens – GSW to right leg (amputated).

Lieutenant J. D'arcy Clark, Sherwood Foresters – GSW to left arm and abdomen.

Lieutenant Collins, Indian Army – GSW to right side of face.

Lieutenant W.K. Esson (NZ), Otago Regiment – GSW to buttock, exit by stomach.

Lieutenant P. Elliott, North Fusiliers – GSW to knee.

Lieutenant J.F. Forster, Green Howards – GSW to left leg and splinter on right leg.

Lieutenant R.C. Foulkes, RAC – GSW to left ankle.

Captain K.A. Fraser, RAOC – leg wounds (left leg amputated).

Lieutenant J. Hayward, REME – GSW to buttock.

Lieutenant A.P Henderson, Black Watch – GSW to left forearm.

Lieutenant H.H. Henderson (Australian).

Lieutenant H.R. Horne, Royal Artillery – wound to right foot (right leg amputated).

Lieutenant A.E Horton, RA – GSW to right leg.

Lieutenant G. How, RAC – GSW to right arm.

Captain A. Kennett, Royal Signals – GSW to left leg.

Lieutenant E.N. Layton, Royal Signals – grazed nose.

Lieutenant N.A. McGilp, RAOC – GSW to right buttock (two).

Lieutenant McLean, RM – GSW to left arm.

Lieutenant D.H. McLennan, North Fusiliers – GSW to right shoulder.

Lieutenant I.M. Mennie, Seaforth Highlanders – GSW to left buttock.

Flight Lieutenant Meredith, RAF – GSW to right forearm.

Captain G.N. Money (Canadian) – GSW to right side of face.

Lieutenant C.R. Mullings, Royal Artillery – wound to right foot (right leg amputated).

Lieutenant Peyanovitch (Russian) – graze.

Lieutenant J.J.T. Roberts, Norfolk Regiment – GSW to right leg, below knee.

Lieutenant S. Saunders, KRRC – GSW to right buttock.

Lieutenant R.A. Sim, Royal Artillery – GSW to left arm.

Lieutenant R.O. Smith, RASC – GSW to right cheek, posterior.

Lieutenant. L.G. Stewart, Cameron Highlanders – GSW to right leg.

Captain R. Stewart, RASC – GSW to right buttock.

Lieutenant van Trotzenburg – scalp wound.

Lieutenant G.H.W. Troughton, OBLI – graze to right hand.

Captain K.A. Waugh, Royal Signals – GSW to right leg and shrapnel in
  right arm.
Captain J.L. Whitehouse, Royal Engineers – GSW to right arm.
Lieutenant P.H. Williams, Royal Artillery – GSW to left shoulder.
Lieutenant J.K. Wilson, RASC – GSW to back.

Bibliography

Books Referenced

Bonner, Norman, *War Diary 1939–1941*, Privately printed (1985).

Mansel, John, *The Mansel Diaries*, Burgess & Co., Oxford (1977).

Murland, Jerry, *Cassel and Hazebrouck 1940*, Pen & Sword (2017)

Reis, Helmut, *Chronik der Jagerkaserne in Eichstätt, 1933–1952*.

Slater, Frank, *As You Were: A Book of Caricatures*, Hutchinson, London (1949).

Wylie, Neville, *Barbed Wire Diplomacy: Britain, Germany and the Politics of Prisoners of War, 1939–1945* (2010), Oxford University Press, Oxford.

Yarrow, C.D., *The ABC: An Address Book of PoWs at Oflag VI-b Eichstätt*, Germany, Privately printed (1949)

Sources

The John Blomfield Dixon Collection

Herefordshire Archive and Records Centre – Papers of John William Hobday (Ref: BZ29/2/2)

The National Archives, Kew – WO 167 & WO 416 Series

Websites

140th-field-regiment-ra-1940.co.uk

Ancestry.com

British Newspapers.com

Findmypast.com

Forces War Records.com

The War Graves Photographic Project (twgpp).com

Traces of Evil.com

Index

Personalities

(The following names are those associated with the life of John Blomfield Dixon outside of his immediate family, whose entries in his diaries are too numerous to list.)

Military Units/Ships

Dear Reader,

We hope you have enjoyed this book, but why not share your views on social media? You can also follow our pages to see more about our other products: facebook.com/penandswordbooks or follow us on X @penswordbooks

You can also view our products at www.pen-and-sword.co.uk (UK and ROW) or www.penandswordbooks.com (North America).

To keep up to date with our latest releases and online catalogues, please sign up to our newsletter at: www.pen-and-sword.co.uk/newsletter

If you would like a printed catalogue with our latest books, then please email: enquiries@pen-and-sword.co.uk or telephone: 01226 734555 (UK and ROW) or email: uspen-and-sword@casematepublishers.com or telephone: (610) 853-9131 (North America).

We respect your privacy and we will only use personal information to send you information about our products.

Thank you!